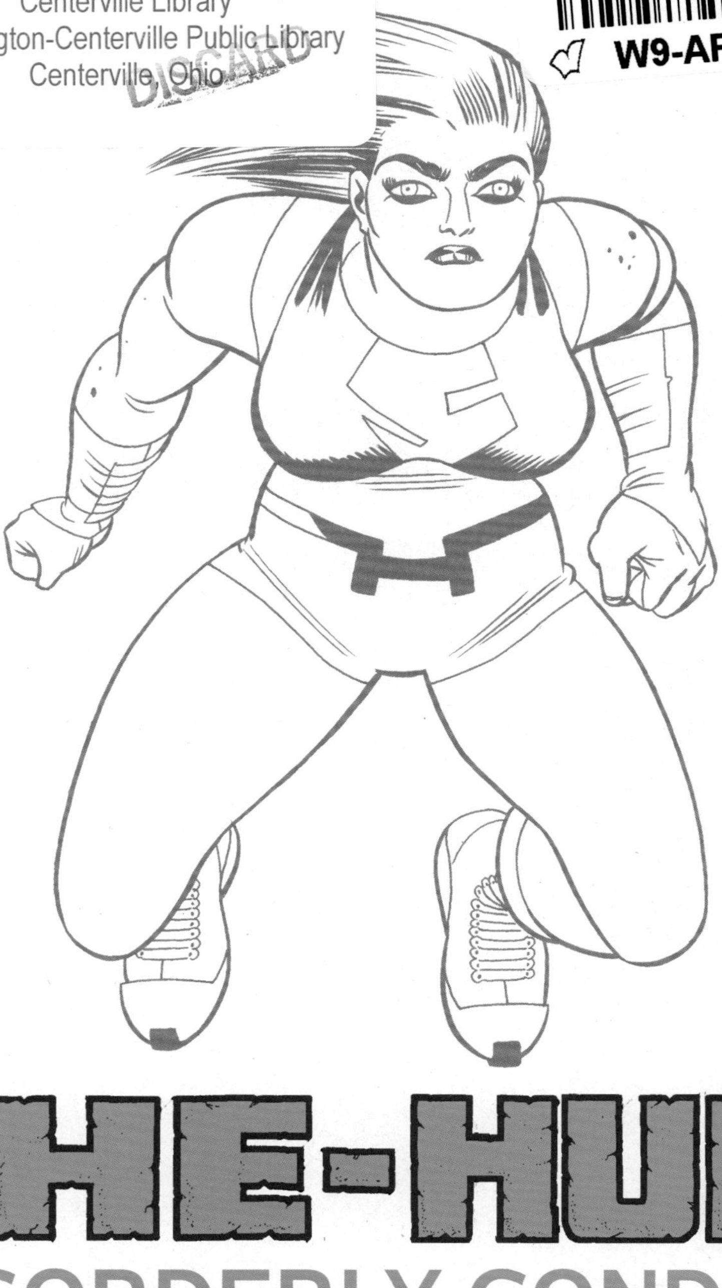

SHE-HULK
DISORDERLY CONDUCT

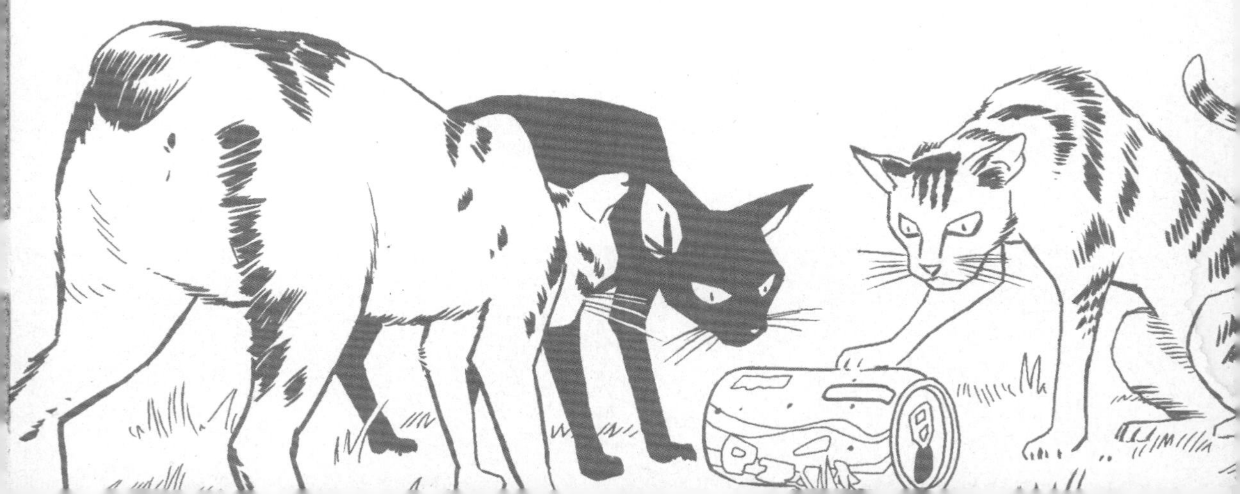

WRITER
CHARLES SOULE

STORYTELLER
JAVIER PULIDO

COLOR ARTIST
MUNTSA VICENTE

LETTERER
VC'S CLAYTON COWLES

COVER ART
KEVIN WADA

EDITOR
JEANINE SCHAEFER

COLLECTION EDITOR: JENNIFER GRÜNWALD
ASSISTANT EDITOR: SARAH BRUNSTAD
ASSOCIATE MANAGING EDITOR: ALEX STARBUCK
EDITOR, SPECIAL PROJECTS: MARK D. BEAZLEY
SENIOR EDITOR, SPECIAL PROJECTS: JEFF YOUNGQUIST
SVP PRINT, SALES & MARKETING: DAVID GABRIEL
BOOK DESIGN: JEFF POWELL

EDITOR IN CHIEF: AXEL ALONSO
CHIEF CREATIVE OFFICER: JOE QUESADA
PUBLISHER: DAN BUCKLEY
EXECUTIVE PRODUCER: ALAN FINE

SHE-HULK VOL. 2: DISORDERLY CONDUCT. Contains material originally published in magazine form as SHE-HULK #7-12. First printing 2015. ISBN# 978-0-7851-9020-2. Published by MARVEL WORLDWIDE, INC., a subsidiary of MARVEL ENTERTAINMENT, LLC. OFFICE OF PUBLICATION: 135 West 50th Street, New York, NY 10020. Copyright © 2014 and 2015 Marvel Characters, Inc. All rights reserved. All characters featured in this issue and the distinctive names and likenesses thereof, and all related indicia are trademarks of Marvel Characters, Inc. No similarity between any of the names, characters, persons, and/or institutions in this magazine with those of any living or dead person or institution is intended, and any such similarity which may exist is purely coincidental. **Printed in Canada.** ALAN FINE, EVP - Office of the President, Marvel Worldwide, Inc. and EVP & CMO Marvel Characters B.V.; DAN BUCKLEY, Publisher & President - Print, Animation & Digital Divisions; JOE QUESADA, Chief Creative Officer; TOM BREVOORT, SVP of Publishing; DAVID BOGART, SVP of Operations & Procurement, Publishing; C.B. CEBULSKI, SVP of Creator & Content Development; DAVID GABRIEL, SVP Print, Sales & Marketing; JIM O'KEEFE, VP of Operations & Logistics; DAN CARR, Executive Director of Publishing Technology; SUSAN CRESPI, Editorial Operations Manager; ALEX MORALES, Publishing Operations Manager; STAN LEE, Chairman Emeritus. For information regarding advertising in Marvel Comics or on Marvel.com, please contact Niza Disla, Director of Marvel Partnerships, at ndisla@marvel.com. For Marvel subscription inquiries, please call 800-217-9158. **Manufactured between 1/30/2015 and 3/9/2015 by SOLISCO PRINTERS, SCOTT, QC, CANADA.**

10 9 8 7 6 5 4 3 2 1

Jennifer Walters was a shy attorney, good at her job and quiet in her life, when she found herself gunned down by criminals. A gamma-irradiated blood transfusion from her cousin, Dr. Bruce Banner, a.k.a. the Incredible Hulk, didn't just give her a second chance at life, it gave her super-strength and bulletproof green skin.

Wherever justice is threatened, you can bet on the gamma-powered gal with the brain and brawn to right some wrong, the Sensational…

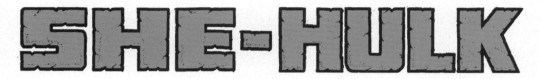

Ever since Jen left the boys' club of her last law firm, life has been tumultuous to say the least. But since she's opened up her own law firm and taken matters into her own hands — from interrogating Iron Man to showing even Doctor Doom a thing or two — things have mostly been on the upswing.

Mostly. Because, well, sure, there's the Blue File that she hasn't quite been able to figure out and it seems to have left a trail of destruction behind it!

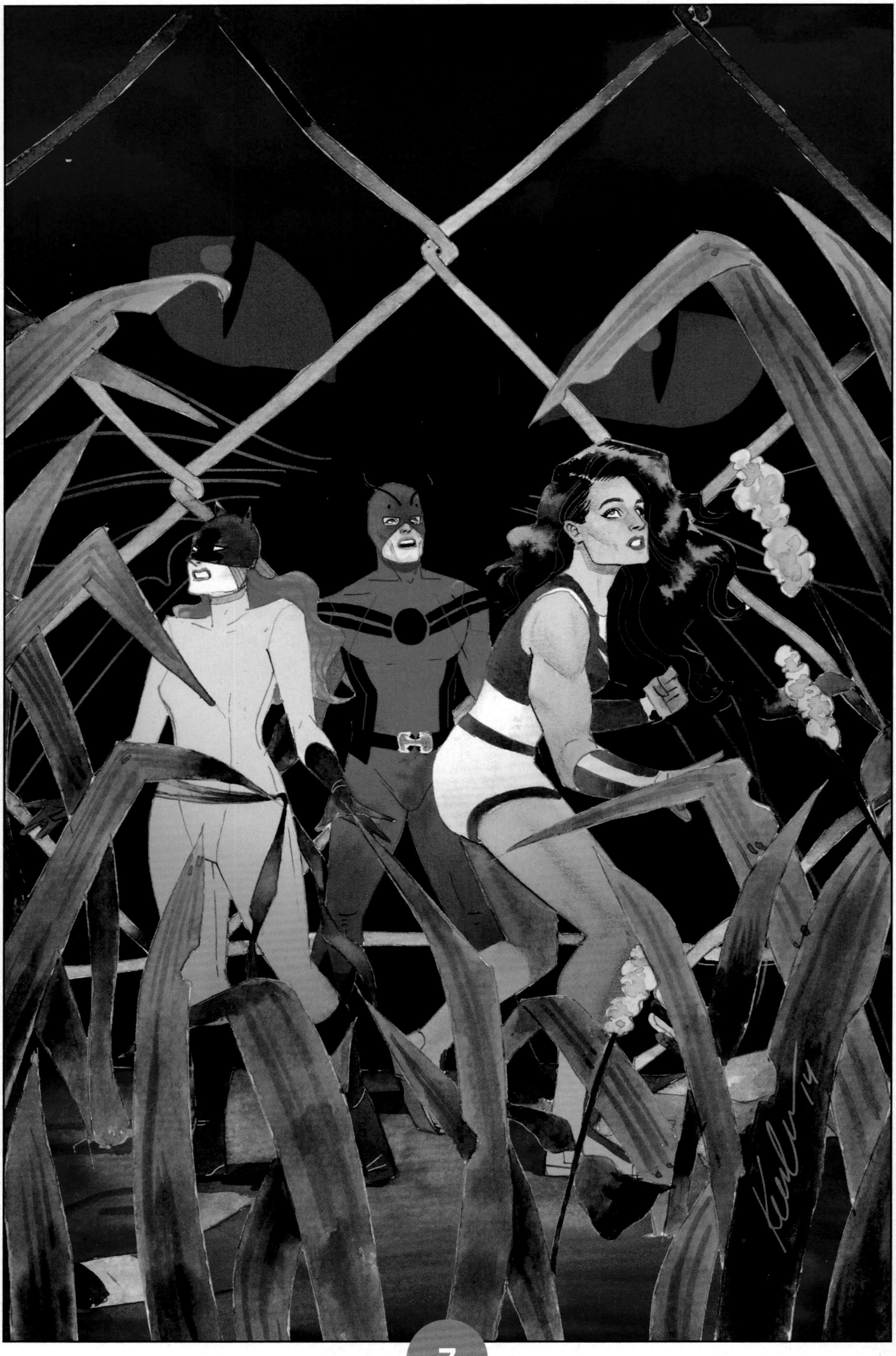

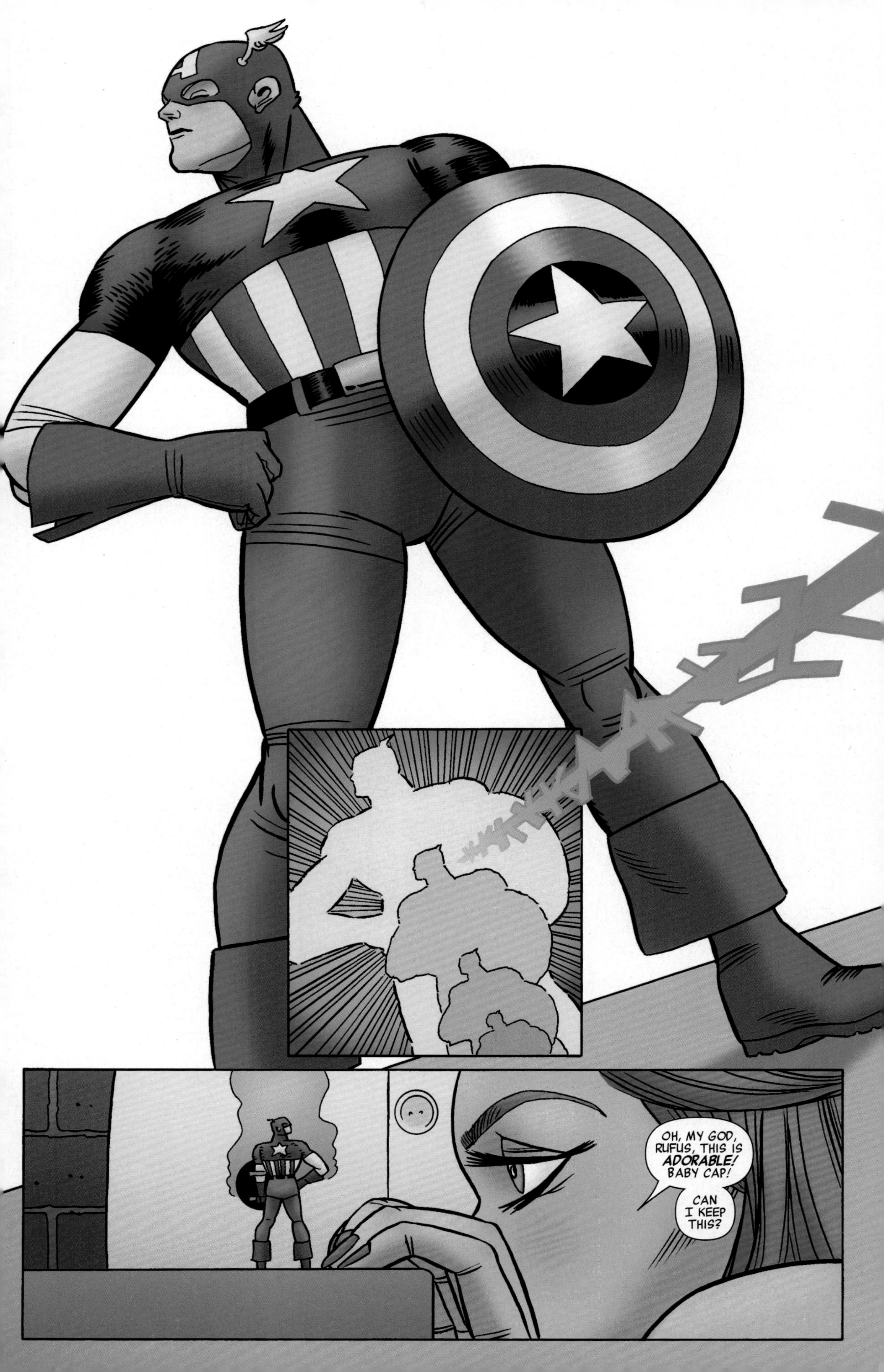
OH, MY GOD, RUFUS, THIS IS ADORABLE! BABY CAP!
CAN I KEEP THIS?

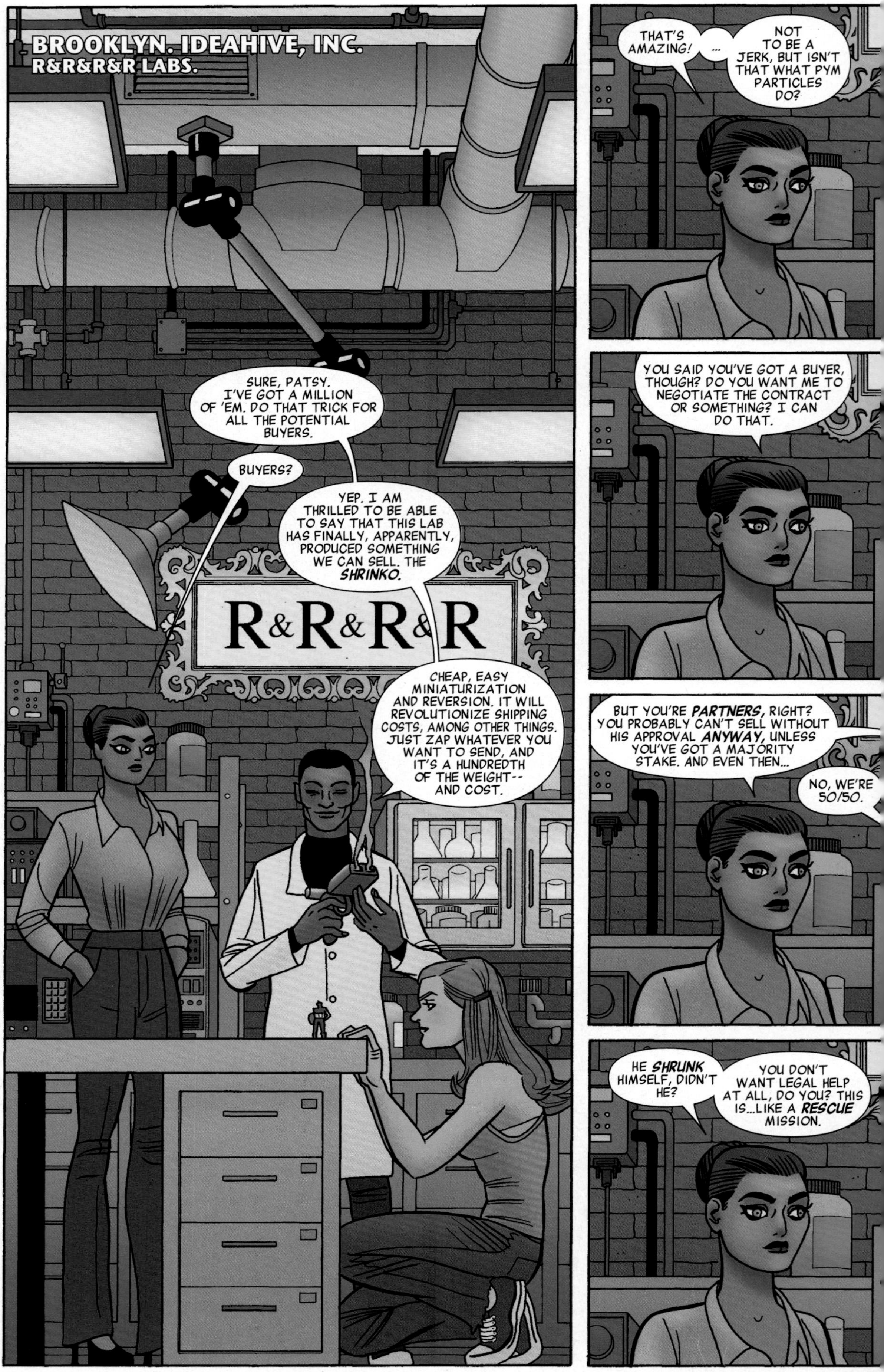
BROOKLYN. IDEAHIVE, INC.
R&R&R&R LABS.
SURE, PATSY. I'VE GOT A MILLION OF 'EM. DO THAT TRICK FOR ALL THE POTENTIAL BUYERS.
BUYERS?
YEP. I AM THRILLED TO BE ABLE TO SAY THAT THIS LAB HAS FINALLY, APPARENTLY, PRODUCED SOMETHING WE CAN SELL. THE SHRINKO.
R&R&R&R
CHEAP, EASY MINIATURIZATION AND REVERSION. IT WILL REVOLUTIONIZE SHIPPING COSTS, AMONG OTHER THINGS. JUST ZAP WHATEVER YOU WANT TO SEND, AND IT'S A HUNDREDTH OF THE WEIGHT-- AND COST.
THAT'S AMAZING!
...
NOT TO BE A JERK, BUT ISN'T THAT WHAT PYM PARTICLES DO?
YOU SAID YOU'VE GOT A BUYER, THOUGH? DO YOU WANT ME TO NEGOTIATE THE CONTRACT OR SOMETHING? I CAN DO THAT.
BUT YOU'RE PARTNERS, RIGHT? YOU PROBABLY CAN'T SELL WITHOUT HIS APPROVAL ANYWAY, UNLESS YOU'VE GOT A MAJORITY STAKE. AND EVEN THEN...
NO, WE'RE 50/50.
HE SHRUNK HIMSELF, DIDN'T HE?
YOU DON'T WANT LEGAL HELP AT ALL, DO YOU? THIS IS...LIKE A RESCUE MISSION.

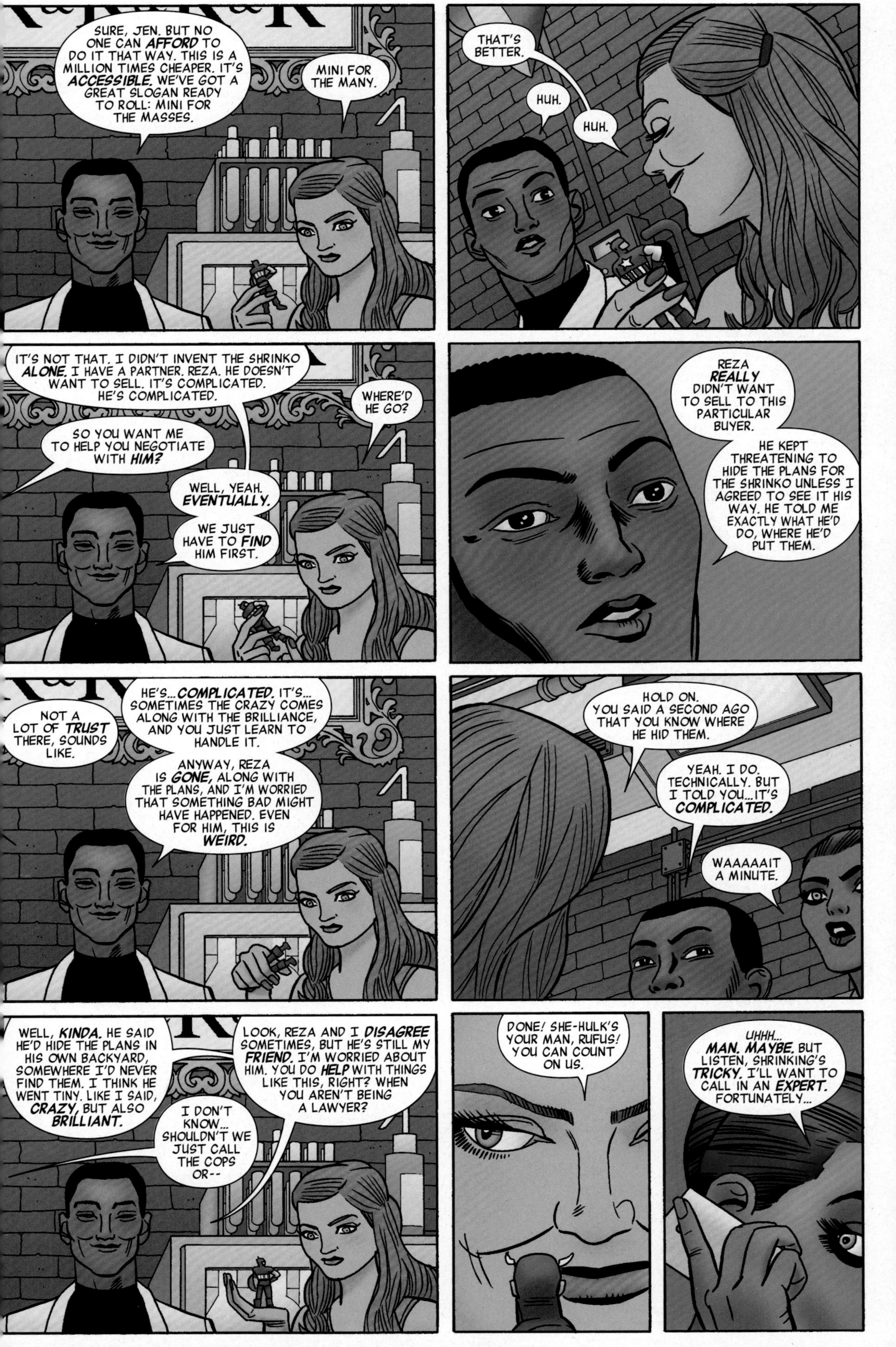

SURE, JEN. BUT NO ONE CAN AFFORD TO DO IT THAT WAY. THIS IS A MILLION TIMES CHEAPER. IT'S ACCESSIBLE. WE'VE GOT A GREAT SLOGAN READY TO ROLL: MINI FOR THE MASSES.
MINI FOR THE MANY.
THAT'S BETTER.
HUH.
HUH.
IT'S NOT THAT. I DIDN'T INVENT THE SHRINKO ALONE. I HAVE A PARTNER. REZA. HE DOESN'T WANT TO SELL. IT'S COMPLICATED. HE'S COMPLICATED.
SO YOU WANT ME TO HELP YOU NEGOTIATE WITH HIM?
WHERE'D HE GO?
WELL, YEAH. EVENTUALLY.
WE JUST HAVE TO FIND HIM FIRST.
REZA REALLY DIDN'T WANT TO SELL TO THIS PARTICULAR BUYER.
HE KEPT THREATENING TO HIDE THE PLANS FOR THE SHRINKO UNLESS I AGREED TO SEE IT HIS WAY. HE TOLD ME EXACTLY WHAT HE'D DO, WHERE HE'D PUT THEM.
NOT A LOT OF TRUST THERE, SOUNDS LIKE.
HE'S...COMPLICATED. IT'S... SOMETIMES THE CRAZY COMES ALONG WITH THE BRILLIANCE, AND YOU JUST LEARN TO HANDLE IT.
ANYWAY, REZA IS GONE, ALONG WITH THE PLANS, AND I'M WORRIED THAT SOMETHING BAD MIGHT HAVE HAPPENED. EVEN FOR HIM, THIS IS WEIRD.
HOLD ON. YOU SAID A SECOND AGO THAT YOU KNOW WHERE HE HID THEM.
YEAH. I DO. TECHNICALLY. BUT I TOLD YOU...IT'S COMPLICATED.
WAAAAAIT A MINUTE.
WELL, KINDA. HE SAID HE'D HIDE THE PLANS IN HIS OWN BACKYARD, SOMEWHERE I'D NEVER FIND THEM. I THINK HE WENT TINY. LIKE I SAID, CRAZY, BUT ALSO BRILLIANT.
LOOK, REZA AND I DISAGREE SOMETIMES, BUT HE'S STILL MY FRIEND. I'M WORRIED ABOUT HIM. YOU DO HELP WITH THINGS LIKE THIS, RIGHT? WHEN YOU AREN'T BEING A LAWYER?
I DON'T KNOW... SHOULDN'T WE JUST CALL THE COPS OR--
DONE! SHE-HULK'S YOUR MAN, RUFUS! YOU CAN COUNT ON US.
UHHH... MAN. MAYBE. BUT LISTEN, SHRINKING'S TRICKY. I'LL WANT TO CALL IN AN EXPERT. FORTUNATELY...

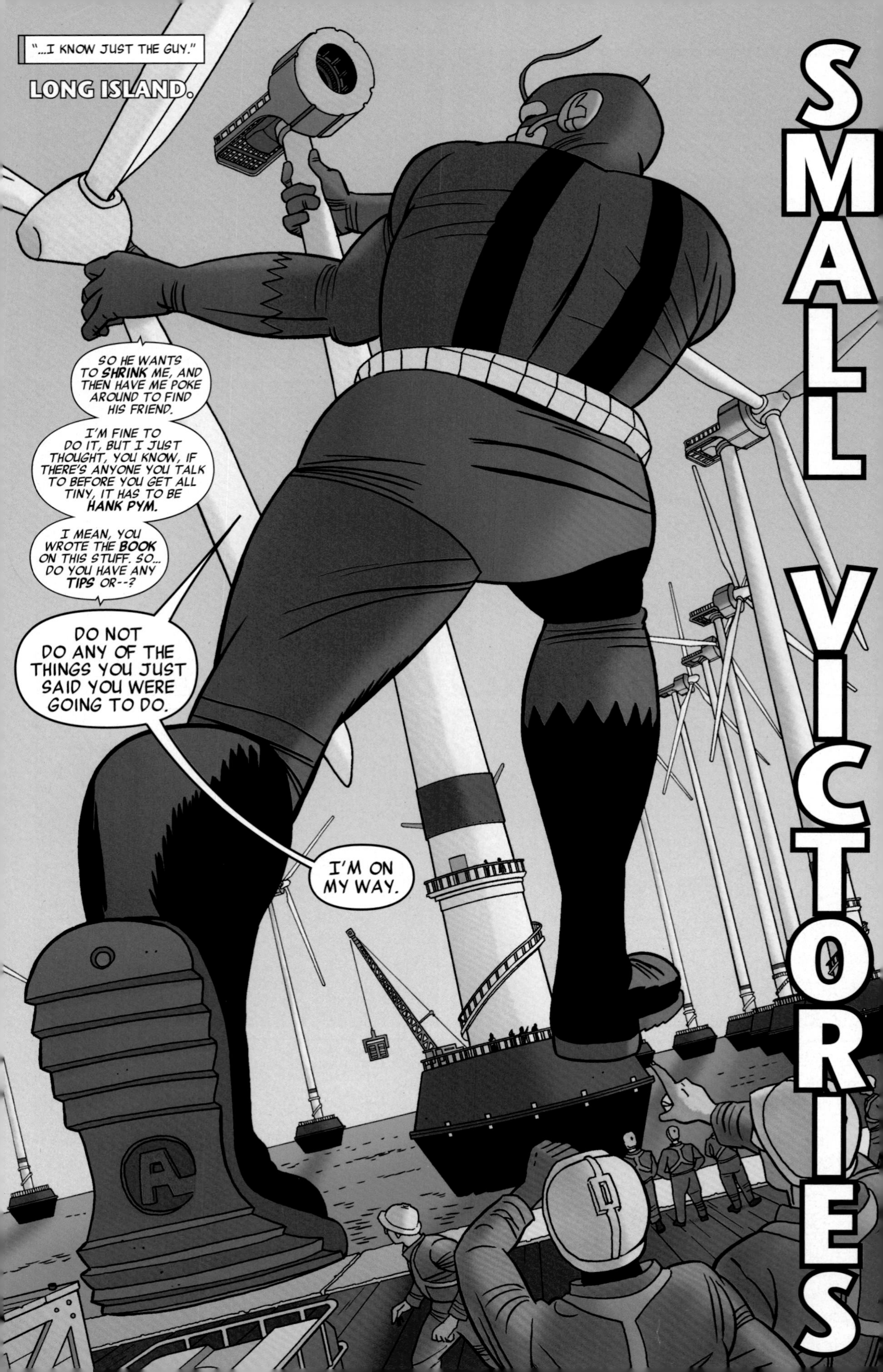

"...I KNOW JUST THE GUY."
LONG ISLAND.
SMALL VICTORIES
SO HE WANTS TO SHRINK ME, AND THEN HAVE ME POKE AROUND TO FIND HIS FRIEND.
I'M FINE TO DO IT, BUT I JUST THOUGHT, YOU KNOW, IF THERE'S ANYONE YOU TALK TO BEFORE YOU GET ALL TINY, IT HAS TO BE HANK PYM.
I MEAN, YOU WROTE THE BOOK ON THIS STUFF. SO... DO YOU HAVE ANY TIPS OR--?
DO NOT DO ANY OF THE THINGS YOU JUST SAID YOU WERE GOING TO DO.
I'M ON MY WAY.

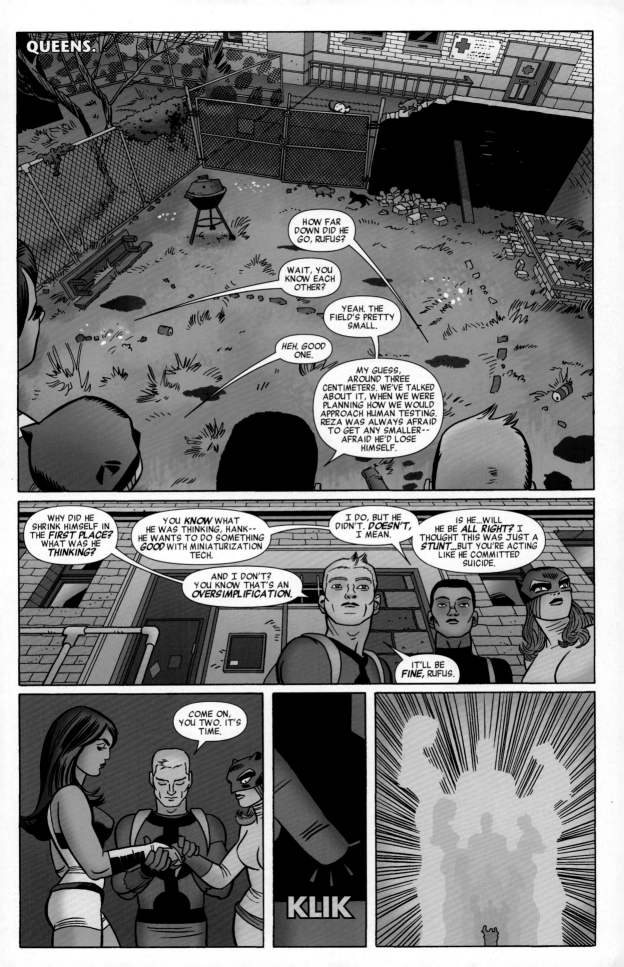

QUEENS.

HOW FAR DOWN DID HE GO, RUFUS?

WAIT, YOU KNOW EACH OTHER?

YEAH. THE FIELD'S PRETTY SMALL.

HEH. GOOD ONE.

MY GUESS, AROUND THREE CENTIMETERS. WE'VE TALKED ABOUT IT, WHEN WE WERE PLANNING HOW WE WOULD APPROACH HUMAN TESTING. REZA WAS ALWAYS AFRAID TO GET ANY SMALLER-- AFRAID HE'D LOSE HIMSELF.

WHY DID HE SHRINK HIMSELF IN THE *FIRST PLACE?* WHAT WAS HE *THINKING?*

YOU *KNOW* WHAT HE WAS THINKING, HANK-- HE WANTS TO DO SOMETHING *GOOD* WITH MINIATURIZATION TECH.

AND I DON'T? YOU KNOW THAT'S AN *OVERSIMPLIFICATION.*

I DO, BUT HE DIDN'T. *DOESN'T,* I MEAN.

IS HE...WILL HE BE *ALL RIGHT?* I THOUGHT THIS WAS JUST A *STUNT...*BUT YOU'RE ACTING LIKE HE COMMITTED SUICIDE.

IT'LL BE *FINE,* RUFUS.

COME ON, YOU TWO. IT'S TIME.

KLIK

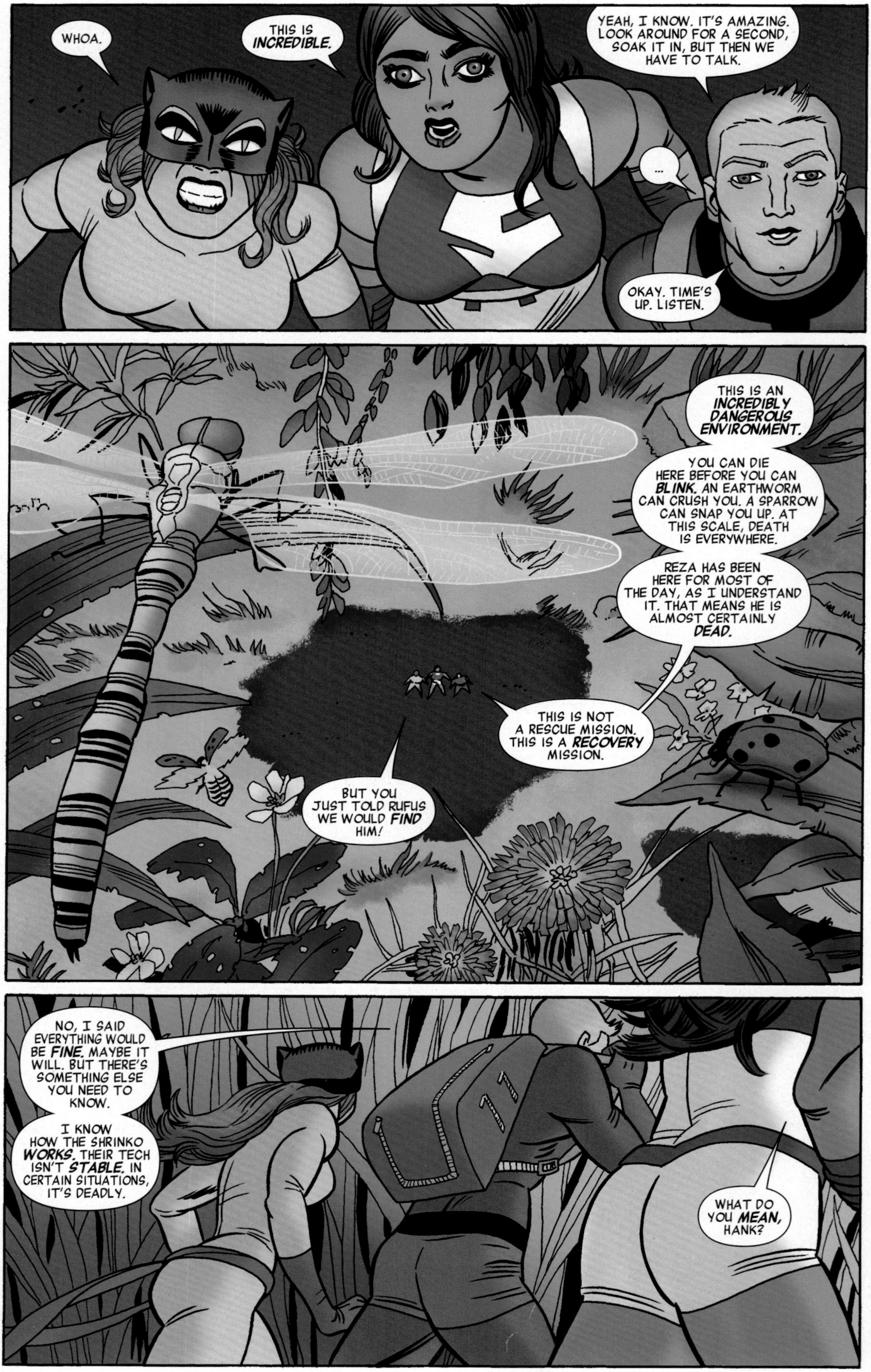
WHOA.
THIS IS INCREDIBLE.
YEAH, I KNOW. IT'S AMAZING. LOOK AROUND FOR A SECOND, SOAK IT IN, BUT THEN WE HAVE TO TALK.
...
OKAY. TIME'S UP. LISTEN.
THIS IS AN INCREDIBLY DANGEROUS ENVIRONMENT.
YOU CAN DIE HERE BEFORE YOU CAN BLINK. AN EARTHWORM CAN CRUSH YOU. A SPARROW CAN SNAP YOU UP. AT THIS SCALE, DEATH IS EVERYWHERE.
REZA HAS BEEN HERE FOR MOST OF THE DAY, AS I UNDERSTAND IT. THAT MEANS HE IS ALMOST CERTAINLY DEAD.
THIS IS NOT A RESCUE MISSION. THIS IS A RECOVERY MISSION.
BUT YOU JUST TOLD RUFUS WE WOULD FIND HIM!
NO, I SAID EVERYTHING WOULD BE FINE. MAYBE IT WILL. BUT THERE'S SOMETHING ELSE YOU NEED TO KNOW.
I KNOW HOW THE SHRINKO WORKS. THEIR TECH ISN'T STABLE. IN CERTAIN SITUATIONS, IT'S DEADLY.
WHAT DO YOU MEAN, HANK?

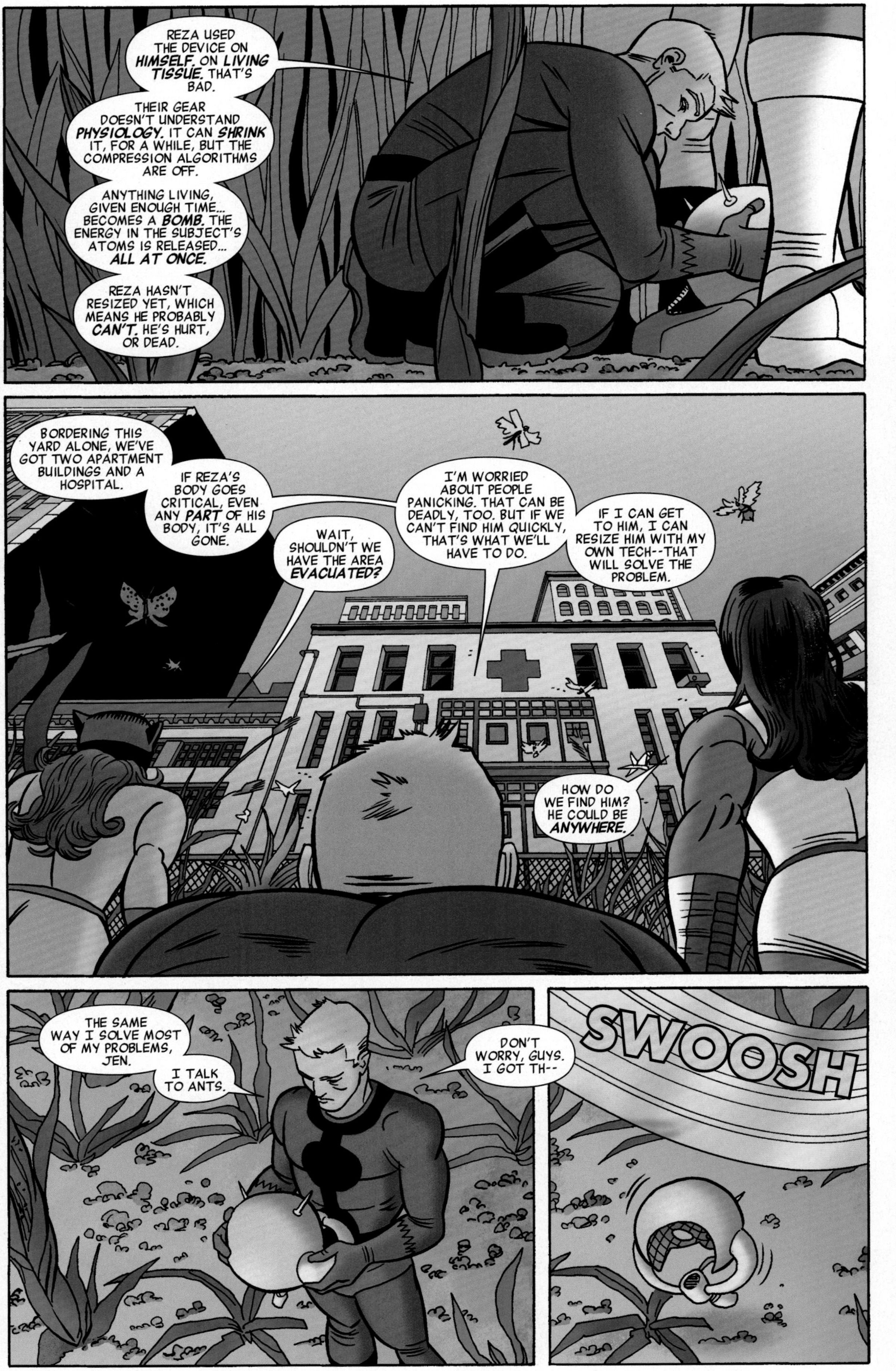

REZA USED THE DEVICE ON HIMSELF. ON LIVING TISSUE. THAT'S BAD.
THEIR GEAR DOESN'T UNDERSTAND PHYSIOLOGY. IT CAN SHRINK IT, FOR A WHILE, BUT THE COMPRESSION ALGORITHMS ARE OFF.
ANYTHING LIVING, GIVEN ENOUGH TIME... BECOMES A BOMB. THE ENERGY IN THE SUBJECT'S ATOMS IS RELEASED... ALL AT ONCE.
REZA HASN'T RESIZED YET, WHICH MEANS HE PROBABLY CAN'T. HE'S HURT, OR DEAD.
BORDERING THIS YARD ALONE, WE'VE GOT TWO APARTMENT BUILDINGS AND A HOSPITAL.
IF REZA'S BODY GOES CRITICAL, EVEN ANY PART OF HIS BODY, IT'S ALL GONE.
WAIT, SHOULDN'T WE HAVE THE AREA EVACUATED?
I'M WORRIED ABOUT PEOPLE PANICKING. THAT CAN BE DEADLY, TOO. BUT IF WE CAN'T FIND HIM QUICKLY, THAT'S WHAT WE'LL HAVE TO DO.
IF I CAN GET TO HIM, I CAN RESIZE HIM WITH MY OWN TECH--THAT WILL SOLVE THE PROBLEM.
HOW DO WE FIND HIM? HE COULD BE ANYWHERE.
THE SAME WAY I SOLVE MOST OF MY PROBLEMS, JEN.
I TALK TO ANTS.
DON'T WORRY, GUYS. I GOT TH--
SWOOSH

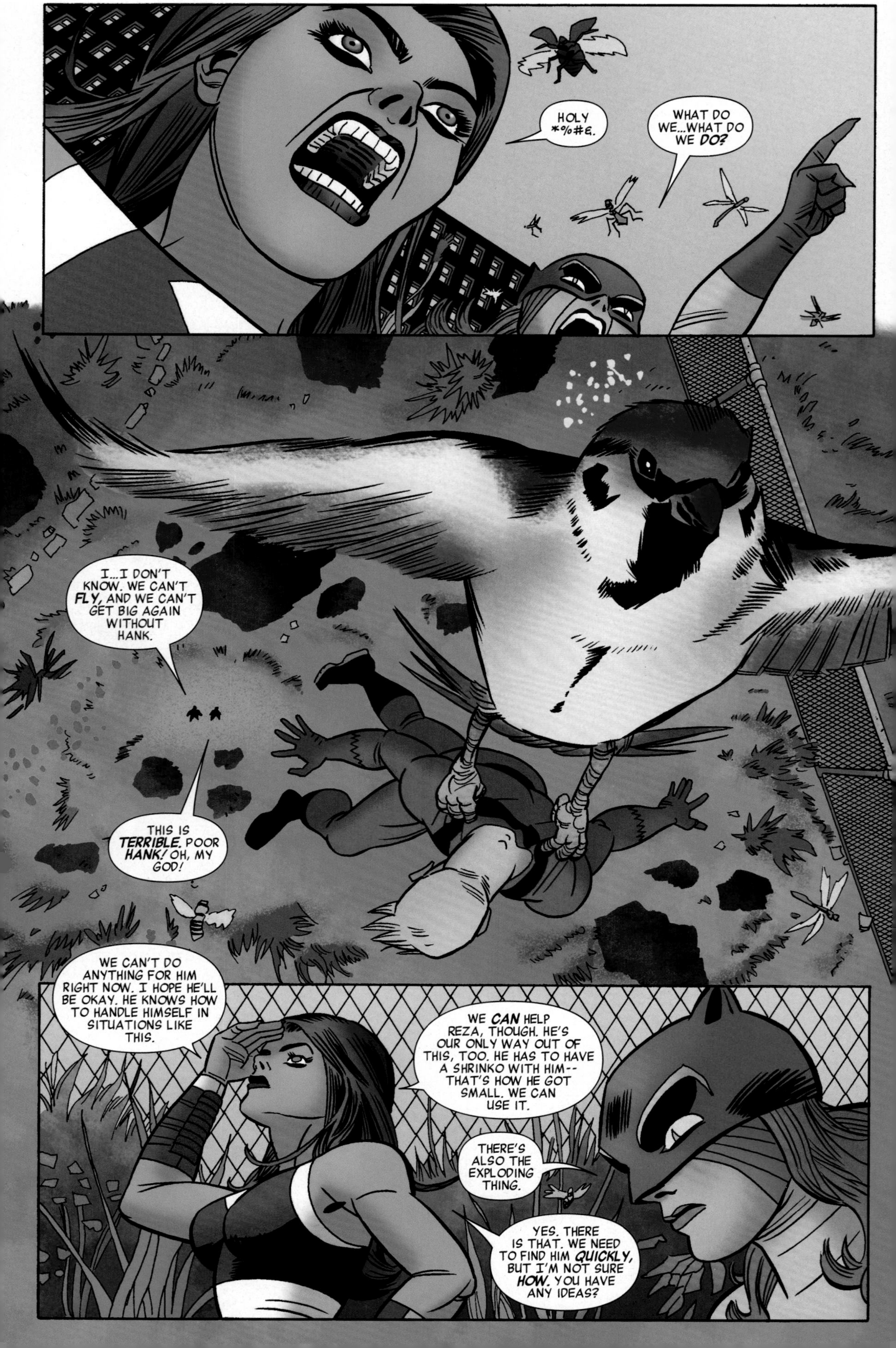
HOLY *%#€.
WHAT DO WE...WHAT DO WE DO?
I...I DON'T KNOW. WE CAN'T FLY, AND WE CAN'T GET BIG AGAIN WITHOUT HANK.
THIS IS TERRIBLE. POOR HANK! OH, MY GOD!
WE CAN'T DO ANYTHING FOR HIM RIGHT NOW. I HOPE HE'LL BE OKAY. HE KNOWS HOW TO HANDLE HIMSELF IN SITUATIONS LIKE THIS.
WE CAN HELP REZA, THOUGH. HE'S OUR ONLY WAY OUT OF THIS, TOO. HE HAS TO HAVE A SHRINKO WITH HIM--THAT'S HOW HE GOT SMALL. WE CAN USE IT.
THERE'S ALSO THE EXPLODING THING.
YES. THERE IS THAT. WE NEED TO FIND HIM QUICKLY, BUT I'M NOT SURE HOW. YOU HAVE ANY IDEAS?

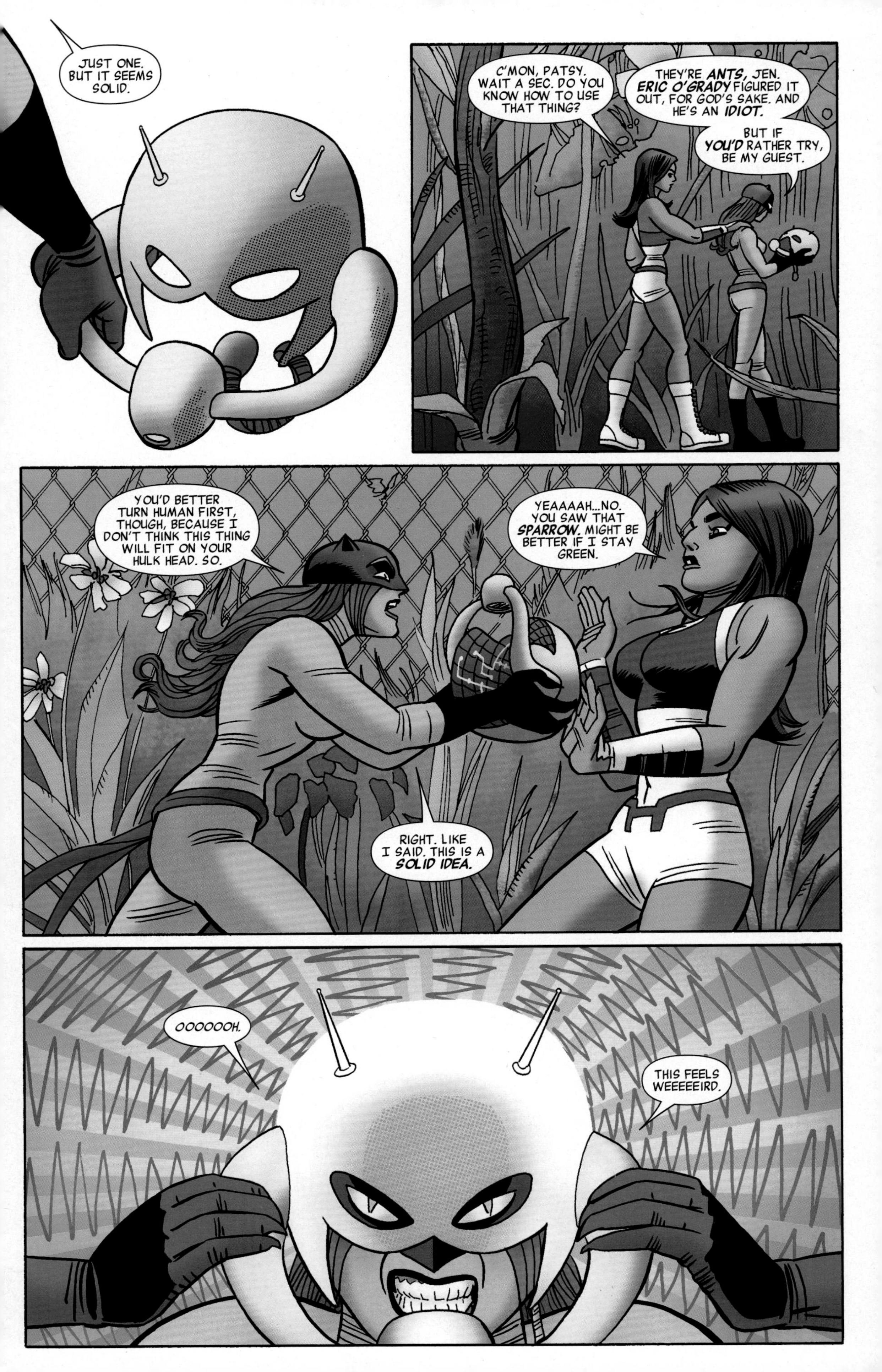

JUST ONE. BUT IT SEEMS SOLID.
C'MON, PATSY. WAIT A SEC. DO YOU KNOW HOW TO USE THAT THING?
THEY'RE ANTS, JEN. ERIC O'GRADY FIGURED IT OUT, FOR GOD'S SAKE. AND HE'S AN IDIOT.
BUT IF YOU'D RATHER TRY, BE MY GUEST.
YOU'D BETTER TURN HUMAN FIRST, THOUGH, BECAUSE I DON'T THINK THIS THING WILL FIT ON YOUR HULK HEAD. SO.
YEAAAAH...NO. YOU SAW THAT SPARROW. MIGHT BE BETTER IF I STAY GREEN.
RIGHT. LIKE I SAID. THIS IS A SOLID IDEA.
OOOOOOH.
THIS FEELS WEEEEEIRD.

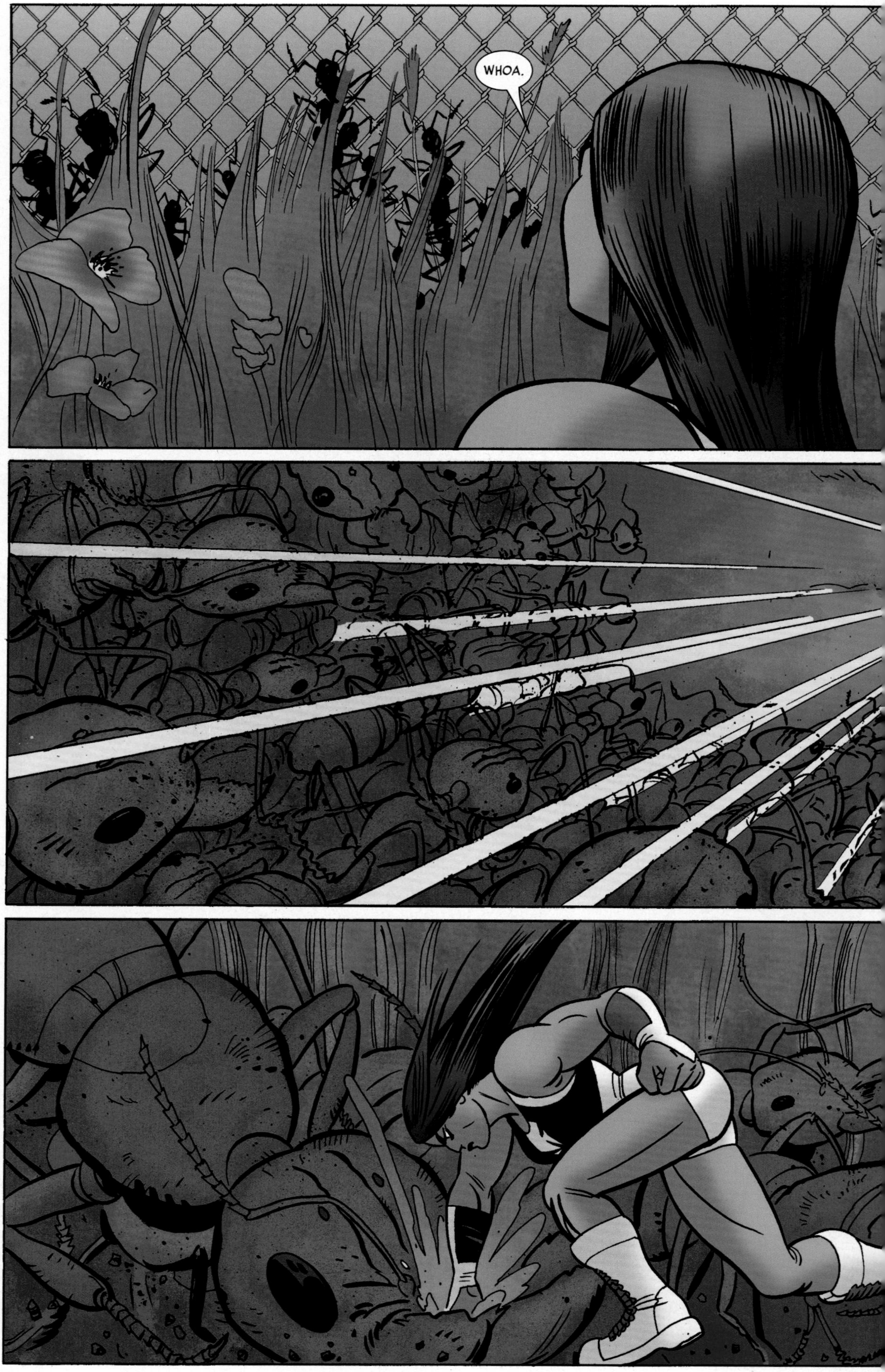
WHOA.

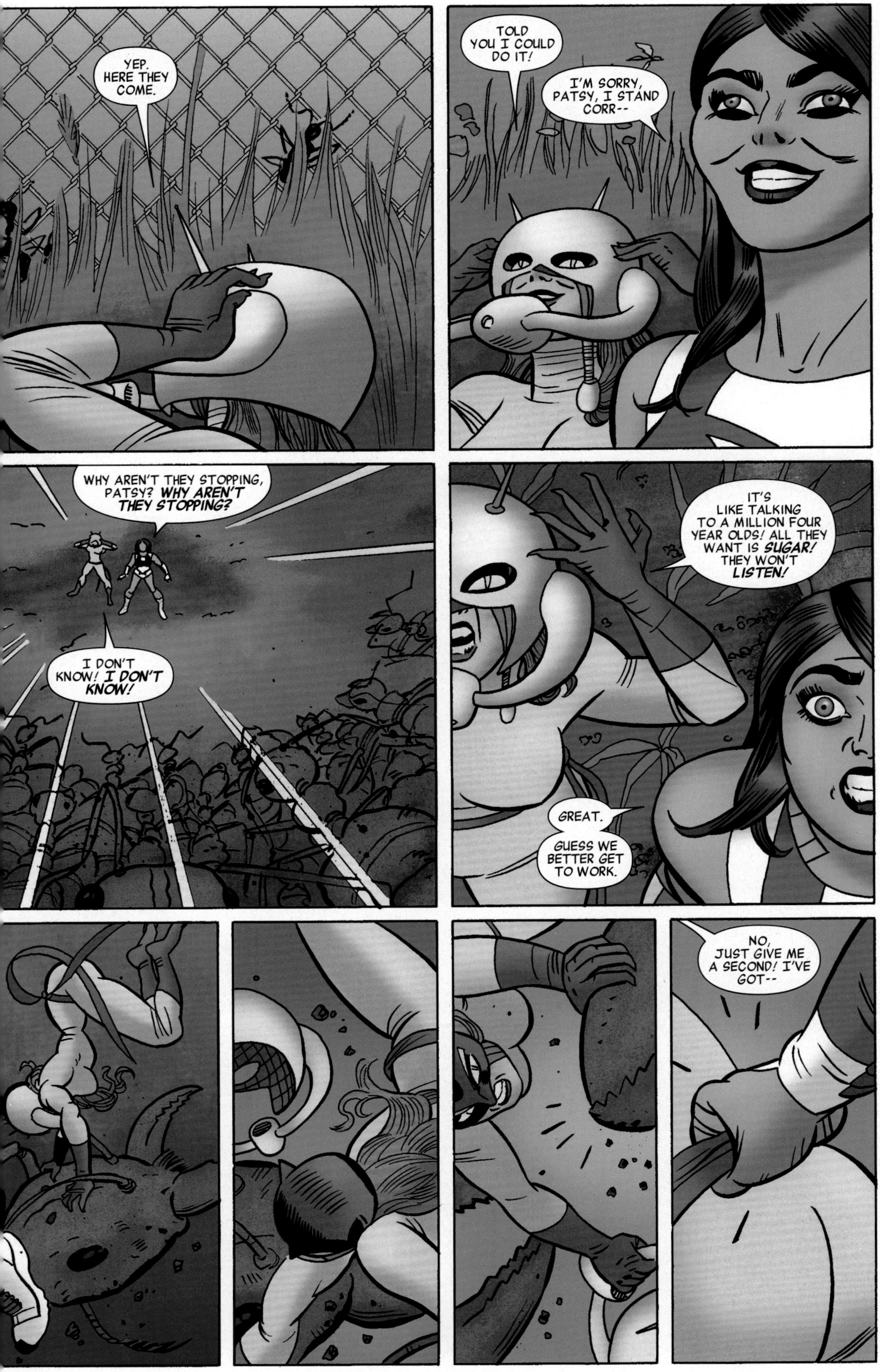
YEP. HERE THEY COME.
TOLD YOU I COULD DO IT!
I'M SORRY, PATSY, I STAND CORR--
WHY AREN'T THEY STOPPING, PATSY? WHY AREN'T THEY STOPPING?
I DON'T KNOW! I DON'T KNOW!
IT'S LIKE TALKING TO A MILLION FOUR YEAR OLDS! ALL THEY WANT IS SUGAR! THEY WON'T LISTEN!
GREAT.
GUESS WE BETTER GET TO WORK.
NO, JUST GIVE ME A SECOND! I'VE GOT--

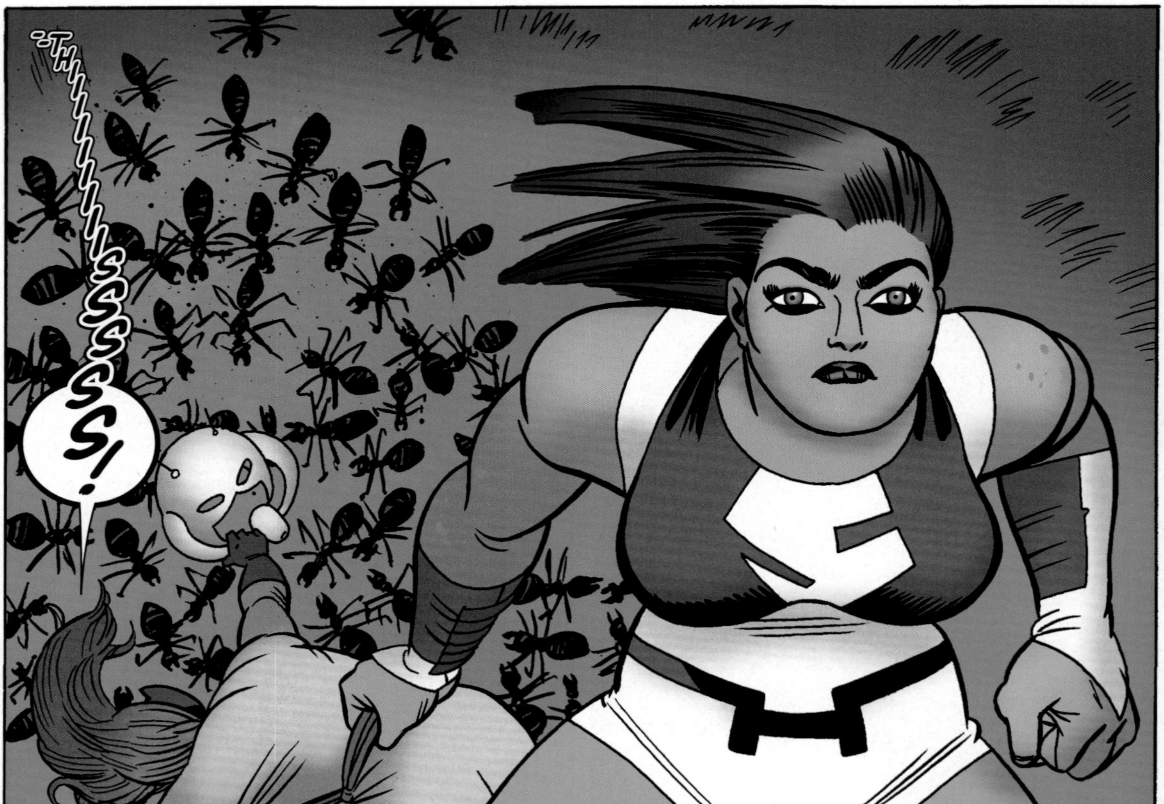
-THIIIIIIIIISSSSSS!

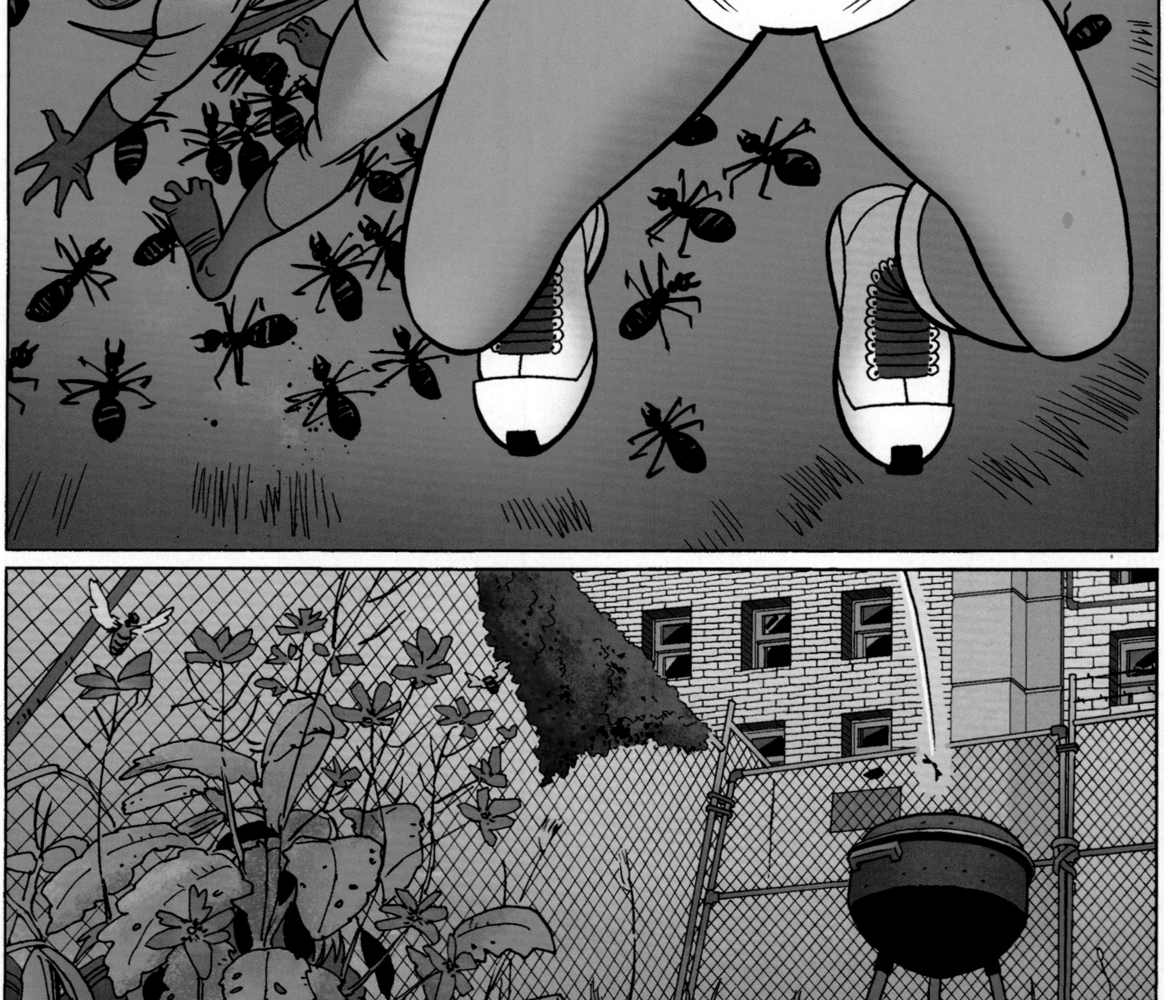

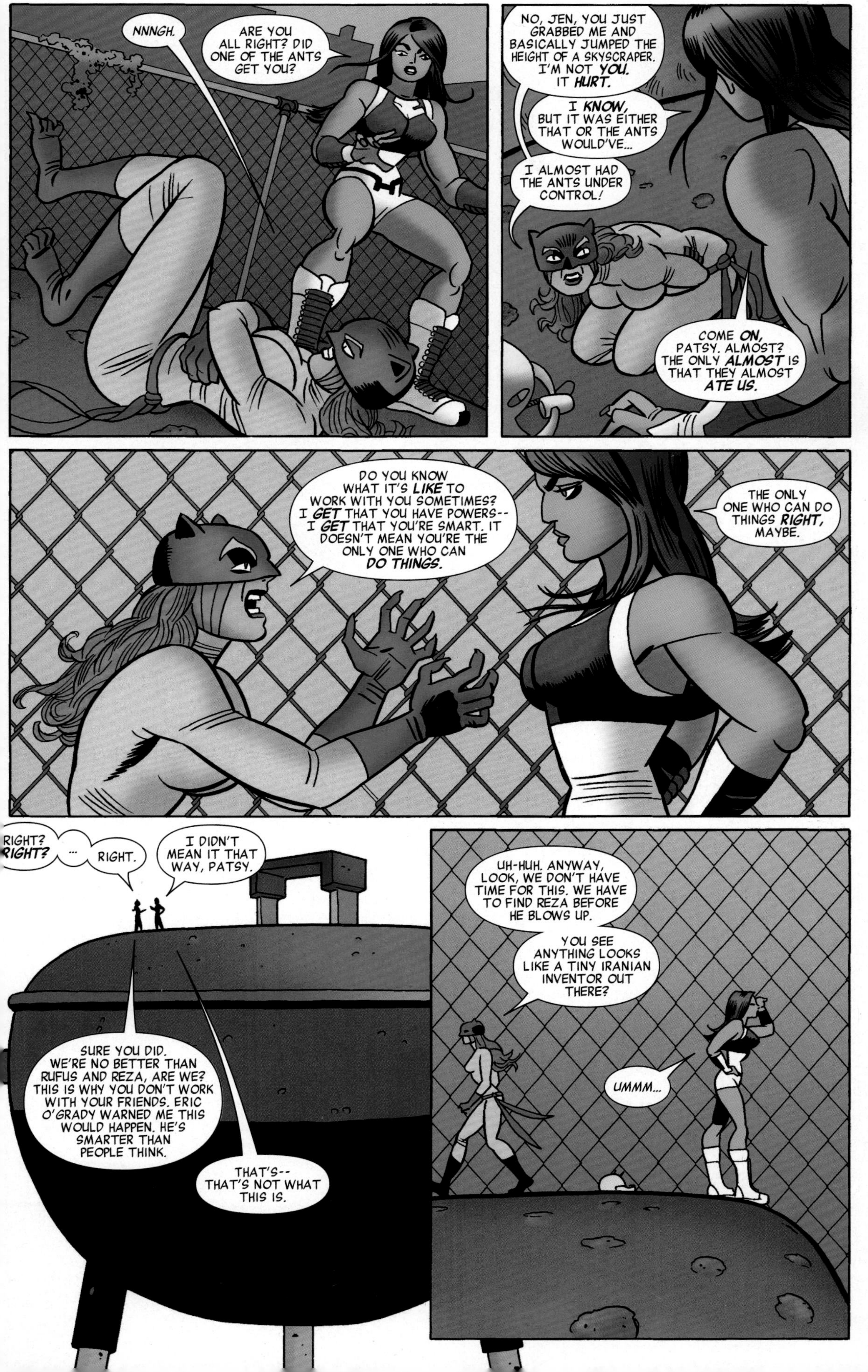
NNNGH.
ARE YOU ALL RIGHT? DID ONE OF THE ANTS GET YOU?
NO, JEN, YOU JUST GRABBED ME AND BASICALLY JUMPED THE HEIGHT OF A SKYSCRAPER. I'M NOT **YOU.** IT **HURT.**
I **KNOW,** BUT IT WAS EITHER THAT OR THE ANTS WOULD'VE...
I ALMOST HAD THE ANTS UNDER CONTROL!
COME **ON,** PATSY. ALMOST? THE ONLY **ALMOST** IS THAT THEY ALMOST **ATE US.**
DO YOU KNOW WHAT IT'S **LIKE** TO WORK WITH YOU SOMETIMES? I **GET** THAT YOU HAVE POWERS-- I **GET** THAT YOU'RE SMART. IT DOESN'T MEAN YOU'RE THE ONLY ONE WHO CAN **DO THINGS.**
THE ONLY ONE WHO CAN DO THINGS **RIGHT,** MAYBE.
RIGHT? **RIGHT?**
...
RIGHT.
I DIDN'T MEAN IT THAT WAY, PATSY.
SURE YOU DID. WE'RE NO BETTER THAN RUFUS AND REZA, ARE WE? THIS IS WHY YOU DON'T WORK WITH YOUR FRIENDS. ERIC O'GRADY WARNED ME THIS WOULD HAPPEN. HE'S SMARTER THAN PEOPLE THINK.
THAT'S-- THAT'S NOT WHAT THIS IS.
UH-HUH. ANYWAY, LOOK, WE DON'T HAVE TIME FOR THIS. WE HAVE TO FIND REZA BEFORE HE BLOWS UP.
YOU SEE ANYTHING LOOKS LIKE A TINY IRANIAN INVENTOR OUT THERE?
UMMM...

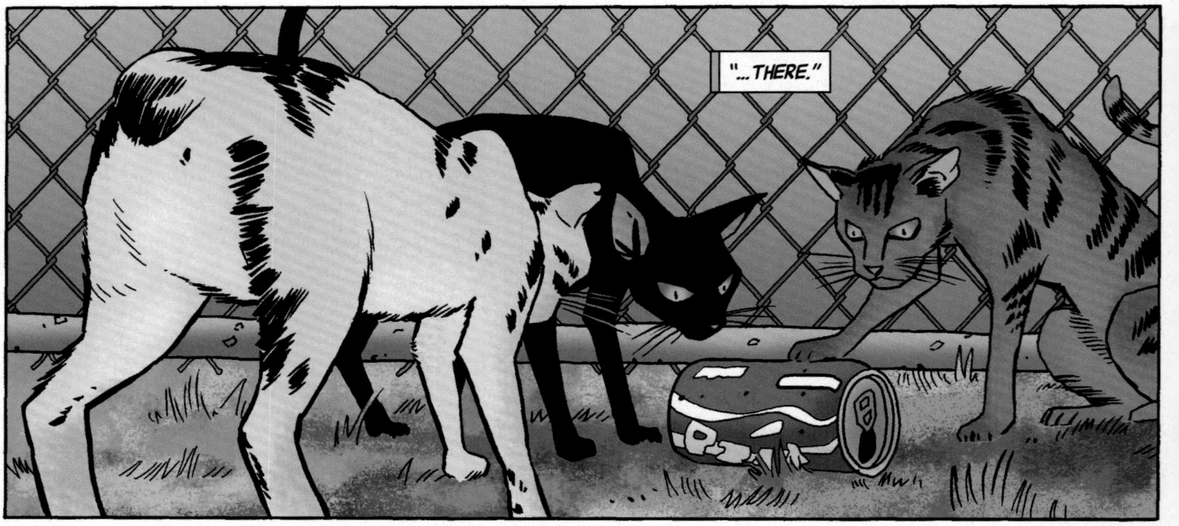
"...THERE."

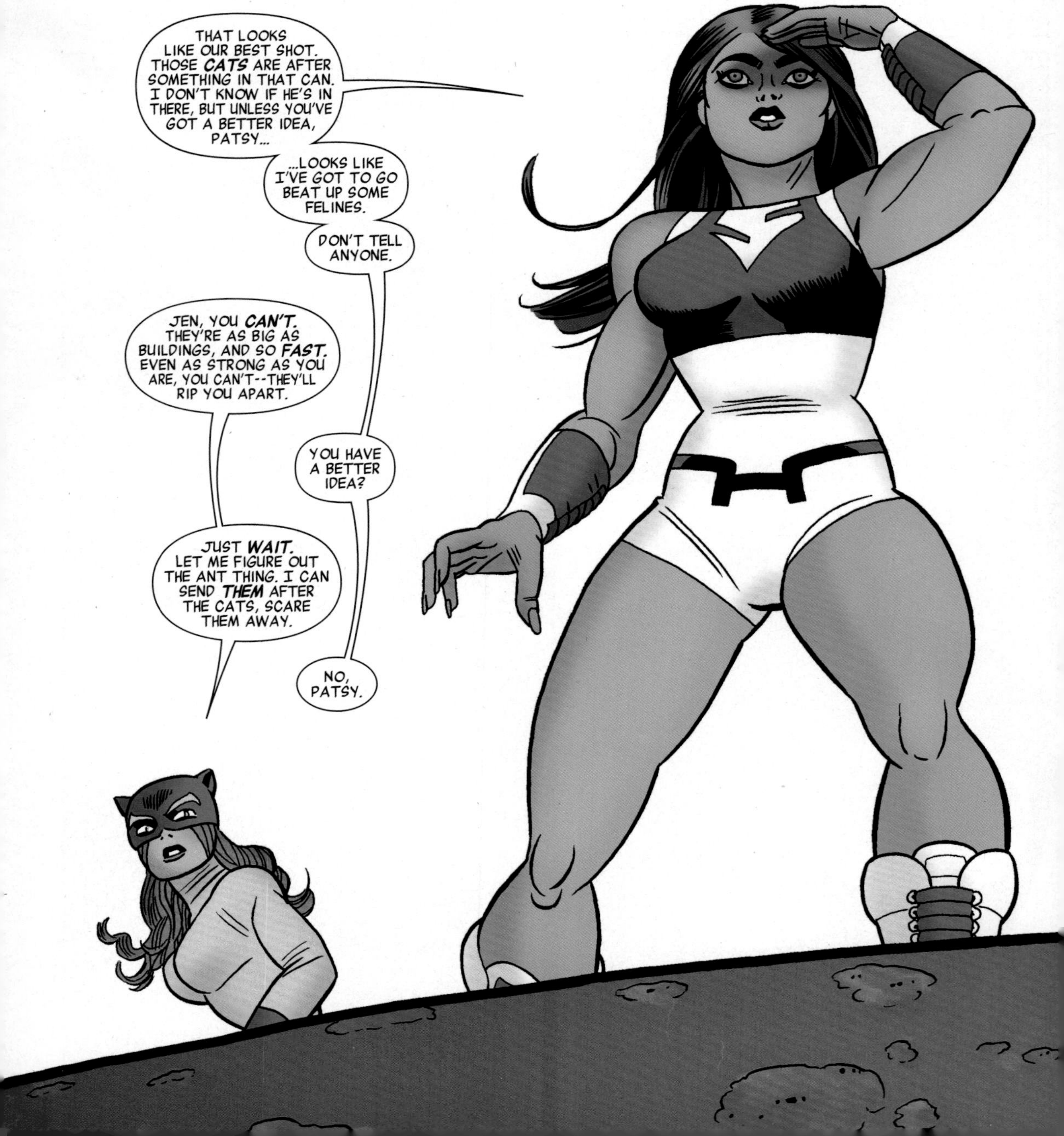
THAT LOOKS LIKE OUR BEST SHOT. THOSE CATS ARE AFTER SOMETHING IN THAT CAN. I DON'T KNOW IF HE'S IN THERE, BUT UNLESS YOU'VE GOT A BETTER IDEA, PATSY...
...LOOKS LIKE I'VE GOT TO GO BEAT UP SOME FELINES.
DON'T TELL ANYONE.
JEN, YOU CAN'T. THEY'RE AS BIG AS BUILDINGS, AND SO FAST. EVEN AS STRONG AS YOU ARE, YOU CAN'T--THEY'LL RIP YOU APART.
YOU HAVE A BETTER IDEA?
JUST WAIT. LET ME FIGURE OUT THE ANT THING. I CAN SEND THEM AFTER THE CATS, SCARE THEM AWAY.
NO, PATSY.

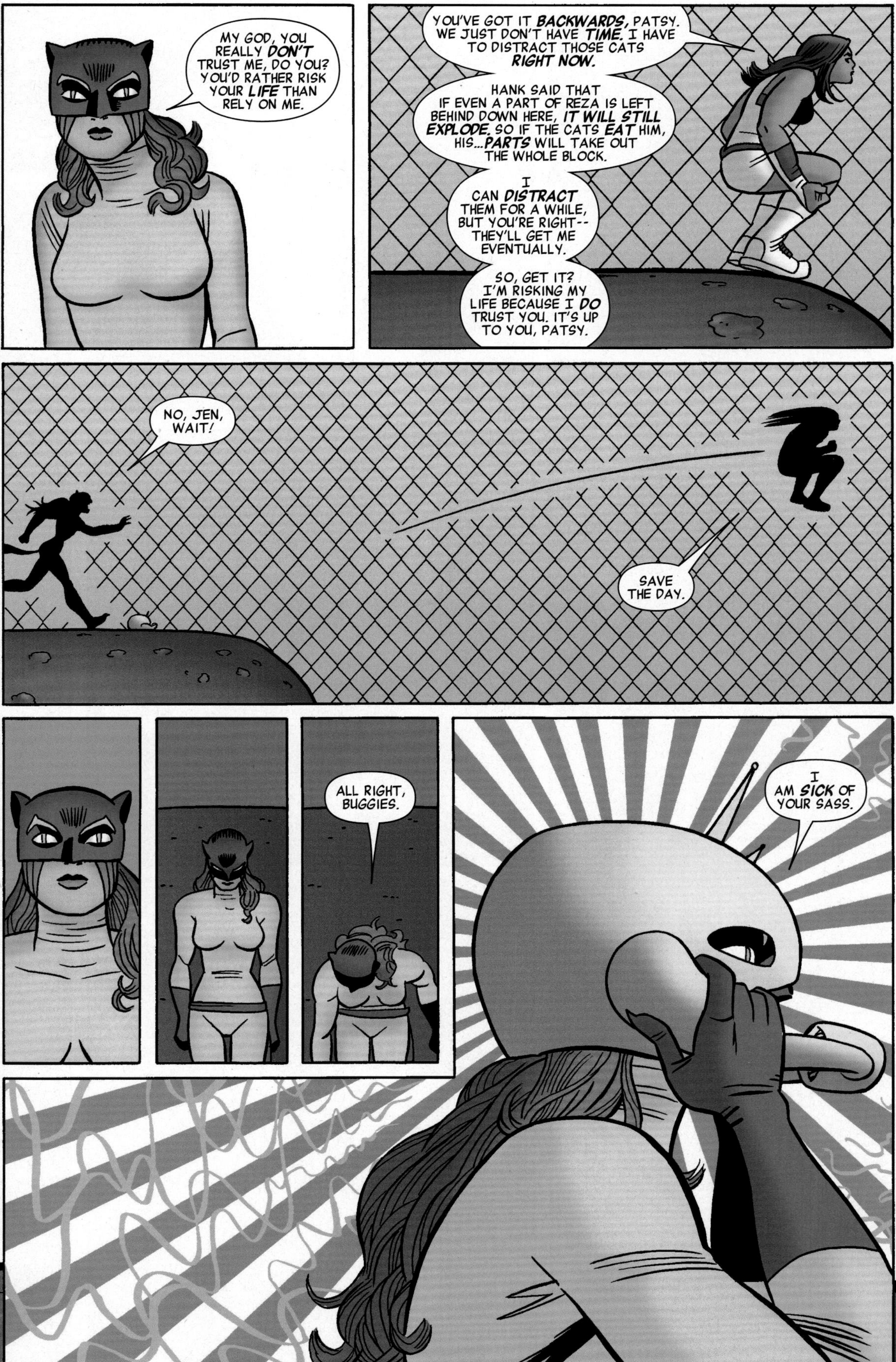

MY GOD, YOU REALLY DON'T TRUST ME, DO YOU? YOU'D RATHER RISK YOUR LIFE THAN RELY ON ME.
YOU'VE GOT IT BACKWARDS, PATSY. WE JUST DON'T HAVE TIME. I HAVE TO DISTRACT THOSE CATS RIGHT NOW.
HANK SAID THAT IF EVEN A PART OF REZA IS LEFT BEHIND DOWN HERE, IT WILL STILL EXPLODE. SO IF THE CATS EAT HIM, HIS...PARTS WILL TAKE OUT THE WHOLE BLOCK.
I CAN DISTRACT THEM FOR A WHILE, BUT YOU'RE RIGHT-- THEY'LL GET ME EVENTUALLY.
SO, GET IT? I'M RISKING MY LIFE BECAUSE I DO TRUST YOU. IT'S UP TO YOU, PATSY.
NO, JEN, WAIT!
SAVE THE DAY.
ALL RIGHT, BUGGIES.
I AM SICK OF YOUR SASS.

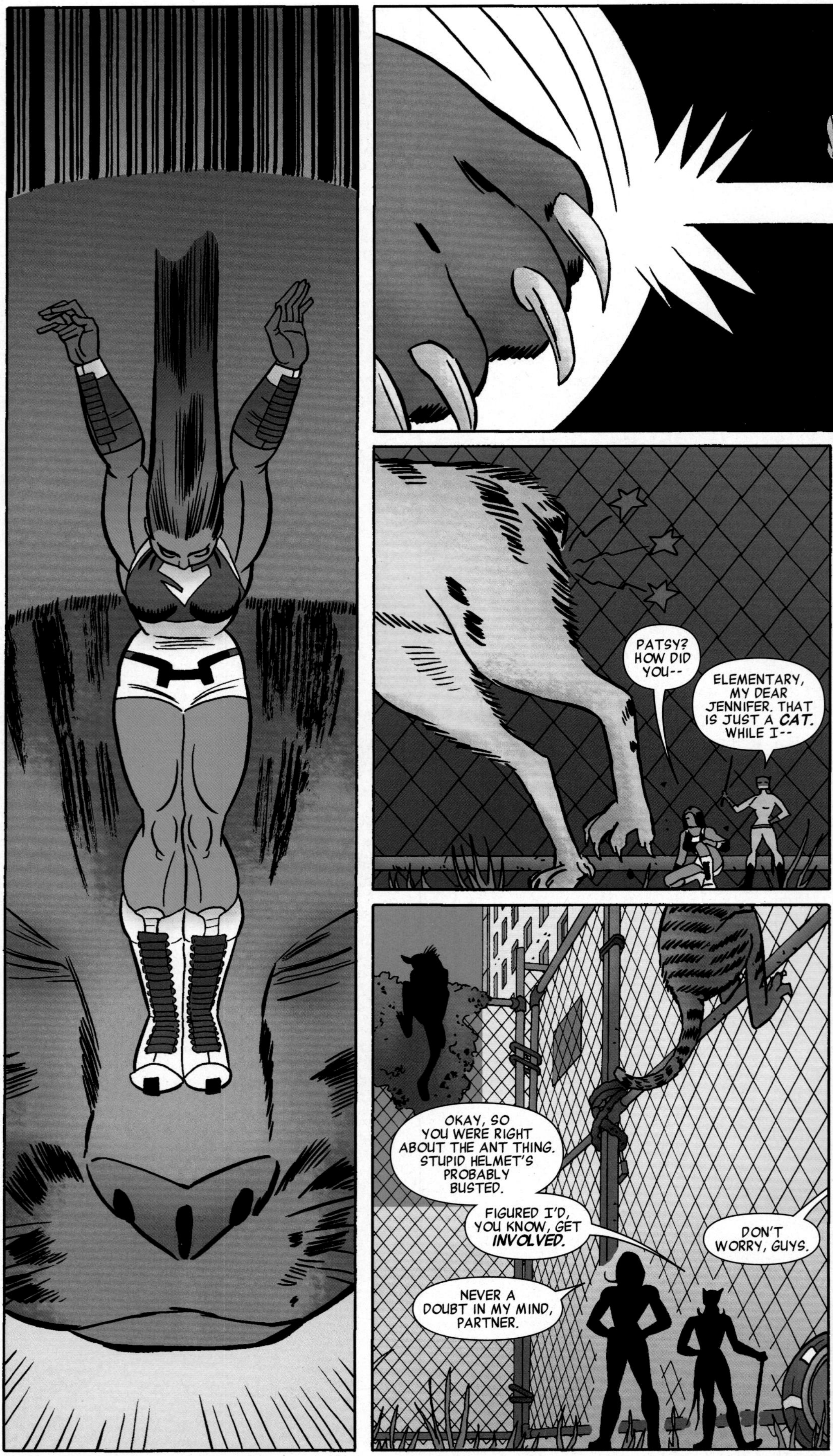
PATSY? HOW DID YOU--
ELEMENTARY, MY DEAR JENNIFER. THAT IS JUST A CAT. WHILE I--
OKAY, SO YOU WERE RIGHT ABOUT THE ANT THING. STUPID HELMET'S PROBABLY BUSTED.
FIGURED I'D, YOU KNOW, GET INVOLVED.
DON'T WORRY, GUYS.
NEVER A DOUBT IN MY MIND, PARTNER.

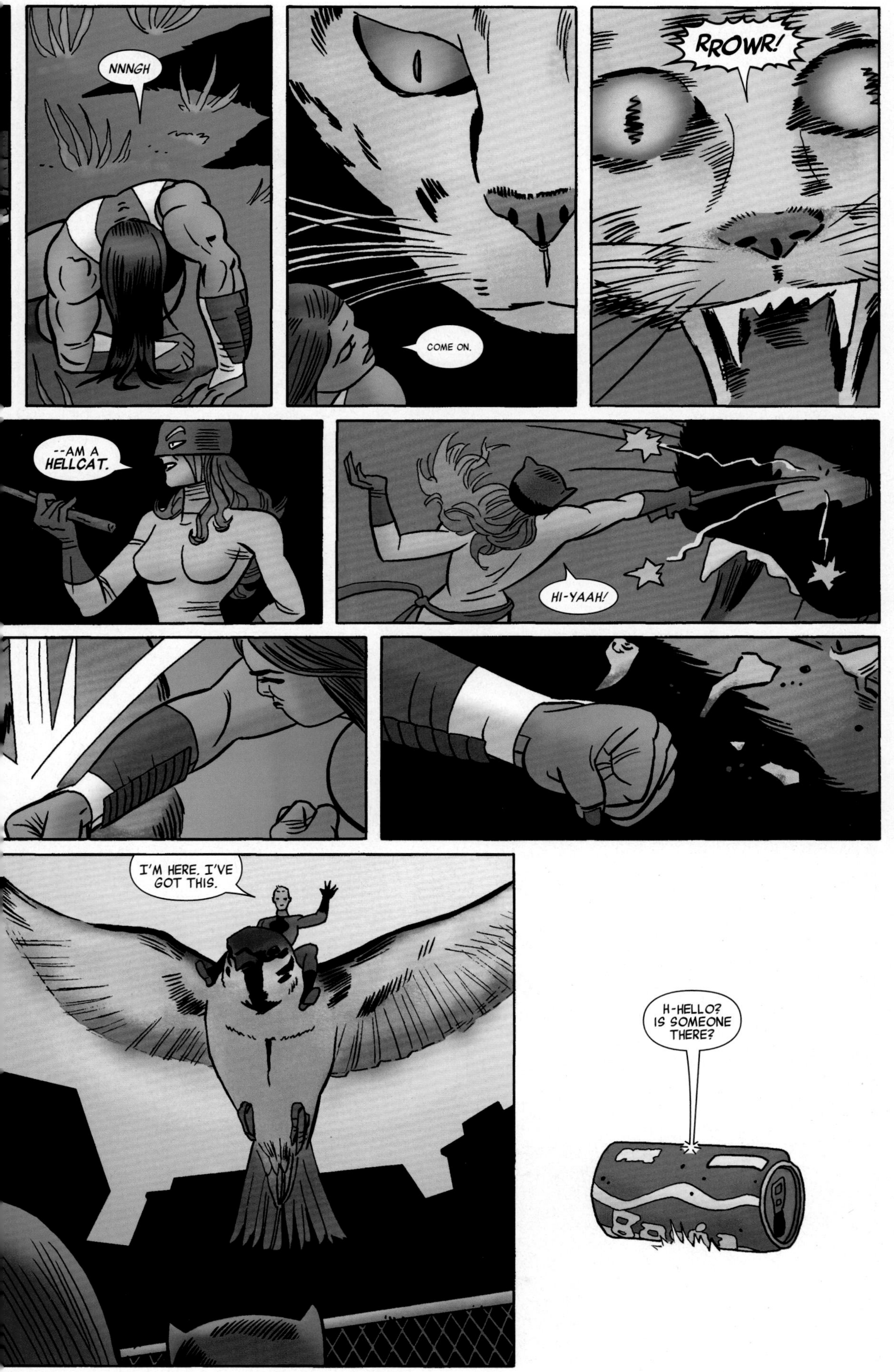
NNNGH
COME ON.
RROWR!
--AM A HELLCAT.
HI-YAAH!
I'M HERE. I'VE GOT THIS.
H-HELLO? IS SOMEONE THERE?

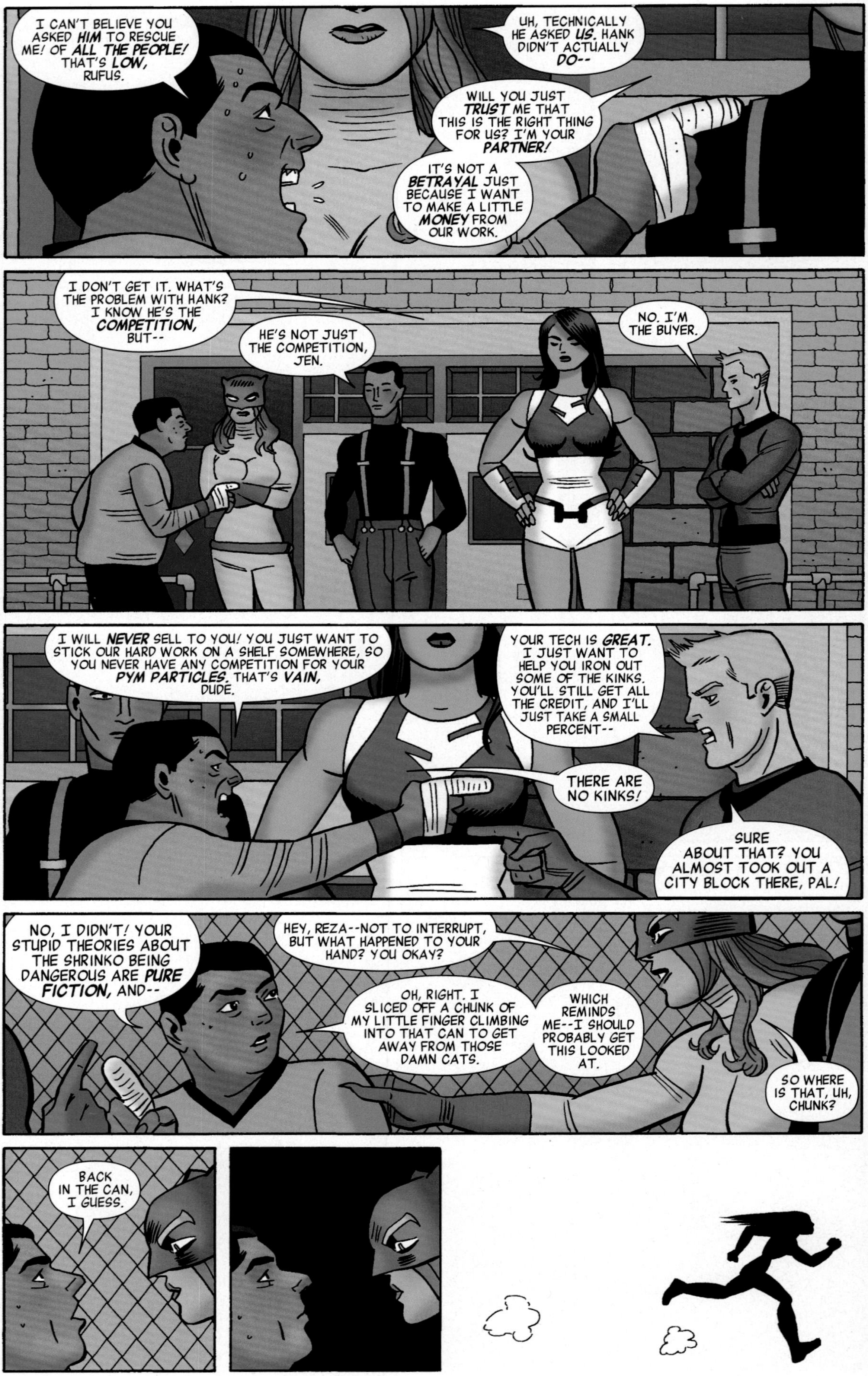
I CAN'T BELIEVE YOU ASKED HIM TO RESCUE ME! OF ALL THE PEOPLE! THAT'S LOW, RUFUS.
UH, TECHNICALLY HE ASKED US. HANK DIDN'T ACTUALLY DO--
WILL YOU JUST TRUST ME THAT THIS IS THE RIGHT THING FOR US? I'M YOUR PARTNER!
IT'S NOT A BETRAYAL JUST BECAUSE I WANT TO MAKE A LITTLE MONEY FROM OUR WORK.
I DON'T GET IT. WHAT'S THE PROBLEM WITH HANK? I KNOW HE'S THE COMPETITION, BUT--
HE'S NOT JUST THE COMPETITION, JEN.
NO. I'M THE BUYER.
I WILL NEVER SELL TO YOU! YOU JUST WANT TO STICK OUR HARD WORK ON A SHELF SOMEWHERE, SO YOU NEVER HAVE ANY COMPETITION FOR YOUR PYM PARTICLES. THAT'S VAIN, DUDE.
YOUR TECH IS GREAT. I JUST WANT TO HELP YOU IRON OUT SOME OF THE KINKS. YOU'LL STILL GET ALL THE CREDIT, AND I'LL JUST TAKE A SMALL PERCENT--
THERE ARE NO KINKS!
SURE ABOUT THAT? YOU ALMOST TOOK OUT A CITY BLOCK THERE, PAL!
NO, I DIDN'T! YOUR STUPID THEORIES ABOUT THE SHRINKO BEING DANGEROUS ARE PURE FICTION, AND--
HEY, REZA--NOT TO INTERRUPT, BUT WHAT HAPPENED TO YOUR HAND? YOU OKAY?
OH, RIGHT. I SLICED OFF A CHUNK OF MY LITTLE FINGER CLIMBING INTO THAT CAN TO GET AWAY FROM THOSE DAMN CATS.
WHICH REMINDS ME--I SHOULD PROBABLY GET THIS LOOKED AT.
SO WHERE IS THAT, UH, CHUNK?
BACK IN THE CAN, I GUESS.

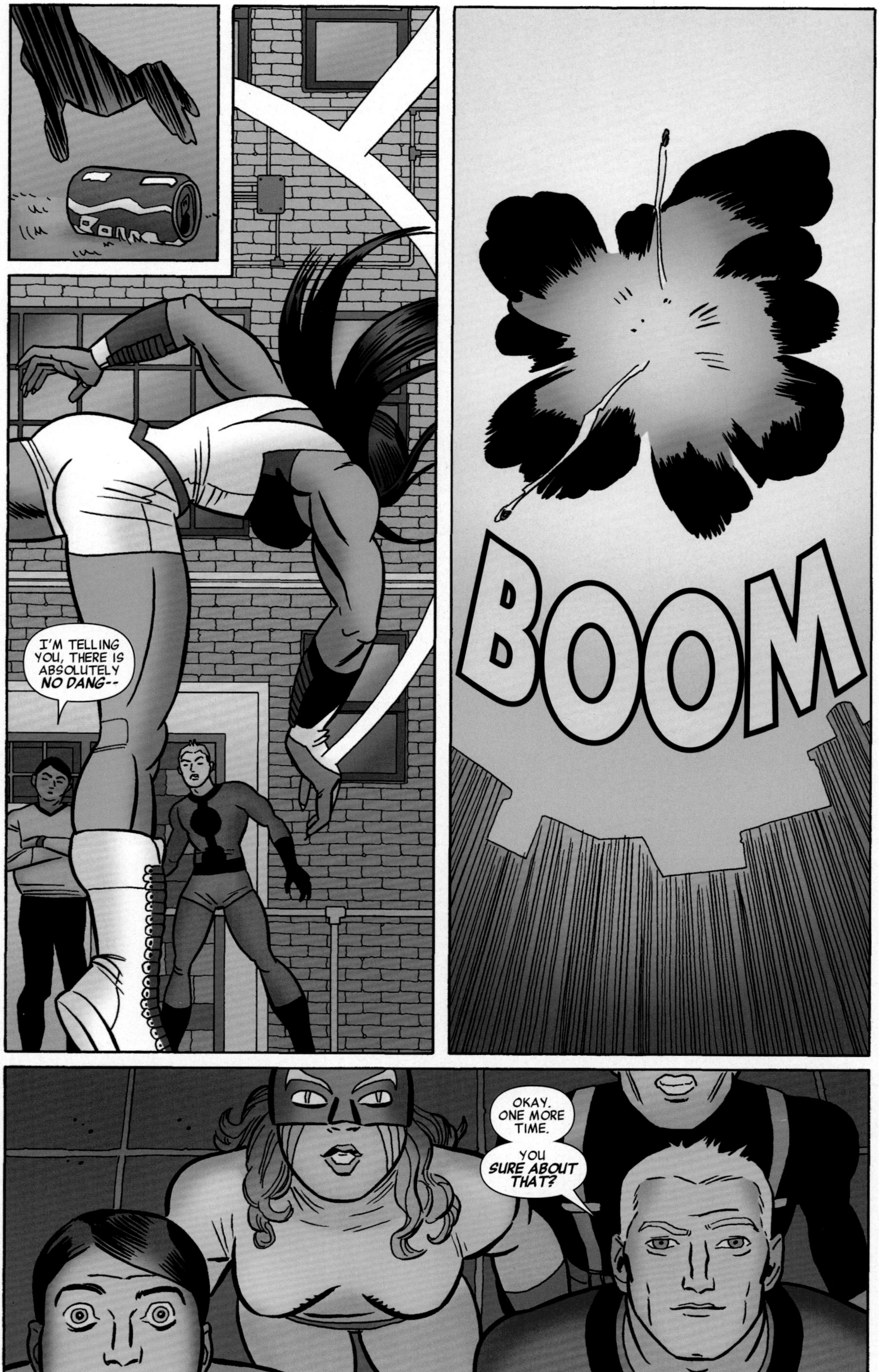

I'M TELLING YOU, THERE IS ABSOLUTELY NO DANG--
BOOM
OKAY. ONE MORE TIME.
YOU SURE ABOUT THAT?

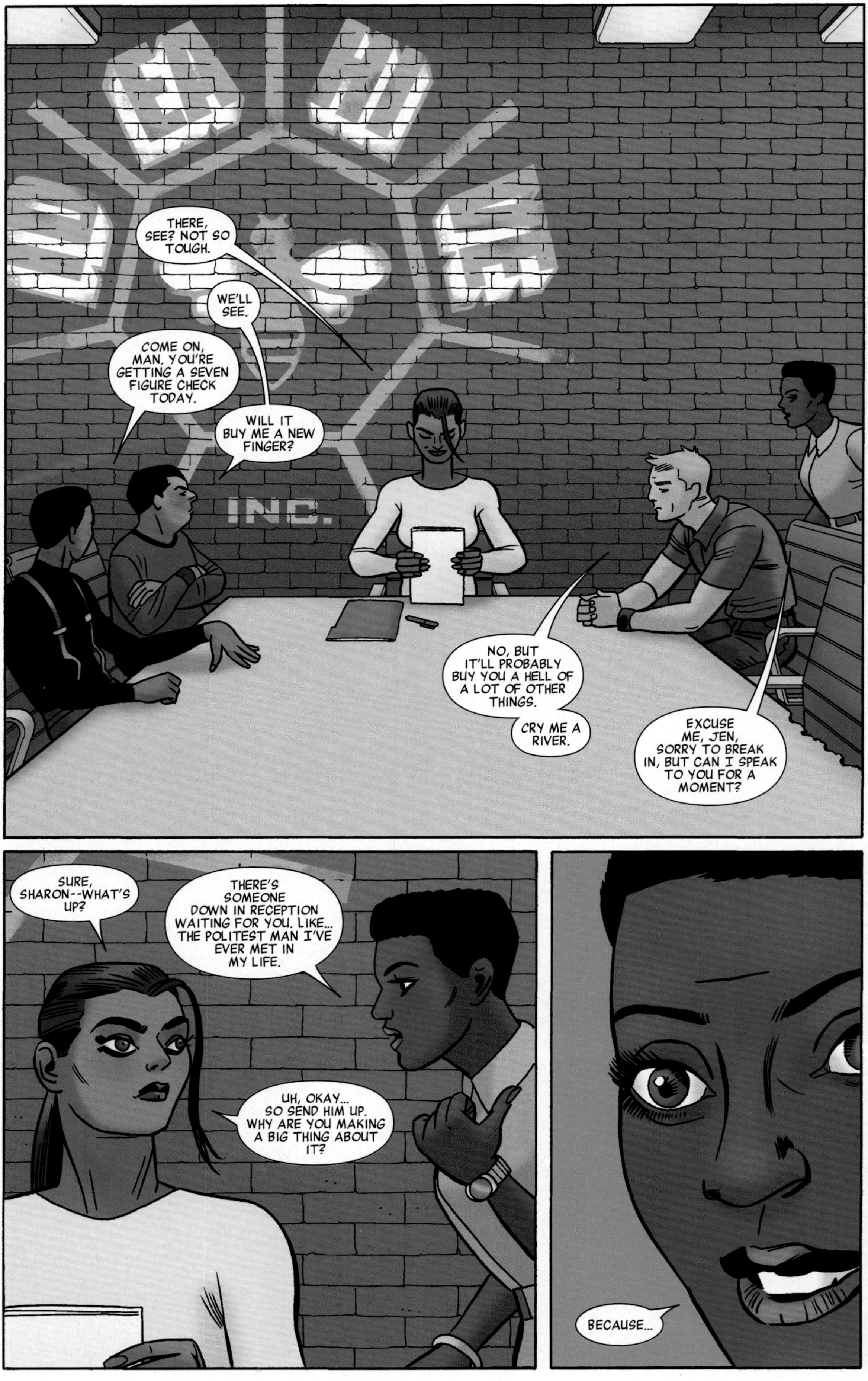
THERE, SEE? NOT SO TOUGH.
WE'LL SEE.
COME ON, MAN. YOU'RE GETTING A SEVEN FIGURE CHECK TODAY.
WILL IT BUY ME A NEW FINGER?
INC.
NO, BUT IT'LL PROBABLY BUY YOU A HELL OF A LOT OF OTHER THINGS.
CRY ME A RIVER.
EXCUSE ME, JEN, SORRY TO BREAK IN, BUT CAN I SPEAK TO YOU FOR A MOMENT?
SURE, SHARON--WHAT'S UP?
THERE'S SOMEONE DOWN IN RECEPTION WAITING FOR YOU. LIKE... THE POLITEST MAN I'VE EVER MET IN MY LIFE.
UH, OKAY... SO SEND HIM UP. WHY ARE YOU MAKING A BIG THING ABOUT IT?
BECAUSE...

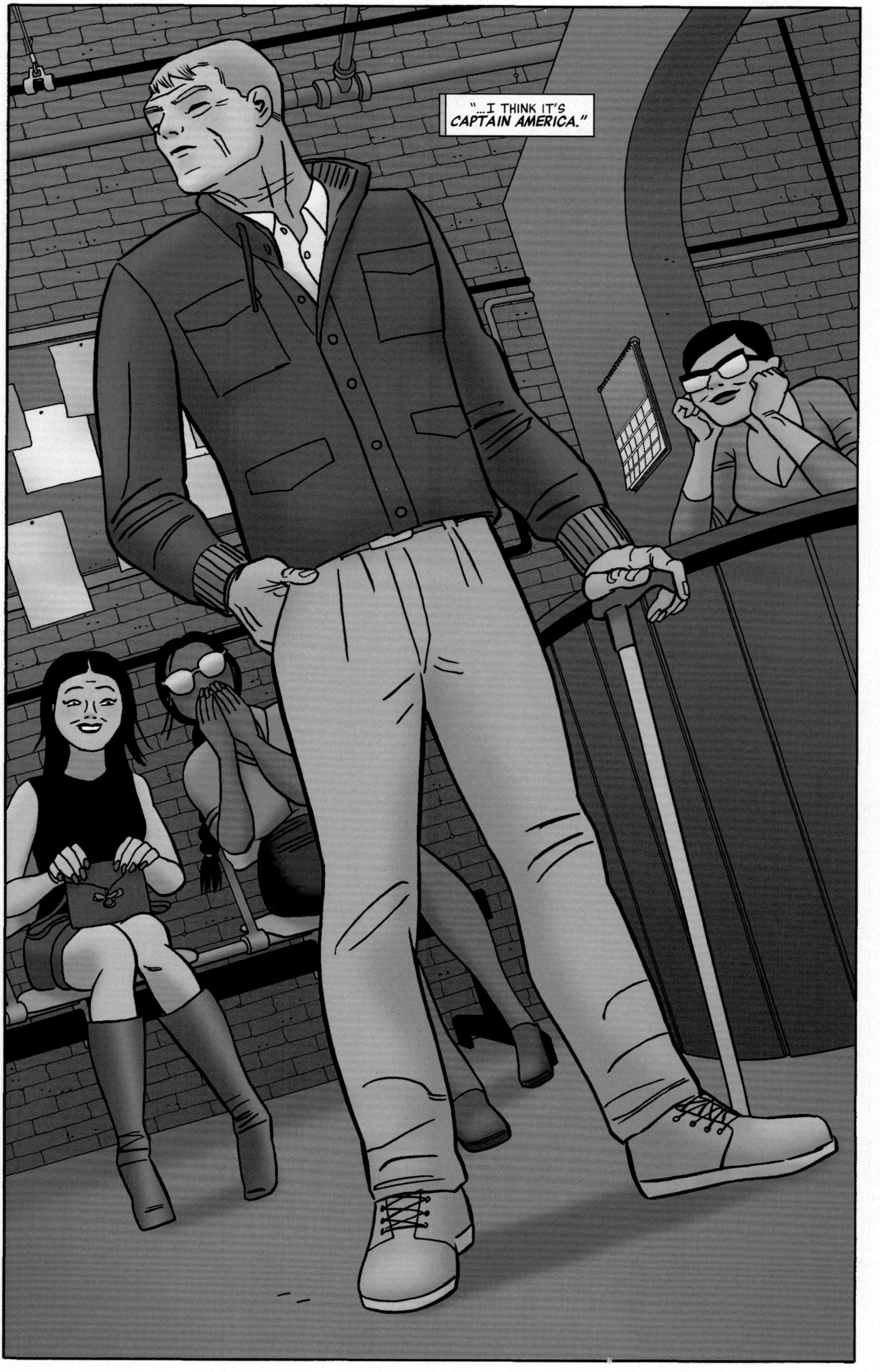
"...I THINK IT'S CAPTAIN AMERICA."

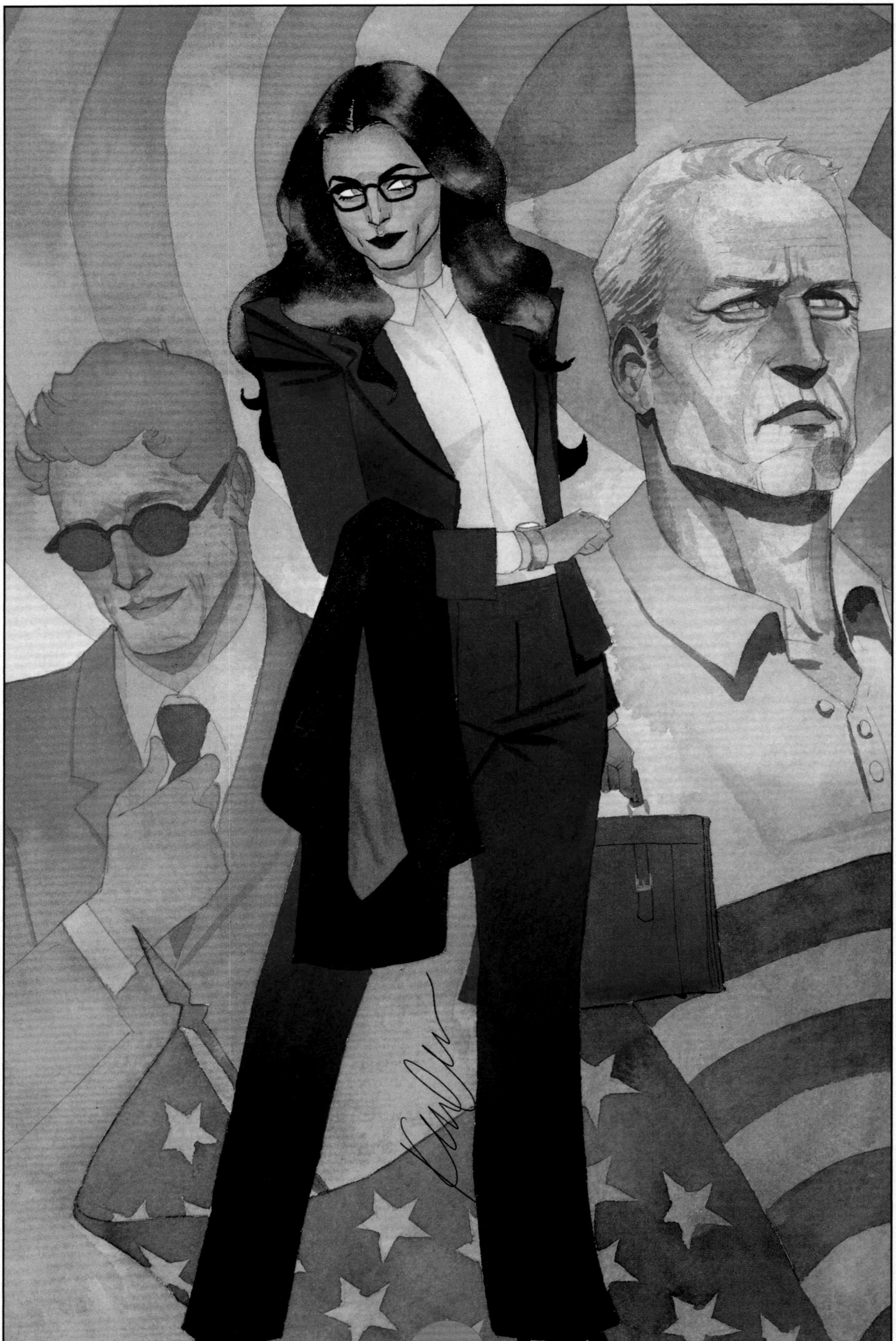

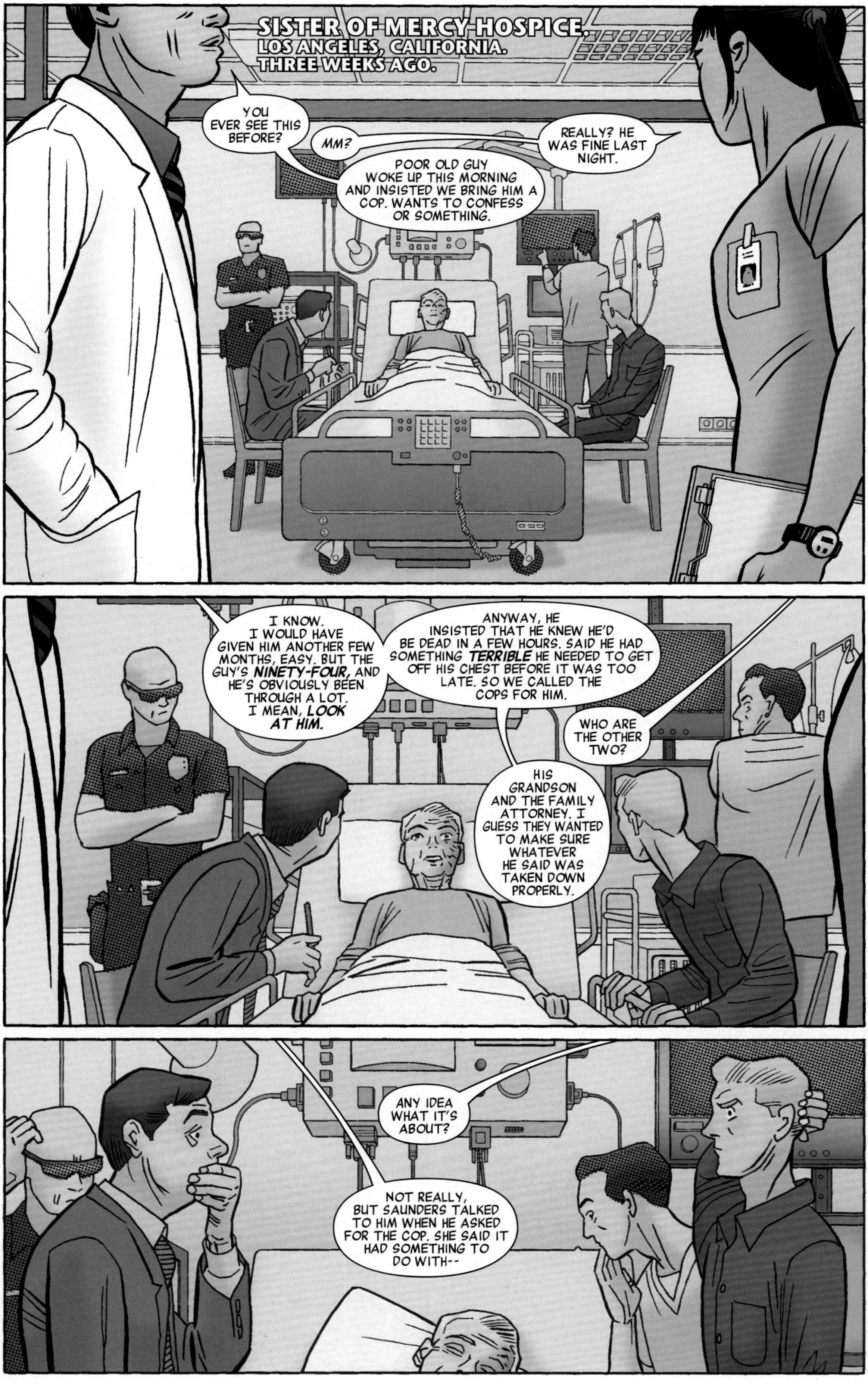
SISTER OF MERCY HOSPICE.
LOS ANGELES, CALIFORNIA.
THREE WEEKS AGO.
YOU EVER SEE THIS BEFORE?
MM?
REALLY? HE WAS FINE LAST NIGHT.
POOR OLD GUY WOKE UP THIS MORNING AND INSISTED WE BRING HIM A COP. WANTS TO CONFESS OR SOMETHING.
I KNOW. I WOULD HAVE GIVEN HIM ANOTHER FEW MONTHS, EASY. BUT THE GUY'S NINETY-FOUR, AND HE'S OBVIOUSLY BEEN THROUGH A LOT. I MEAN, LOOK AT HIM.
ANYWAY, HE INSISTED THAT HE KNEW HE'D BE DEAD IN A FEW HOURS. SAID HE HAD SOMETHING TERRIBLE HE NEEDED TO GET OFF HIS CHEST BEFORE IT WAS TOO LATE. SO WE CALLED THE COPS FOR HIM.
WHO ARE THE OTHER TWO?
HIS GRANDSON AND THE FAMILY ATTORNEY. I GUESS THEY WANTED TO MAKE SURE WHATEVER HE SAID WAS TAKEN DOWN PROPERLY.
ANY IDEA WHAT IT'S ABOUT?
NOT REALLY, BUT SAUNDERS TALKED TO HIM WHEN HE ASKED FOR THE COP. SHE SAID IT HAD SOMETHING TO DO WITH--

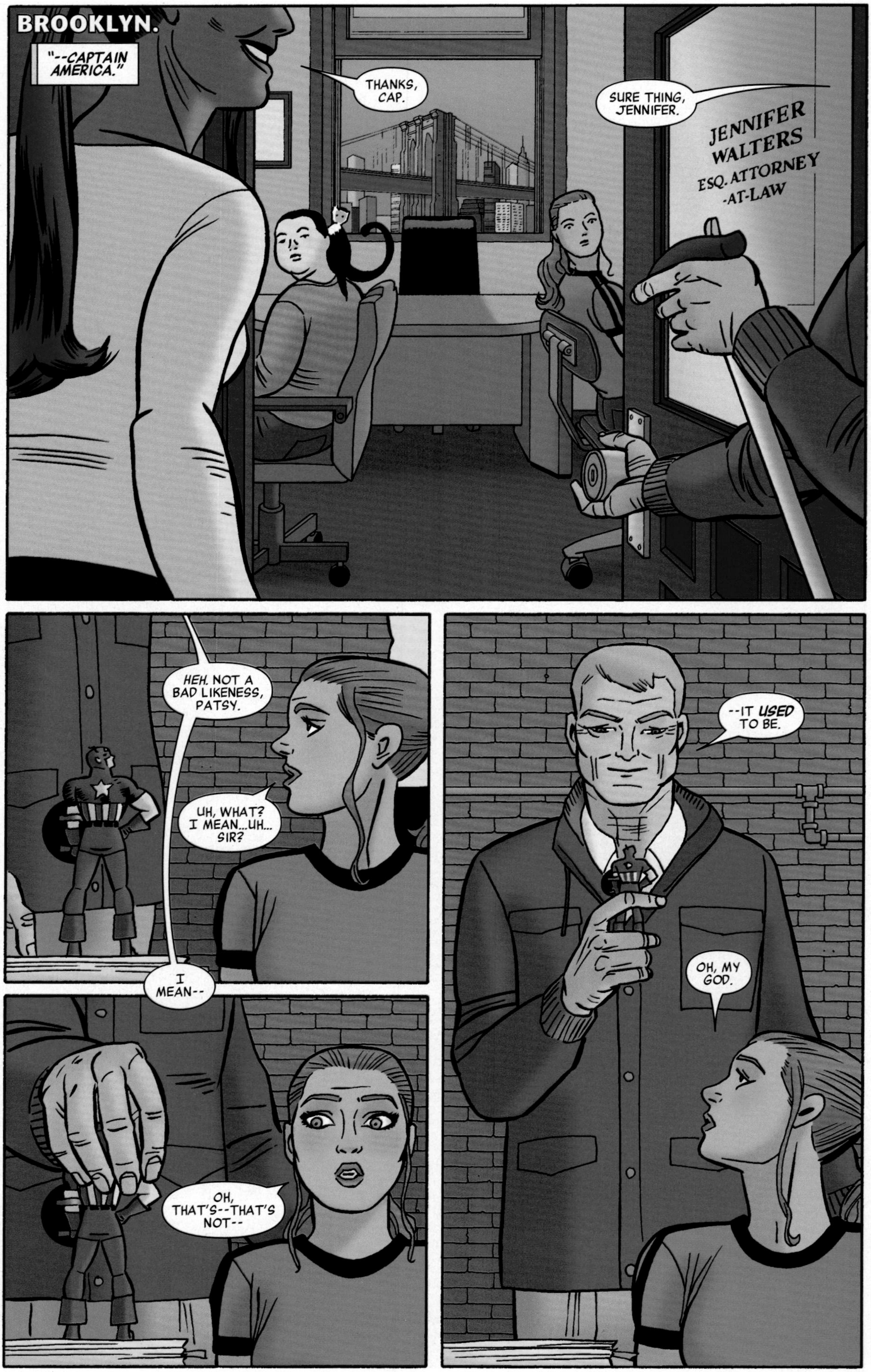
BROOKLYN.
"--CAPTAIN AMERICA."
THANKS, CAP.
SURE THING, JENNIFER.
JENNIFER WALTERS ESQ. ATTORNEY -AT-LAW
HEH. NOT A BAD LIKENESS, PATSY.
UH, WHAT? I MEAN...UH... SIR?
I MEAN--
--IT USED TO BE.
OH, THAT'S--THAT'S NOT--
OH, MY GOD.

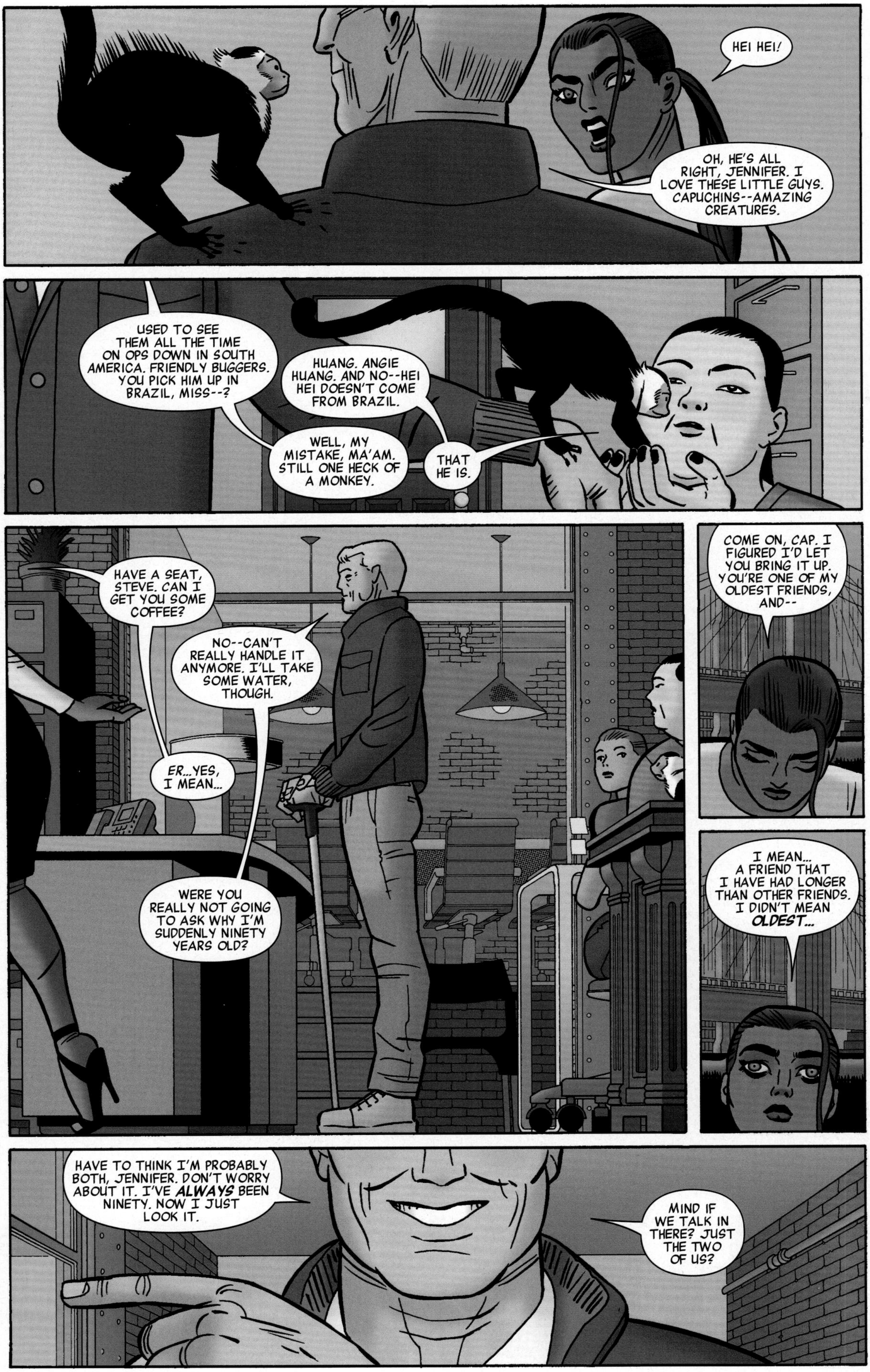
HEI HEI!
OH, HE'S ALL RIGHT, JENNIFER. I LOVE THESE LITTLE GUYS. CAPUCHINS--AMAZING CREATURES.
USED TO SEE THEM ALL THE TIME ON OPS DOWN IN SOUTH AMERICA. FRIENDLY BUGGERS. YOU PICK HIM UP IN BRAZIL, MISS--?
HUANG. ANGIE HUANG. AND NO--HEI HEI DOESN'T COME FROM BRAZIL.
WELL, MY MISTAKE, MA'AM. STILL ONE HECK OF A MONKEY.
THAT HE IS.
HAVE A SEAT, STEVE. CAN I GET YOU SOME COFFEE?
NO--CAN'T REALLY HANDLE IT ANYMORE. I'LL TAKE SOME WATER, THOUGH.
ER...YES, I MEAN...
WERE YOU REALLY NOT GOING TO ASK WHY I'M SUDDENLY NINETY YEARS OLD?
COME ON, CAP. I FIGURED I'D LET YOU BRING IT UP. YOU'RE ONE OF MY OLDEST FRIENDS, AND--
I MEAN... A FRIEND THAT I HAVE HAD LONGER THAN OTHER FRIENDS. I DIDN'T MEAN OLDEST...
HAVE TO THINK I'M PROBABLY BOTH, JENNIFER. DON'T WORRY ABOUT IT. I'VE ALWAYS BEEN NINETY. NOW I JUST LOOK IT.
MIND IF WE TALK IN THERE? JUST THE TWO OF US?

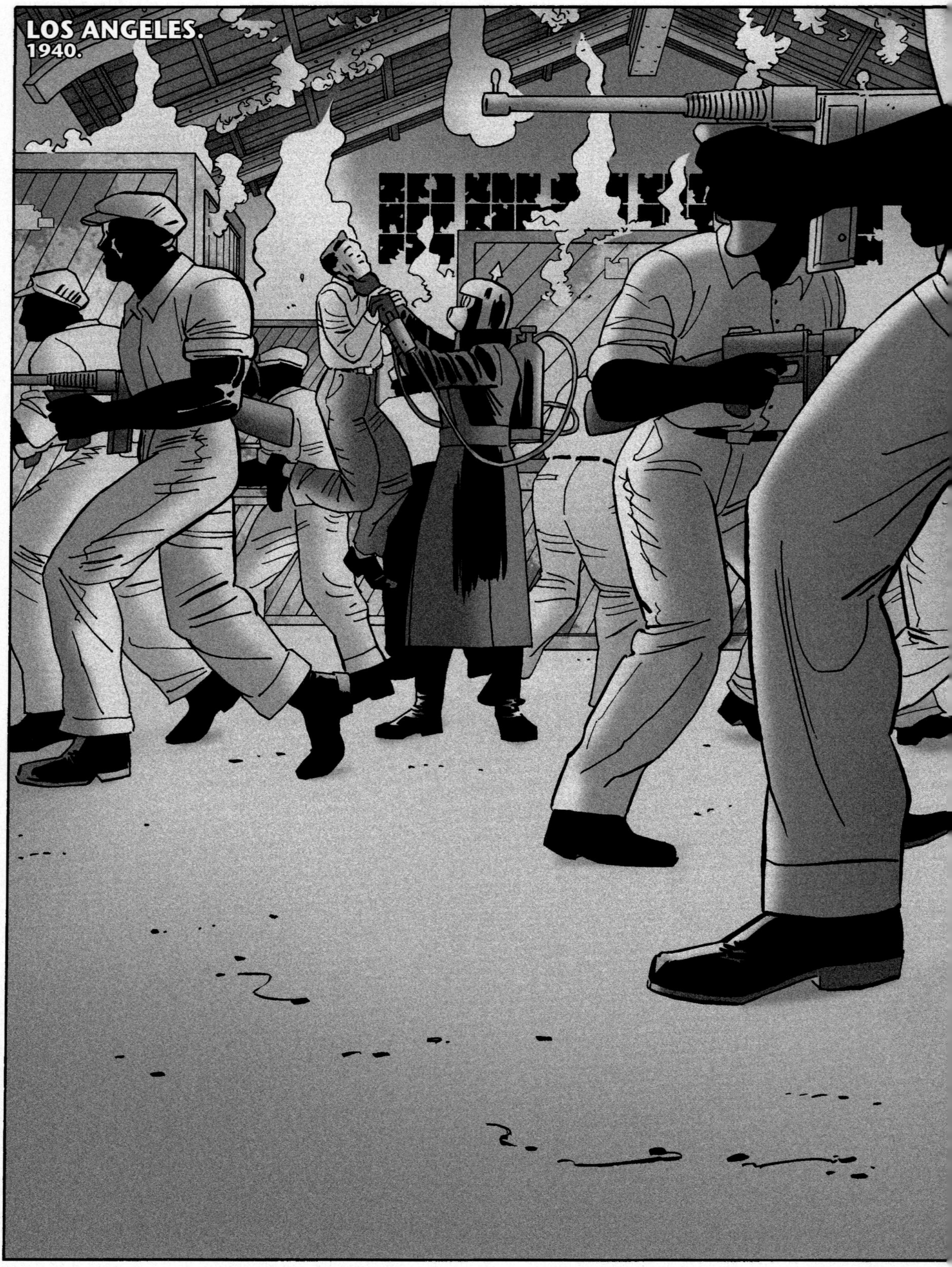
LOS ANGELES.
1940.

THE GOOD O

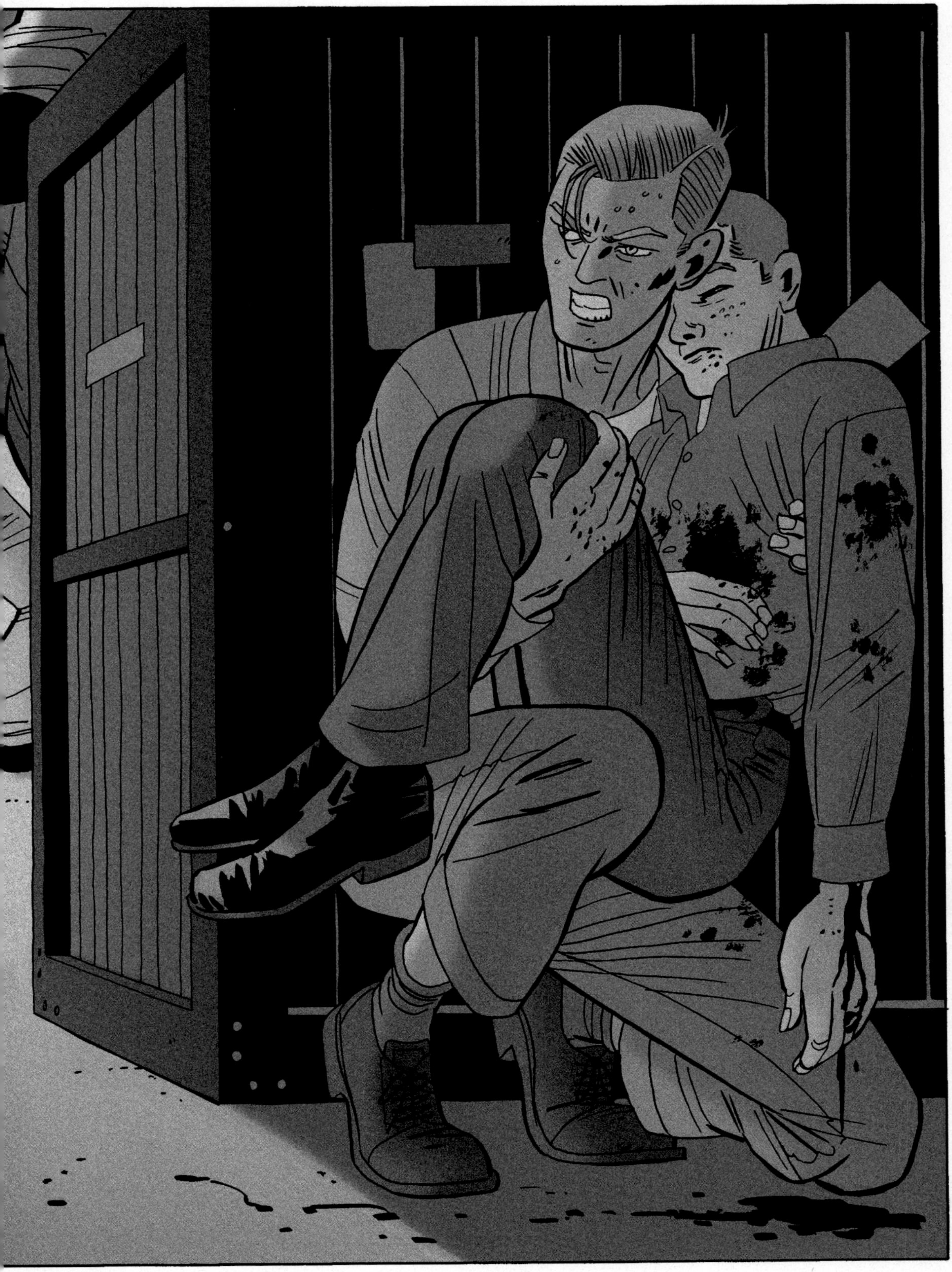

D DAYS Part 1

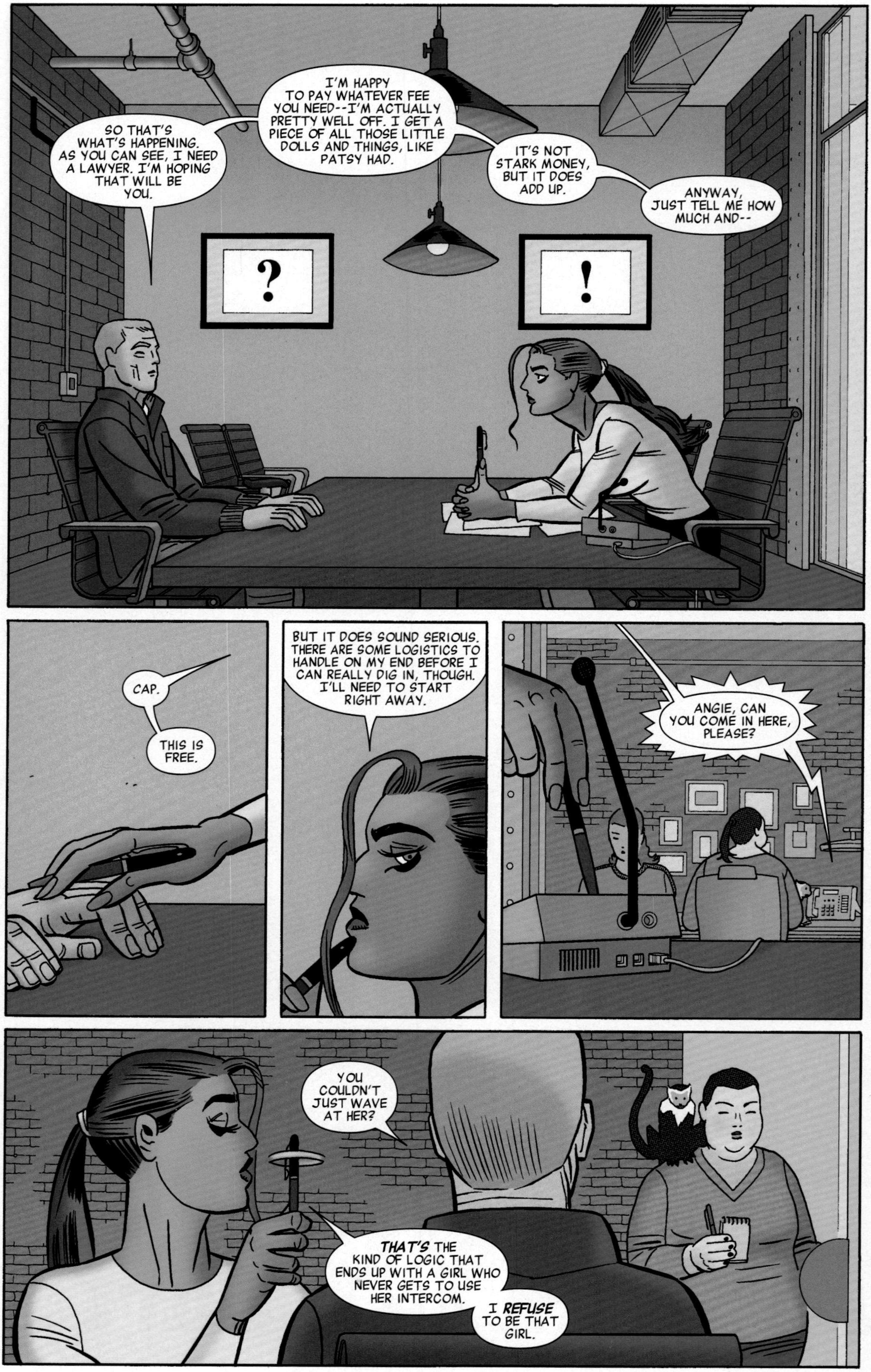
SO THAT'S WHAT'S HAPPENING. AS YOU CAN SEE, I NEED A LAWYER. I'M HOPING THAT WILL BE YOU.
I'M HAPPY TO PAY WHATEVER FEE YOU NEED--I'M ACTUALLY PRETTY WELL OFF. I GET A PIECE OF ALL THOSE LITTLE DOLLS AND THINGS, LIKE PATSY HAD.
IT'S NOT STARK MONEY, BUT IT DOES ADD UP.
ANYWAY, JUST TELL ME HOW MUCH AND--
?
!
CAP.
THIS IS FREE.
BUT IT DOES SOUND SERIOUS. THERE ARE SOME LOGISTICS TO HANDLE ON MY END BEFORE I CAN REALLY DIG IN, THOUGH. I'LL NEED TO START RIGHT AWAY.
ANGIE, CAN YOU COME IN HERE, PLEASE?
YOU COULDN'T JUST WAVE AT HER?
THAT'S THE KIND OF LOGIC THAT ENDS UP WITH A GIRL WHO NEVER GETS TO USE HER INTERCOM.
I REFUSE TO BE THAT GIRL.

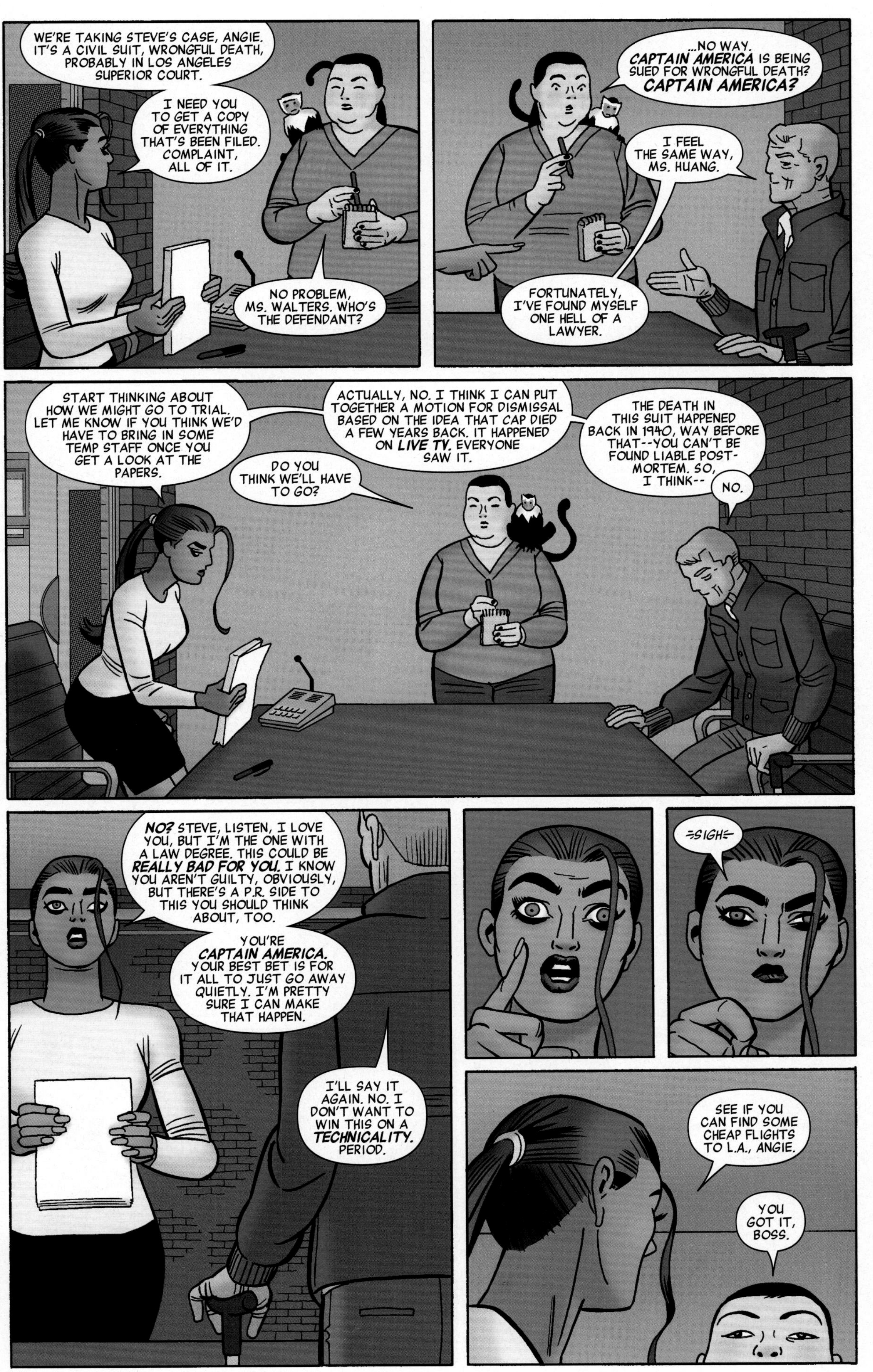
WE'RE TAKING STEVE'S CASE, ANGIE. IT'S A CIVIL SUIT, WRONGFUL DEATH, PROBABLY IN LOS ANGELES SUPERIOR COURT.
I NEED YOU TO GET A COPY OF EVERYTHING THAT'S BEEN FILED. COMPLAINT, ALL OF IT.
NO PROBLEM, MS. WALTERS. WHO'S THE DEFENDANT?
...NO WAY. CAPTAIN AMERICA IS BEING SUED FOR WRONGFUL DEATH? CAPTAIN AMERICA?
I FEEL THE SAME WAY, MS. HUANG.
FORTUNATELY, I'VE FOUND MYSELF ONE HELL OF A LAWYER.
START THINKING ABOUT HOW WE MIGHT GO TO TRIAL. LET ME KNOW IF YOU THINK WE'D HAVE TO BRING IN SOME TEMP STAFF ONCE YOU GET A LOOK AT THE PAPERS.
DO YOU THINK WE'LL HAVE TO GO?
ACTUALLY, NO. I THINK I CAN PUT TOGETHER A MOTION FOR DISMISSAL BASED ON THE IDEA THAT CAP DIED A FEW YEARS BACK. IT HAPPENED ON LIVE TV. EVERYONE SAW IT.
THE DEATH IN THIS SUIT HAPPENED BACK IN 1940, WAY BEFORE THAT--YOU CAN'T BE FOUND LIABLE POST-MORTEM. SO, I THINK--
NO.
NO? STEVE, LISTEN, I LOVE YOU, BUT I'M THE ONE WITH A LAW DEGREE. THIS COULD BE REALLY BAD FOR YOU. I KNOW YOU AREN'T GUILTY, OBVIOUSLY, BUT THERE'S A P.R. SIDE TO THIS YOU SHOULD THINK ABOUT, TOO.
YOU'RE CAPTAIN AMERICA. YOUR BEST BET IS FOR IT ALL TO JUST GO AWAY QUIETLY. I'M PRETTY SURE I CAN MAKE THAT HAPPEN.
I'LL SAY IT AGAIN. NO. I DON'T WANT TO WIN THIS ON A TECHNICALITY. PERIOD.
=SIGH=
SEE IF YOU CAN FIND SOME CHEAP FLIGHTS TO L.A., ANGIE.
YOU GOT IT, BOSS.

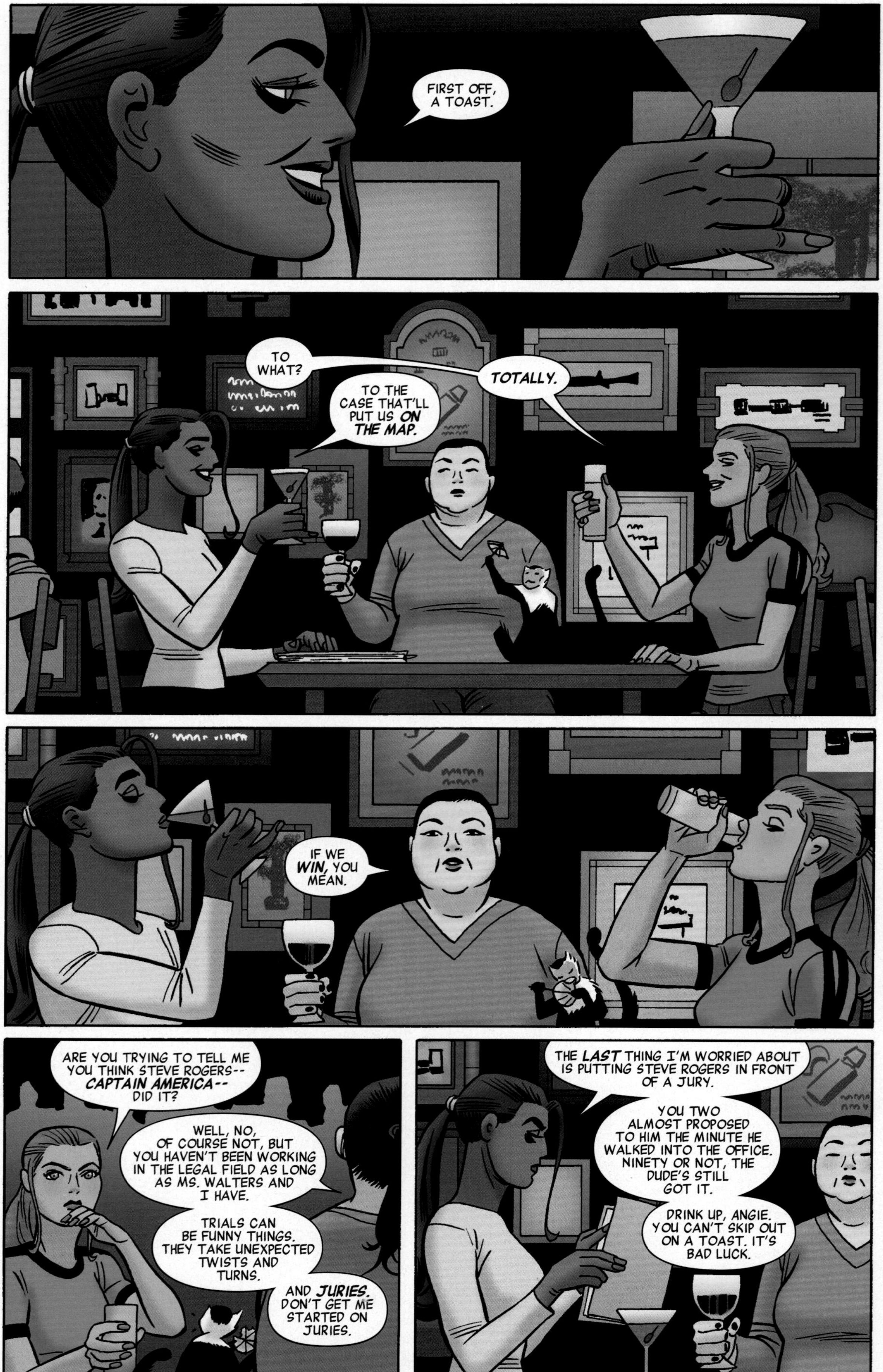
FIRST OFF, A TOAST.
TO WHAT?
TOTALLY.
TO THE CASE THAT'LL PUT US ON THE MAP.
IF WE WIN, YOU MEAN.
ARE YOU TRYING TO TELL ME YOU THINK STEVE ROGERS-- CAPTAIN AMERICA-- DID IT?
WELL, NO, OF COURSE NOT, BUT YOU HAVEN'T BEEN WORKING IN THE LEGAL FIELD AS LONG AS MS. WALTERS AND I HAVE.
TRIALS CAN BE FUNNY THINGS. THEY TAKE UNEXPECTED TWISTS AND TURNS.
AND JURIES. DON'T GET ME STARTED ON JURIES.
THE LAST THING I'M WORRIED ABOUT IS PUTTING STEVE ROGERS IN FRONT OF A JURY.
YOU TWO ALMOST PROPOSED TO HIM THE MINUTE HE WALKED INTO THE OFFICE. NINETY OR NOT, THE DUDE'S STILL GOT IT.
DRINK UP, ANGIE. YOU CAN'T SKIP OUT ON A TOAST. IT'S BAD LUCK.

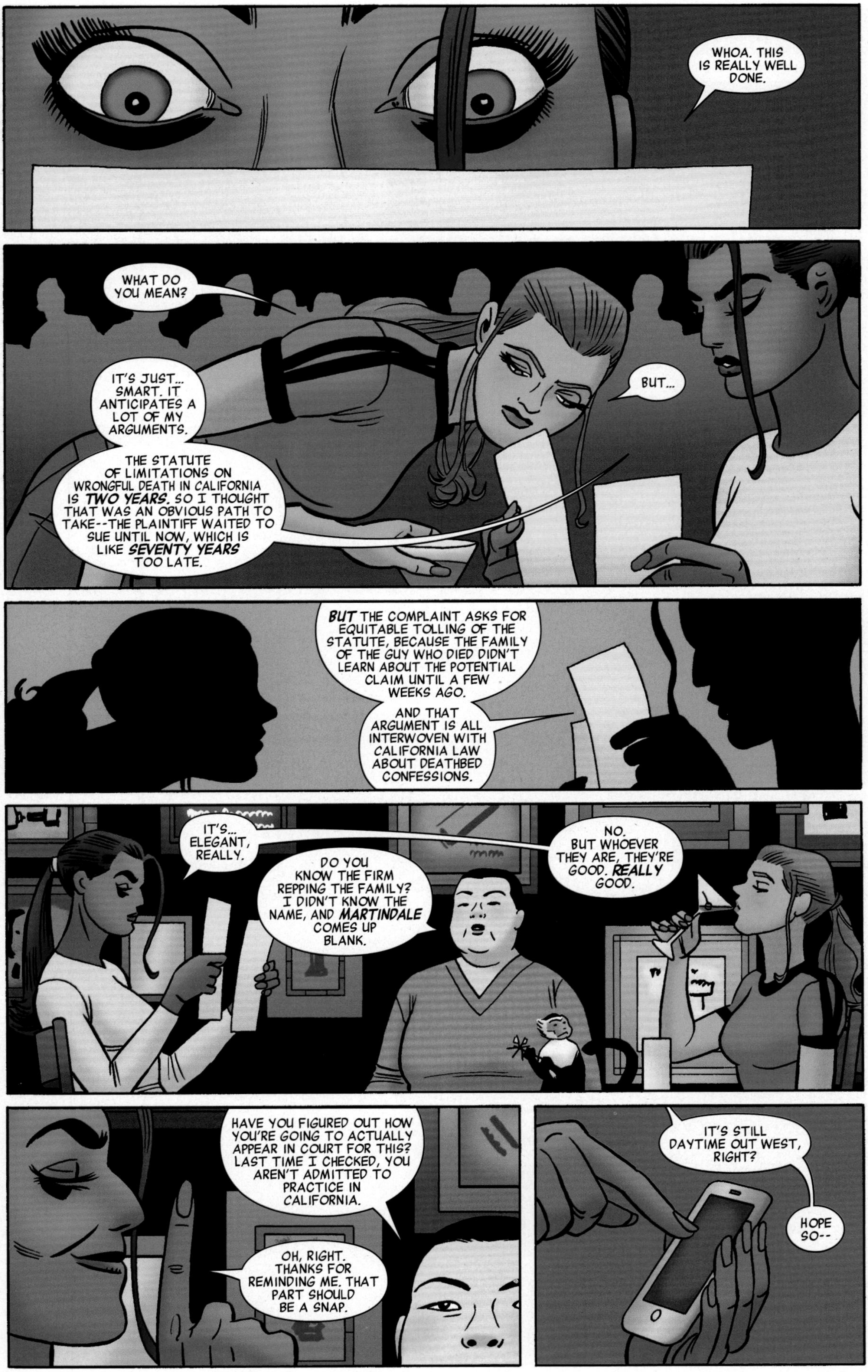
WHOA. THIS IS REALLY WELL DONE.
WHAT DO YOU MEAN?
IT'S JUST... SMART. IT ANTICIPATES A LOT OF MY ARGUMENTS.
BUT...
THE STATUTE OF LIMITATIONS ON WRONGFUL DEATH IN CALIFORNIA IS TWO YEARS. SO I THOUGHT THAT WAS AN OBVIOUS PATH TO TAKE--THE PLAINTIFF WAITED TO SUE UNTIL NOW, WHICH IS LIKE SEVENTY YEARS TOO LATE.
BUT THE COMPLAINT ASKS FOR EQUITABLE TOLLING OF THE STATUTE, BECAUSE THE FAMILY OF THE GUY WHO DIED DIDN'T LEARN ABOUT THE POTENTIAL CLAIM UNTIL A FEW WEEKS AGO.
AND THAT ARGUMENT IS ALL INTERWOVEN WITH CALIFORNIA LAW ABOUT DEATHBED CONFESSIONS.
IT'S... ELEGANT, REALLY.
DO YOU KNOW THE FIRM REPPING THE FAMILY? I DIDN'T KNOW THE NAME, AND MARTINDALE COMES UP BLANK.
NO. BUT WHOEVER THEY ARE, THEY'RE GOOD. REALLY GOOD.
HAVE YOU FIGURED OUT HOW YOU'RE GOING TO ACTUALLY APPEAR IN COURT FOR THIS? LAST TIME I CHECKED, YOU AREN'T ADMITTED TO PRACTICE IN CALIFORNIA.
OH, RIGHT. THANKS FOR REMINDING ME. THAT PART SHOULD BE A SNAP.
IT'S STILL DAYTIME OUT WEST, RIGHT?
HOPE SO--

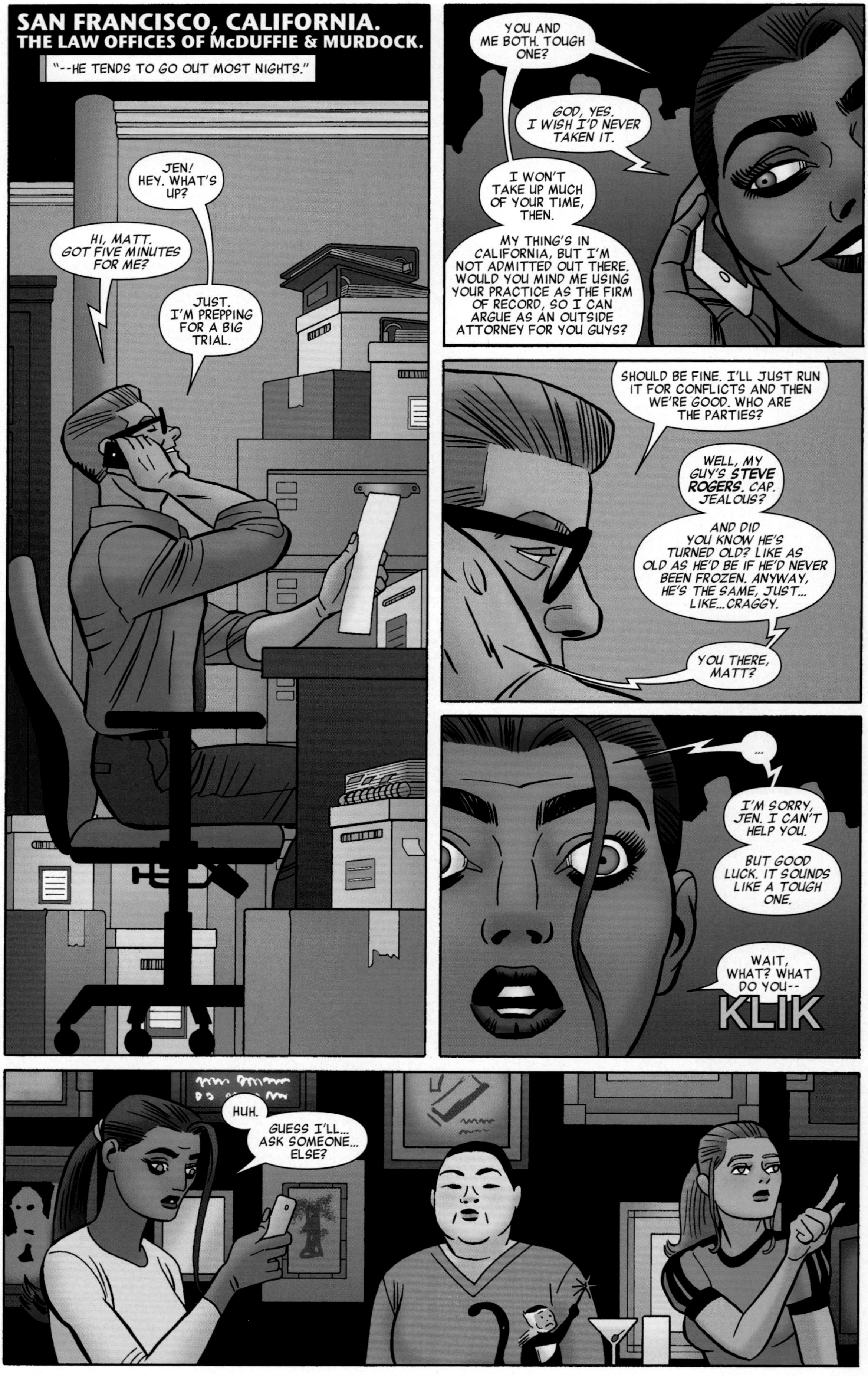
SAN FRANCISCO, CALIFORNIA.
THE LAW OFFICES OF McDUFFIE & MURDOCK.
"--HE TENDS TO GO OUT MOST NIGHTS."
JEN! HEY. WHAT'S UP?
HI, MATT. GOT FIVE MINUTES FOR ME?
JUST. I'M PREPPING FOR A BIG TRIAL.
YOU AND ME BOTH. TOUGH ONE?
GOD, YES. I WISH I'D NEVER TAKEN IT.
I WON'T TAKE UP MUCH OF YOUR TIME, THEN.
MY THING'S IN CALIFORNIA, BUT I'M NOT ADMITTED OUT THERE. WOULD YOU MIND ME USING YOUR PRACTICE AS THE FIRM OF RECORD, SO I CAN ARGUE AS AN OUTSIDE ATTORNEY FOR YOU GUYS?
SHOULD BE FINE. I'LL JUST RUN IT FOR CONFLICTS AND THEN WE'RE GOOD. WHO ARE THE PARTIES?
WELL, MY GUY'S STEVE ROGERS. CAP. JEALOUS?
AND DID YOU KNOW HE'S TURNED OLD? LIKE AS OLD AS HE'D BE IF HE'D NEVER BEEN FROZEN. ANYWAY, HE'S THE SAME, JUST... LIKE...CRAGGY.
YOU THERE, MATT?
...
I'M SORRY, JEN. I CAN'T HELP YOU.
BUT GOOD LUCK. IT SOUNDS LIKE A TOUGH ONE.
WAIT, WHAT? WHAT DO YOU--
KLIK
HUH.
GUESS I'LL... ASK SOMEONE... ELSE?

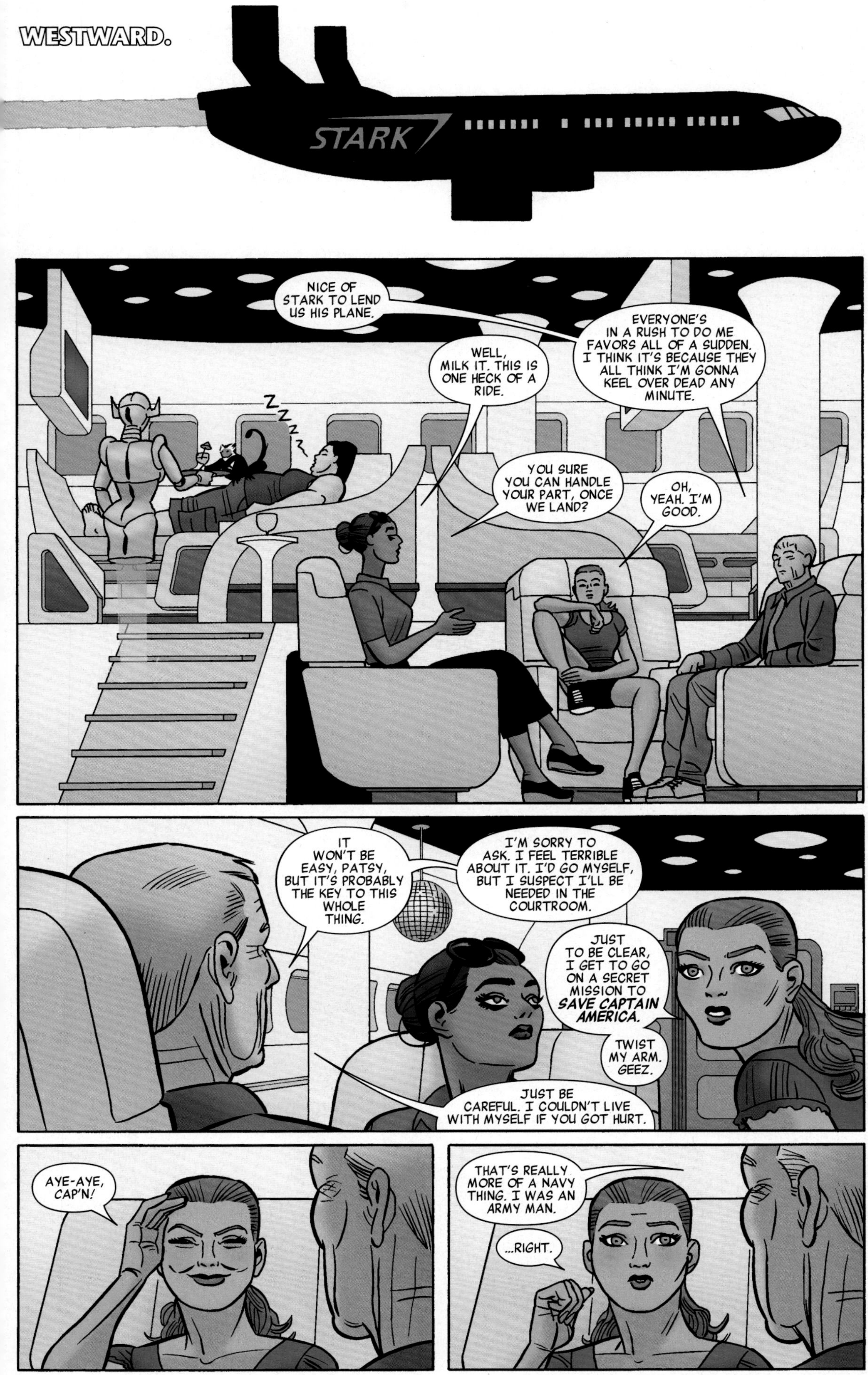
WESTWARD.
STARK
NICE OF STARK TO LEND US HIS PLANE.
EVERYONE'S IN A RUSH TO DO ME FAVORS ALL OF A SUDDEN. I THINK IT'S BECAUSE THEY ALL THINK I'M GONNA KEEL OVER DEAD ANY MINUTE.
WELL, MILK IT. THIS IS ONE HECK OF A RIDE.
ZZZZ
YOU SURE YOU CAN HANDLE YOUR PART, ONCE WE LAND?
OH, YEAH. I'M GOOD.
IT WON'T BE EASY, PATSY, BUT IT'S PROBABLY THE KEY TO THIS WHOLE THING.
I'M SORRY TO ASK. I FEEL TERRIBLE ABOUT IT. I'D GO MYSELF, BUT I SUSPECT I'LL BE NEEDED IN THE COURTROOM.
JUST TO BE CLEAR, I GET TO GO ON A SECRET MISSION TO SAVE CAPTAIN AMERICA.
TWIST MY ARM. GEEZ.
JUST BE CAREFUL. I COULDN'T LIVE WITH MYSELF IF YOU GOT HURT.
AYE-AYE, CAP'N!
THAT'S REALLY MORE OF A NAVY THING. I WAS AN ARMY MAN.
...RIGHT.

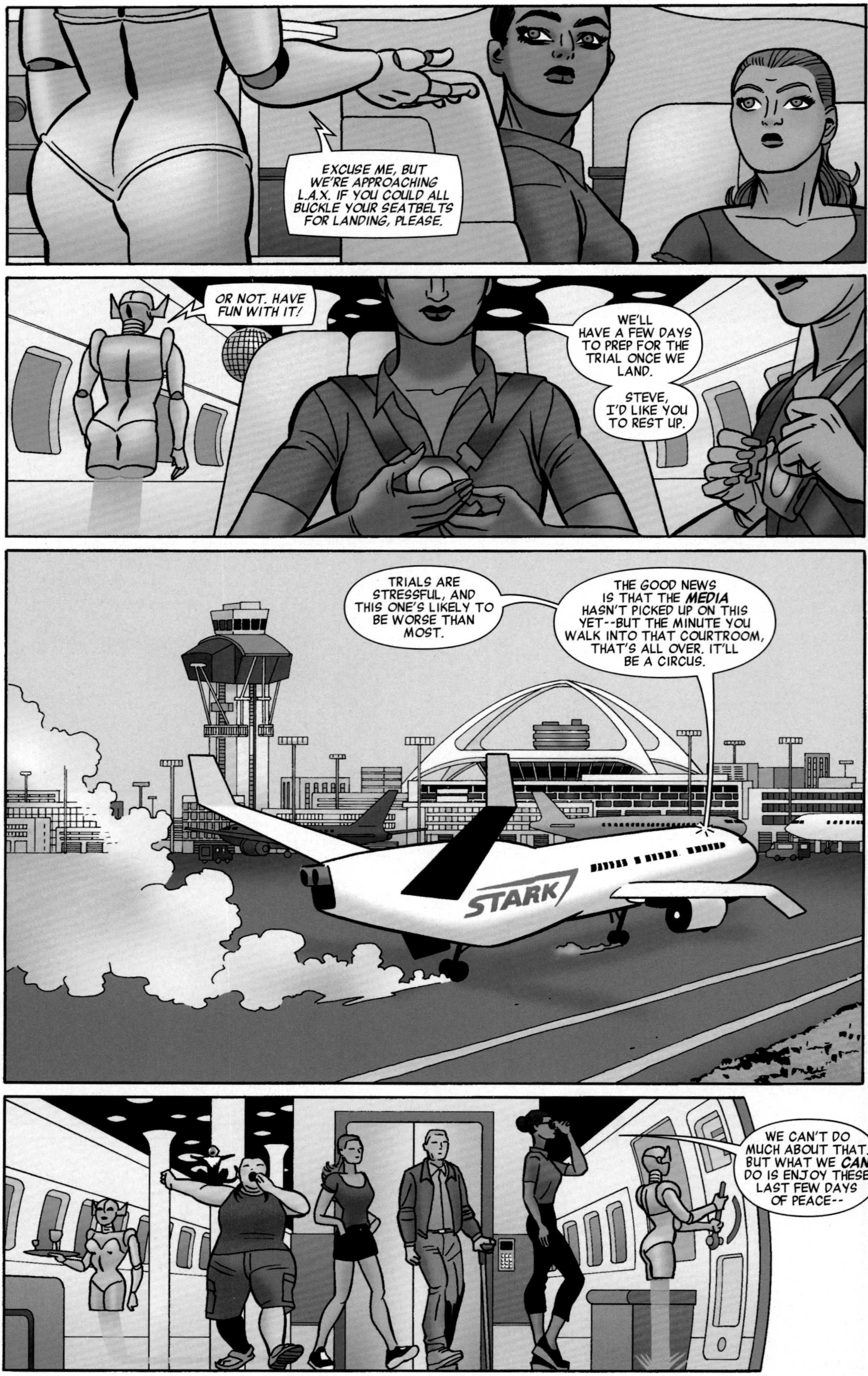
EXCUSE ME, BUT WE'RE APPROACHING L.A.X. IF YOU COULD ALL BUCKLE YOUR SEATBELTS FOR LANDING, PLEASE.
OR NOT. HAVE FUN WITH IT!
WE'LL HAVE A FEW DAYS TO PREP FOR THE TRIAL ONCE WE LAND.
STEVE, I'D LIKE YOU TO REST UP.
TRIALS ARE STRESSFUL, AND THIS ONE'S LIKELY TO BE WORSE THAN MOST.
THE GOOD NEWS IS THAT THE MEDIA HASN'T PICKED UP ON THIS YET--BUT THE MINUTE YOU WALK INTO THAT COURTROOM, THAT'S ALL OVER. IT'LL BE A CIRCUS.
STARK
WE CAN'T DO MUCH ABOUT THAT. BUT WHAT WE CAN DO IS ENJOY THESE LAST FEW DAYS OF PEACE--

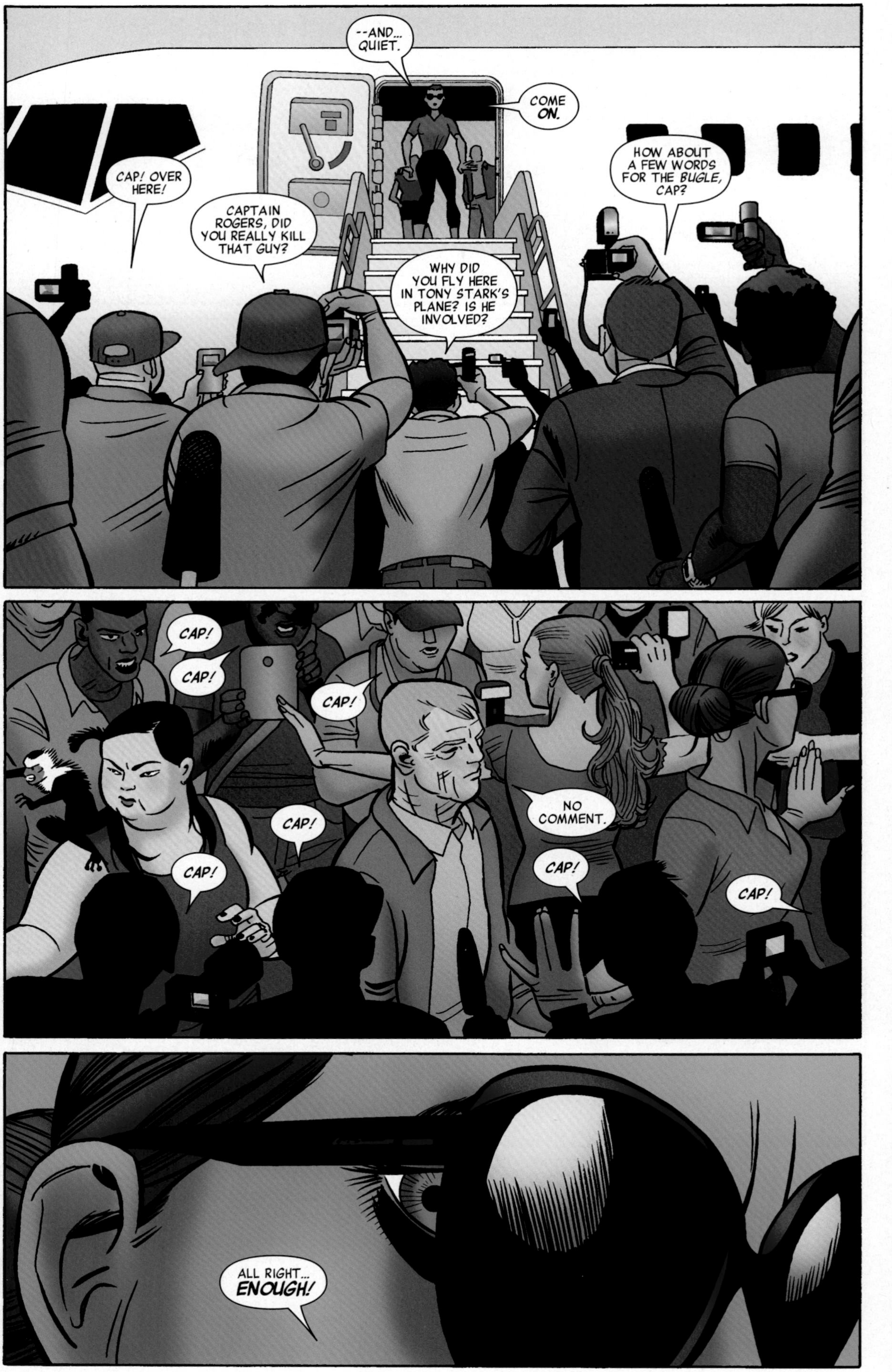
--AND... QUIET.
COME ON.
CAP! OVER HERE!
CAPTAIN ROGERS, DID YOU REALLY KILL THAT GUY?
WHY DID YOU FLY HERE IN TONY STARK'S PLANE? IS HE INVOLVED?
HOW ABOUT A FEW WORDS FOR THE BUGLE, CAP?
CAP!
CAP!
CAP!
NO COMMENT.
CAP!
CAP!
CAP!
CAP!
ALL RIGHT... ENOUGH!

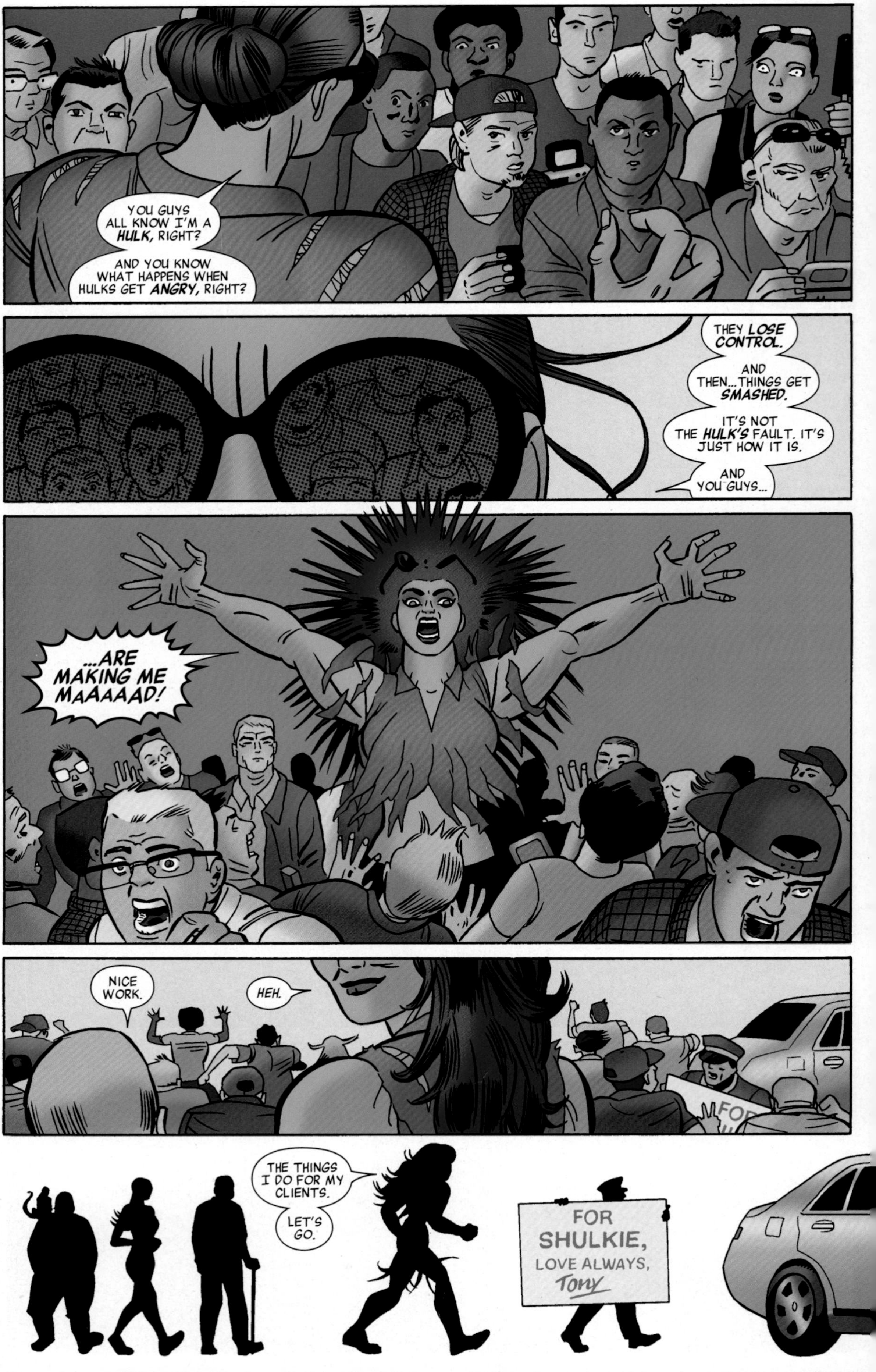

YOU GUYS ALL KNOW I'M A HULK, RIGHT?
AND YOU KNOW WHAT HAPPENS WHEN HULKS GET ANGRY, RIGHT?
THEY LOSE CONTROL.
AND THEN...THINGS GET SMASHED.
IT'S NOT THE HULK'S FAULT. IT'S JUST HOW IT IS.
AND YOU GUYS...
...ARE MAKING ME MAAAAAD!
NICE WORK.
HEH.
THE THINGS I DO FOR MY CLIENTS.
LET'S GO.
FOR SHULKIE, LOVE ALWAYS, Tony

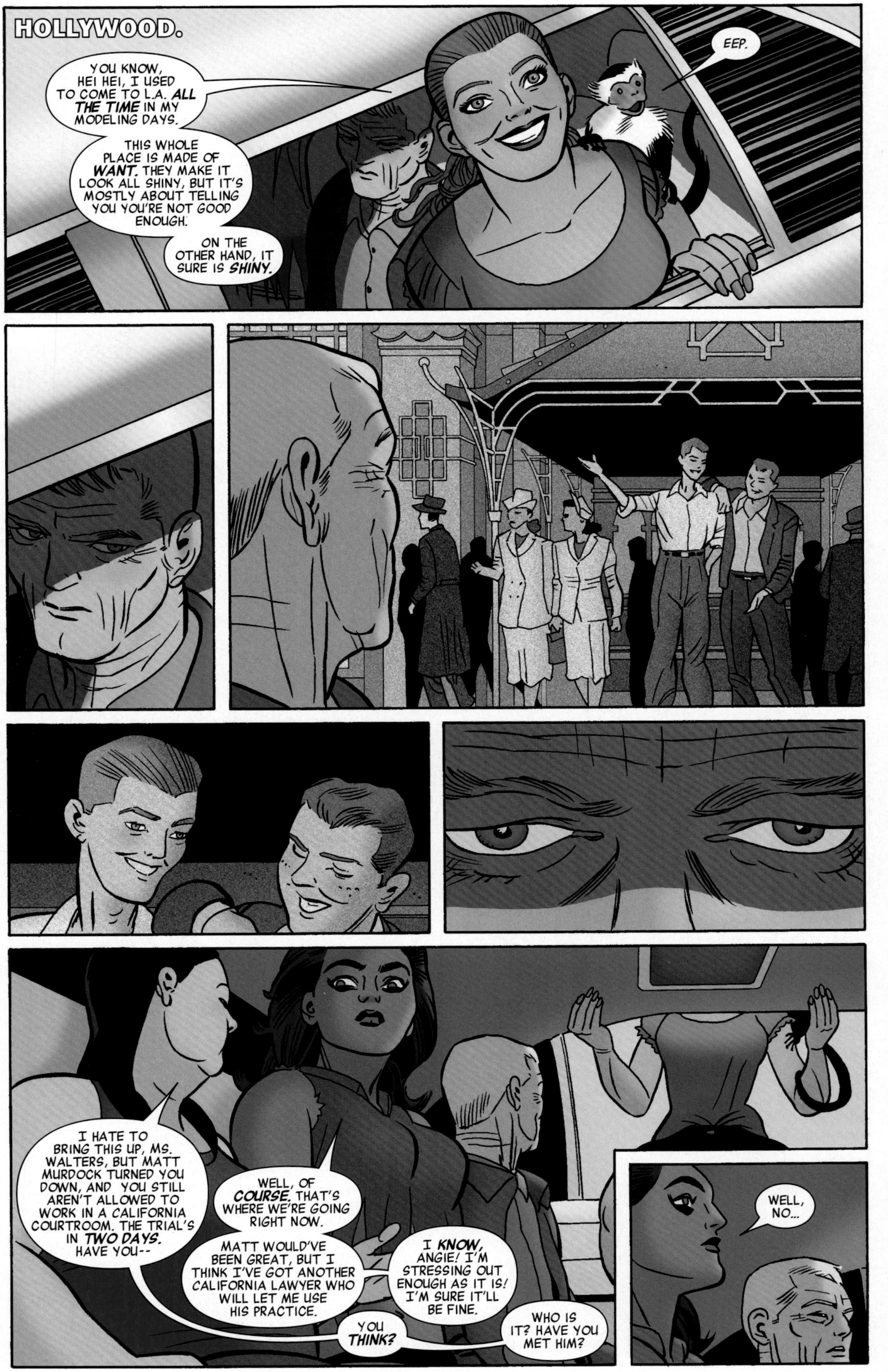
HOLLYWOOD.
YOU KNOW, HEI HEI, I USED TO COME TO L.A. ALL THE TIME IN MY MODELING DAYS.
EEP.
THIS WHOLE PLACE IS MADE OF WANT. THEY MAKE IT LOOK ALL SHINY, BUT IT'S MOSTLY ABOUT TELLING YOU YOU'RE NOT GOOD ENOUGH.
ON THE OTHER HAND, IT SURE IS SHINY.
I HATE TO BRING THIS UP, MS. WALTERS, BUT MATT MURDOCK TURNED YOU DOWN, AND YOU STILL AREN'T ALLOWED TO WORK IN A CALIFORNIA COURTROOM. THE TRIAL'S IN TWO DAYS. HAVE YOU--
WELL, OF COURSE. THAT'S WHERE WE'RE GOING RIGHT NOW.
MATT WOULD'VE BEEN GREAT, BUT I THINK I'VE GOT ANOTHER CALIFORNIA LAWYER WHO WILL LET ME USE HIS PRACTICE.
YOU THINK?
I KNOW, ANGIE! I'M STRESSING OUT ENOUGH AS IT IS! I'M SURE IT'LL BE FINE.
WHO IS IT? HAVE YOU MET HIM?
WELL, NO...

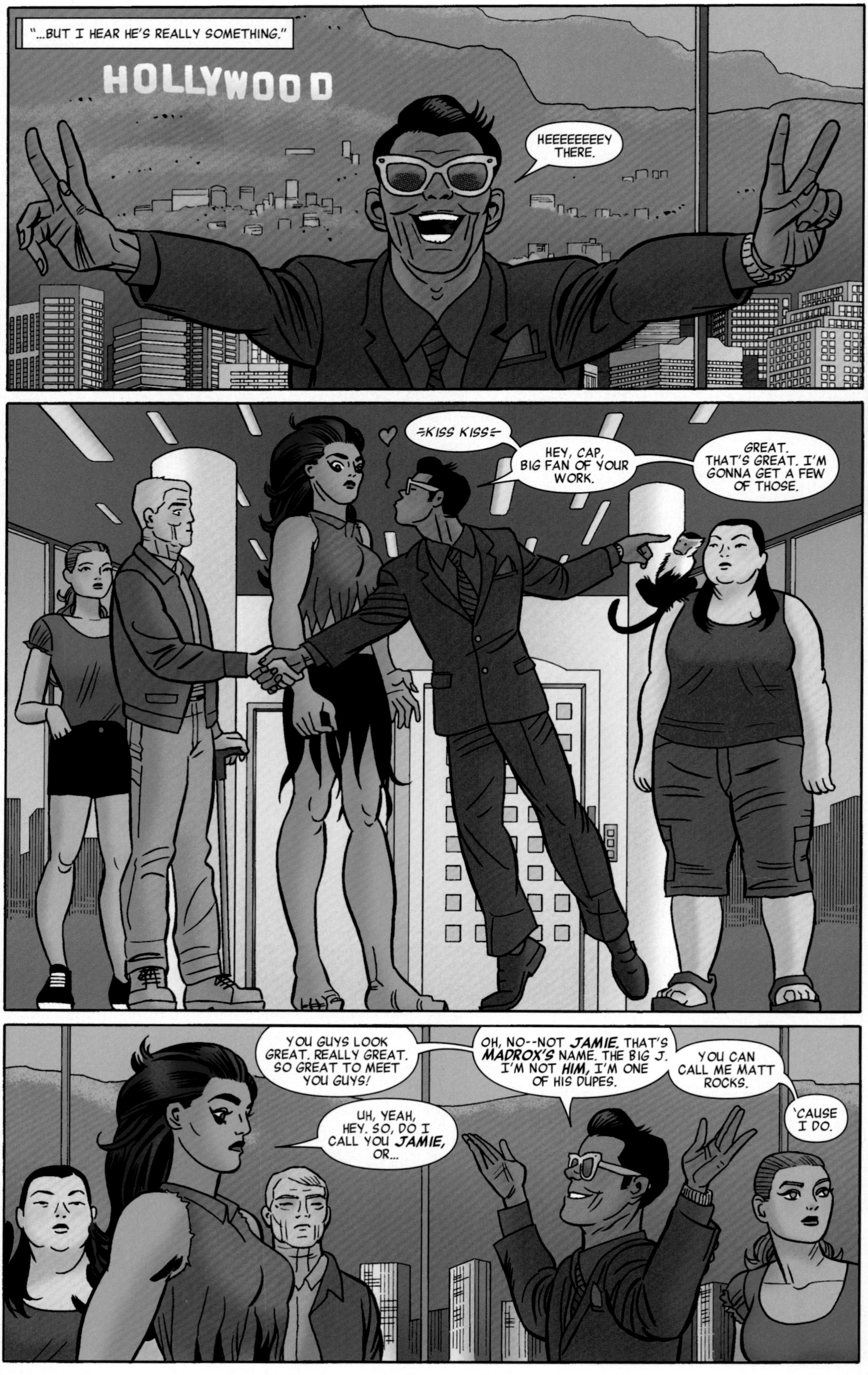
"...BUT I HEAR HE'S REALLY SOMETHING."
HOLLYWOOD
HEEEEEEEEY THERE.
=KISS KISS=
HEY, CAP, BIG FAN OF YOUR WORK.
GREAT. THAT'S GREAT. I'M GONNA GET A FEW OF THOSE.
YOU GUYS LOOK GREAT. REALLY GREAT. SO GREAT TO MEET YOU GUYS!
UH, YEAH, HEY. SO, DO I CALL YOU JAMIE, OR...
OH, NO--NOT JAMIE. THAT'S MADROX'S NAME. THE BIG J. I'M NOT HIM, I'M ONE OF HIS DUPES.
YOU CAN CALL ME MATT ROCKS.
'CAUSE I DO.

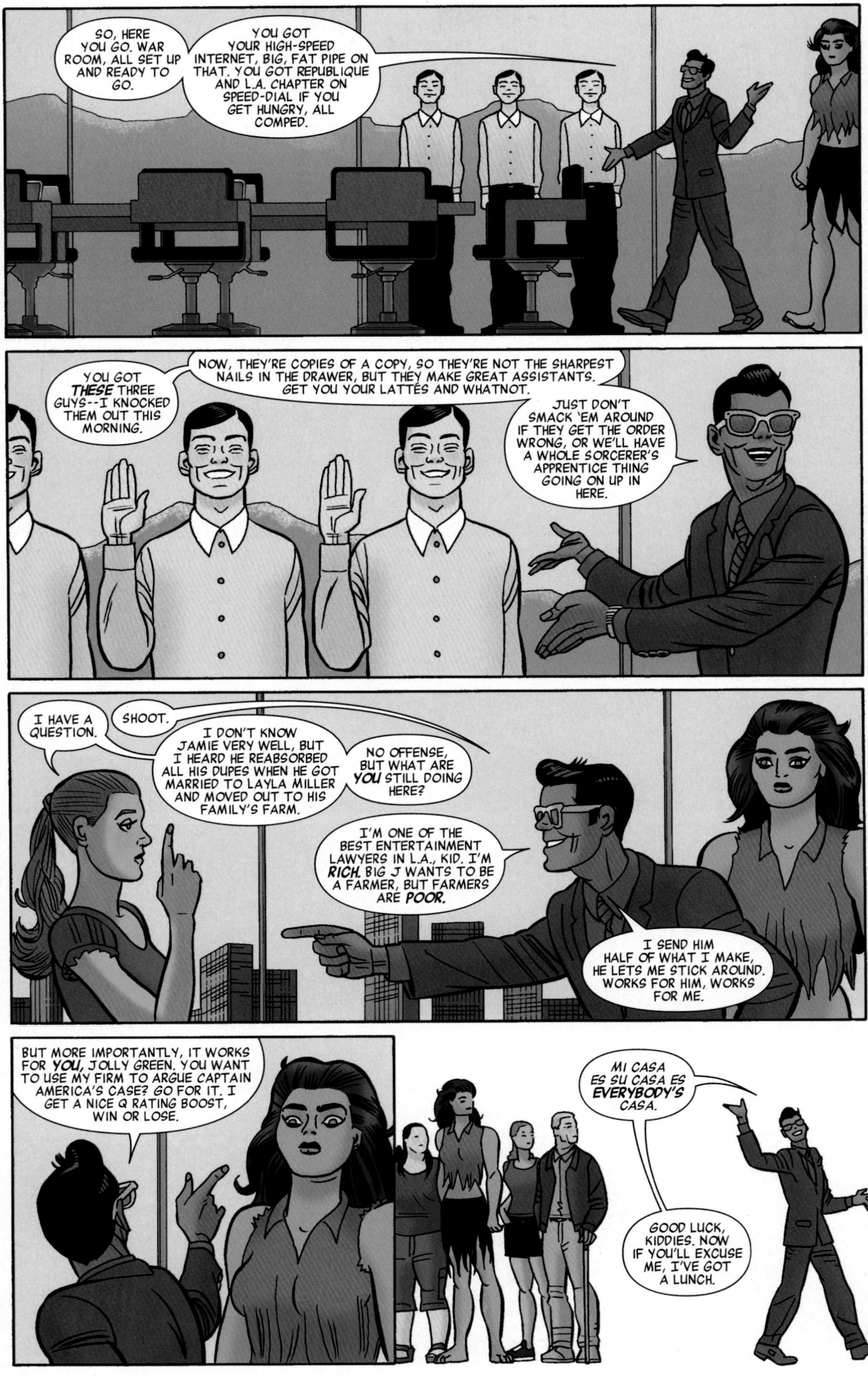
SO, HERE YOU GO. WAR ROOM, ALL SET UP AND READY TO GO.
YOU GOT YOUR HIGH-SPEED INTERNET, BIG, FAT PIPE ON THAT. YOU GOT REPUBLIQUE AND L.A. CHAPTER ON SPEED-DIAL IF YOU GET HUNGRY, ALL COMPED.
YOU GOT *THESE* THREE GUYS--I KNOCKED THEM OUT THIS MORNING.
NOW, THEY'RE COPIES OF A COPY, SO THEY'RE NOT THE SHARPEST NAILS IN THE DRAWER, BUT THEY MAKE GREAT ASSISTANTS. GET YOU YOUR LATTÉS AND WHATNOT.
JUST DON'T SMACK 'EM AROUND IF THEY GET THE ORDER WRONG, OR WE'LL HAVE A WHOLE SORCERER'S APPRENTICE THING GOING ON UP IN HERE.
I HAVE A QUESTION.
SHOOT.
I DON'T KNOW JAMIE VERY WELL, BUT I HEARD HE REABSORBED ALL HIS DUPES WHEN HE GOT MARRIED TO LAYLA MILLER AND MOVED OUT TO HIS FAMILY'S FARM.
NO OFFENSE, BUT WHAT ARE *YOU* STILL DOING HERE?
I'M ONE OF THE BEST ENTERTAINMENT LAWYERS IN L.A., KID. I'M *RICH.* BIG J WANTS TO BE A FARMER, BUT FARMERS ARE *POOR.*
I SEND HIM HALF OF WHAT I MAKE, HE LETS ME STICK AROUND. WORKS FOR HIM, WORKS FOR ME.
BUT MORE IMPORTANTLY, IT WORKS FOR *YOU,* JOLLY GREEN. YOU WANT TO USE MY FIRM TO ARGUE CAPTAIN AMERICA'S CASE? GO FOR IT. I GET A NICE Q RATING BOOST, WIN OR LOSE.
MI CASA ES SU CASA ES *EVERYBODY'S* CASA.
GOOD LUCK, KIDDIES. NOW IF YOU'LL EXCUSE ME, I'VE GOT A LUNCH.

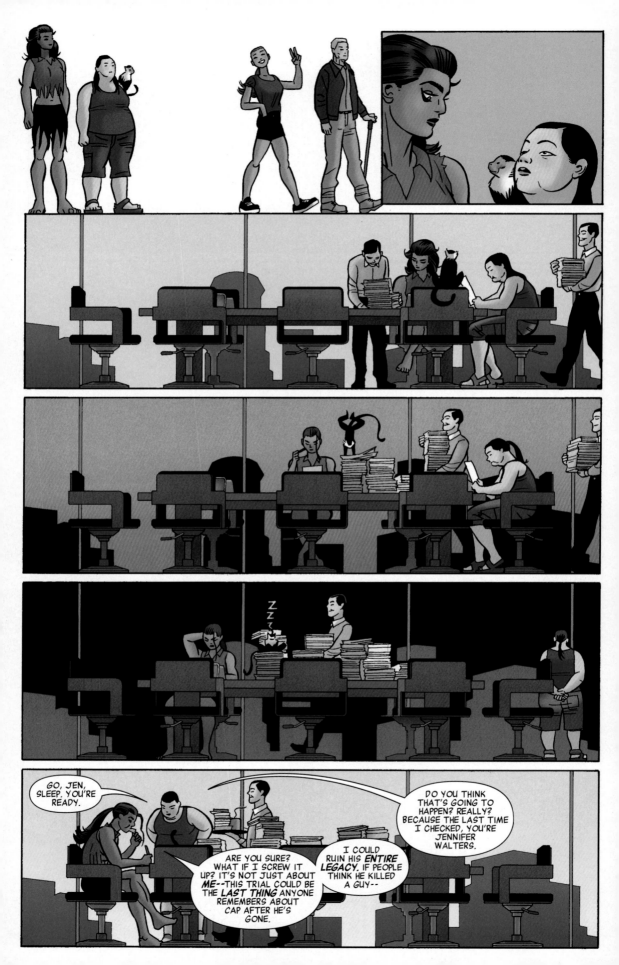

GO, JEN, SLEEP. YOU'RE READY.

DO YOU THINK THAT'S GOING TO HAPPEN? REALLY? BECAUSE THE LAST TIME I CHECKED, YOU'RE JENNIFER WALTERS.

ARE YOU SURE? WHAT IF I SCREW IT UP? IT'S NOT JUST ABOUT ME--THIS TRIAL COULD BE THE LAST THING ANYONE REMEMBERS ABOUT CAP AFTER HE'S GONE.

I COULD RUIN HIS ENTIRE LEGACY. IF PEOPLE THINK HE KILLED A GUY--

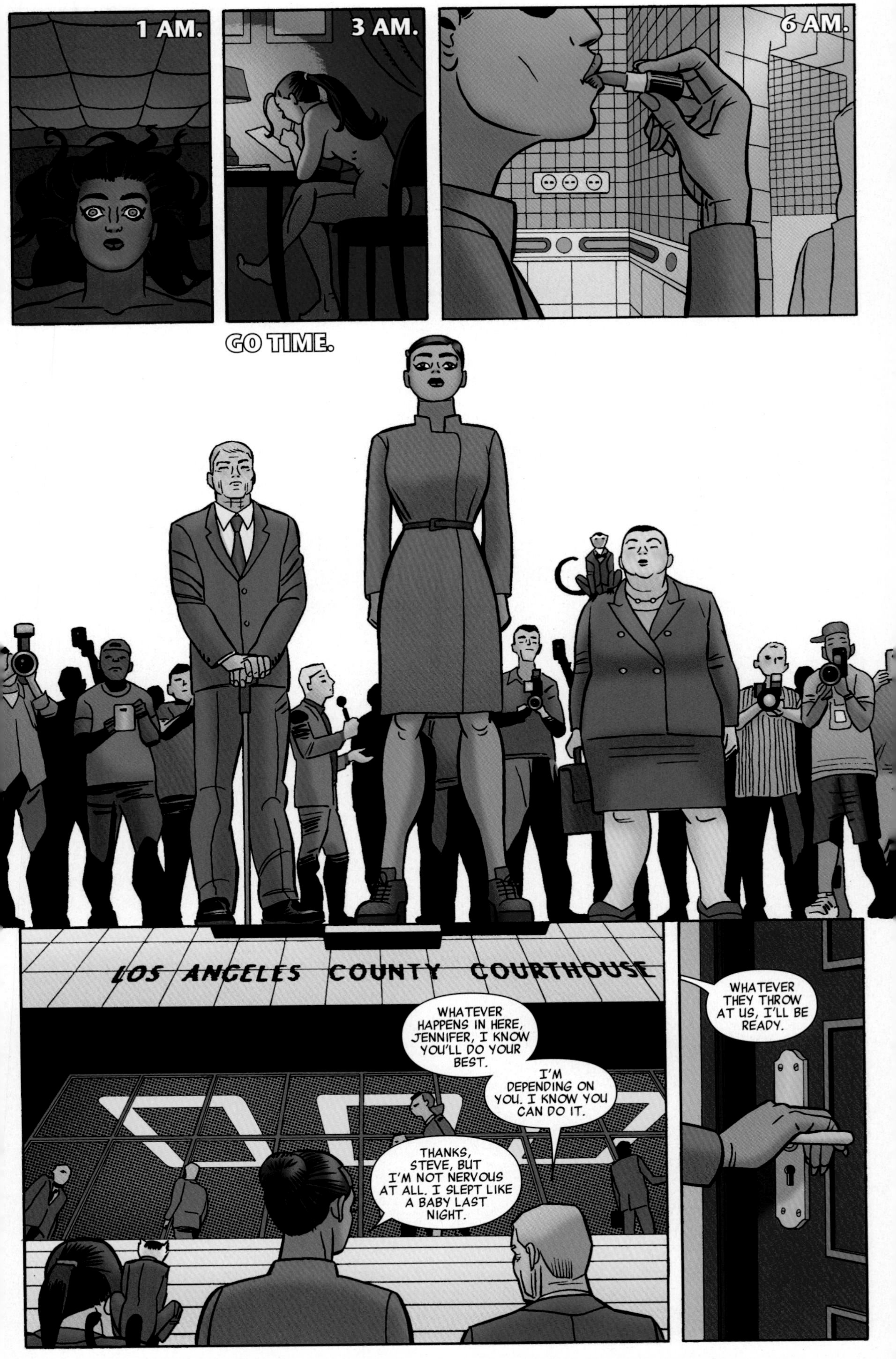
1 AM.
3 AM.
6 AM.
GO TIME.
LOS ANGELES COUNTY COURTHOUSE
WHATEVER HAPPENS IN HERE, JENNIFER, I KNOW YOU'LL DO YOUR BEST.
I'M DEPENDING ON YOU. I KNOW YOU CAN DO IT.
THANKS, STEVE, BUT I'M NOT NERVOUS AT ALL. I SLEPT LIKE A BABY LAST NIGHT.
WHATEVER THEY THROW AT US, I'LL BE READY.

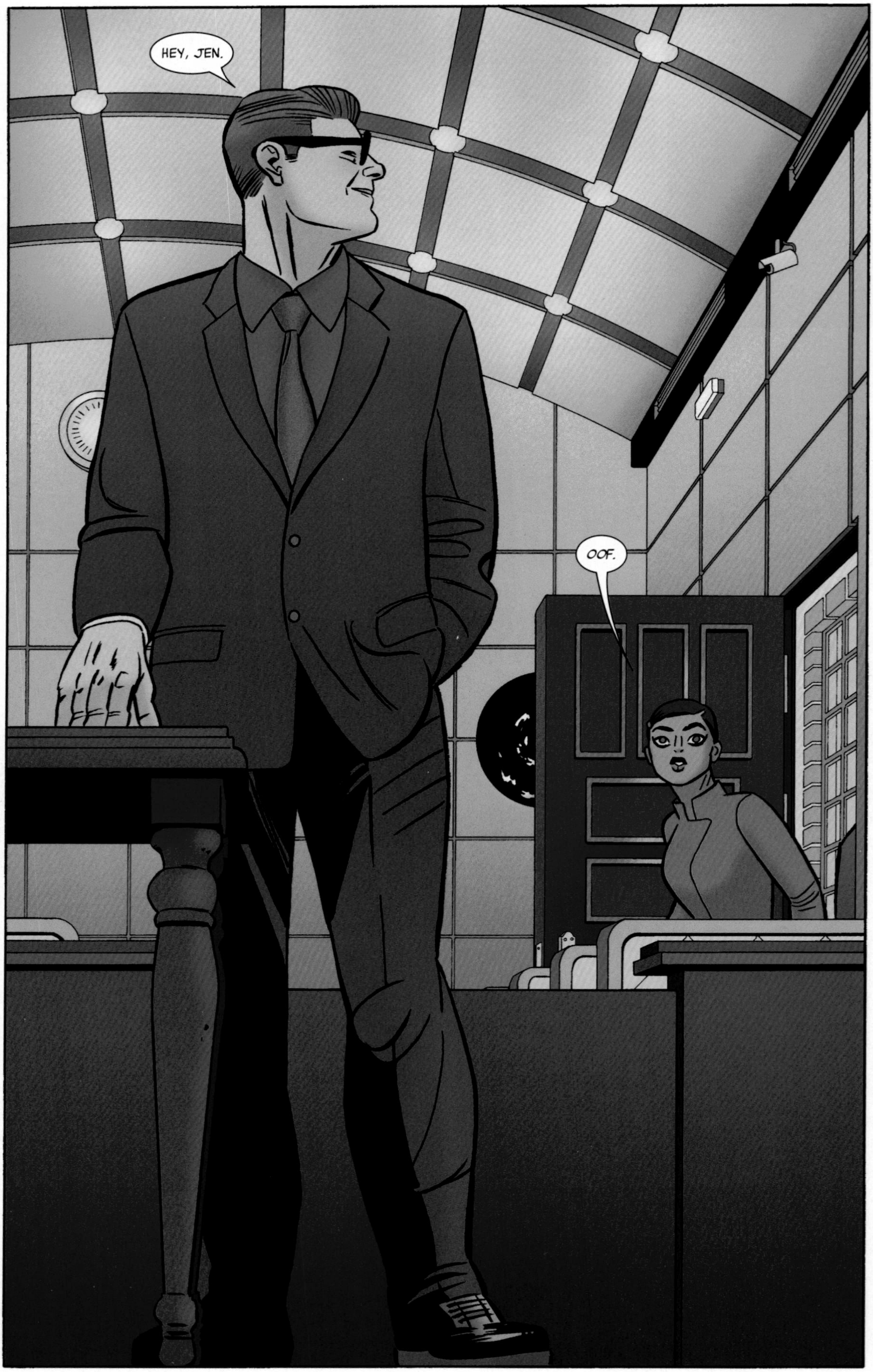
HEY, JEN.
OOF.

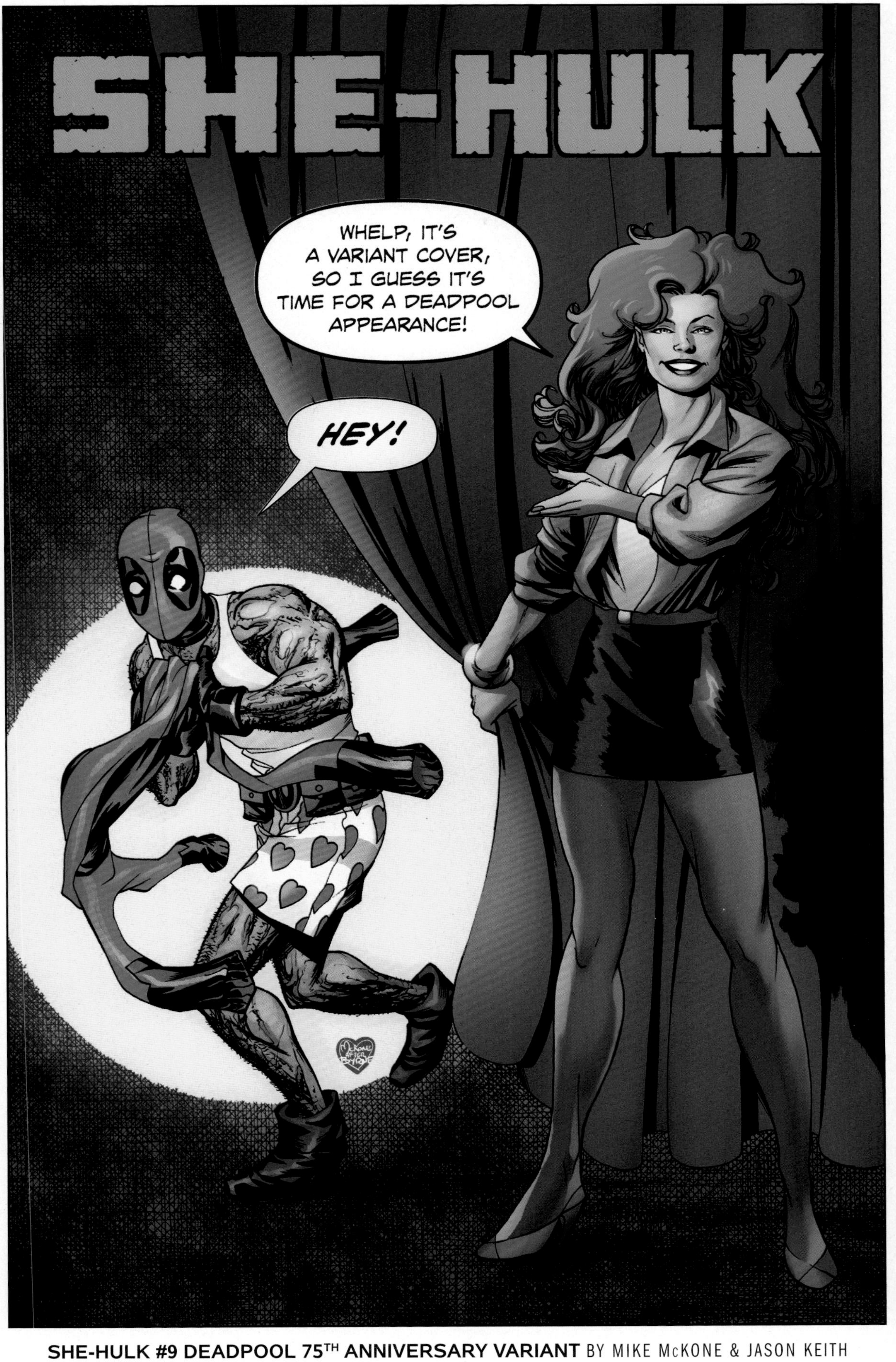
SHE-HULK
WHELP, IT'S A VARIANT COVER, SO I GUESS IT'S TIME FOR A DEADPOOL APPEARANCE!
HEY!

SHE-HULK #9 DEADPOOL 75TH ANNIVERSARY VARIANT BY MIKE McKONE & JASON KEITH

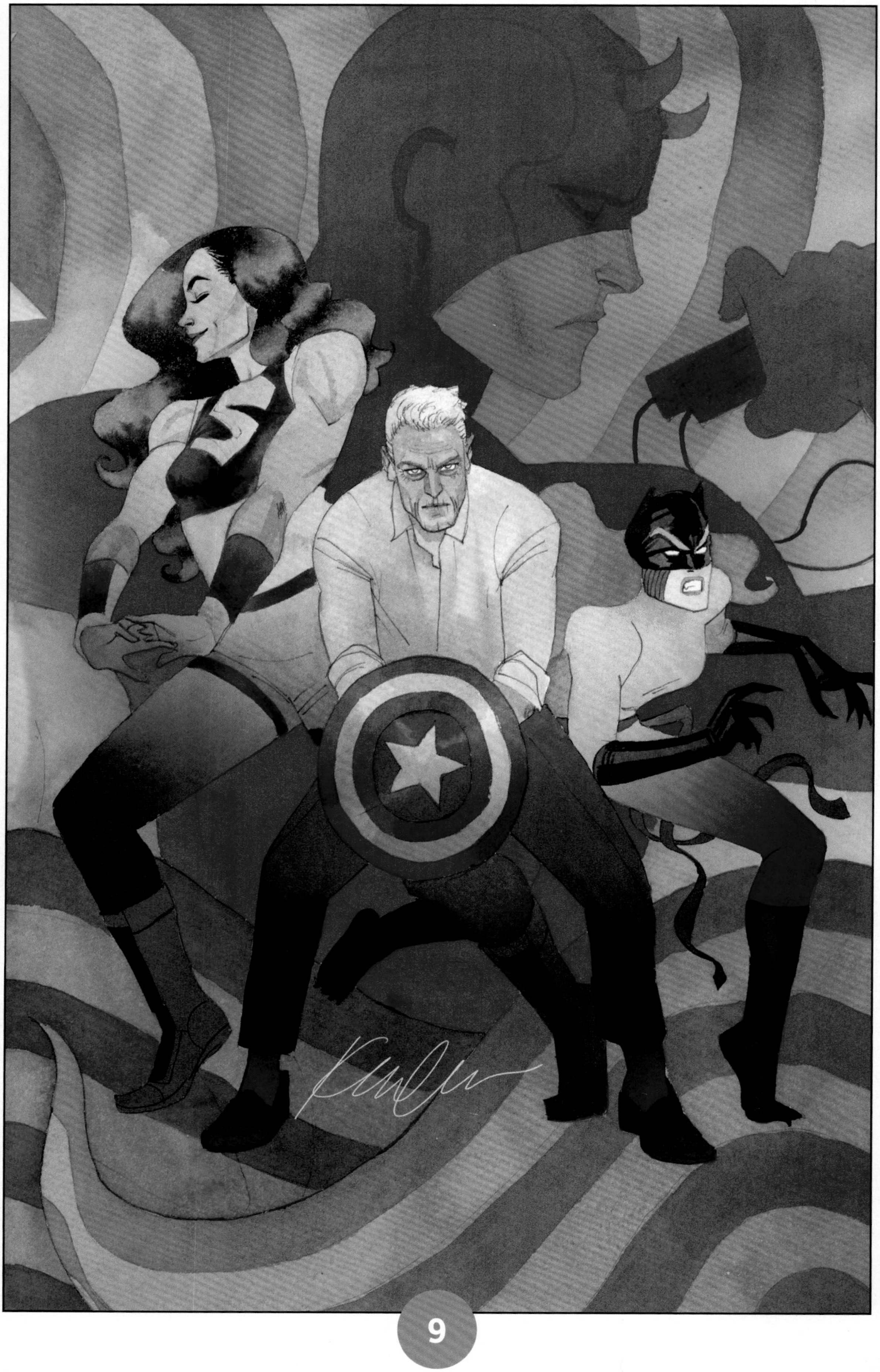

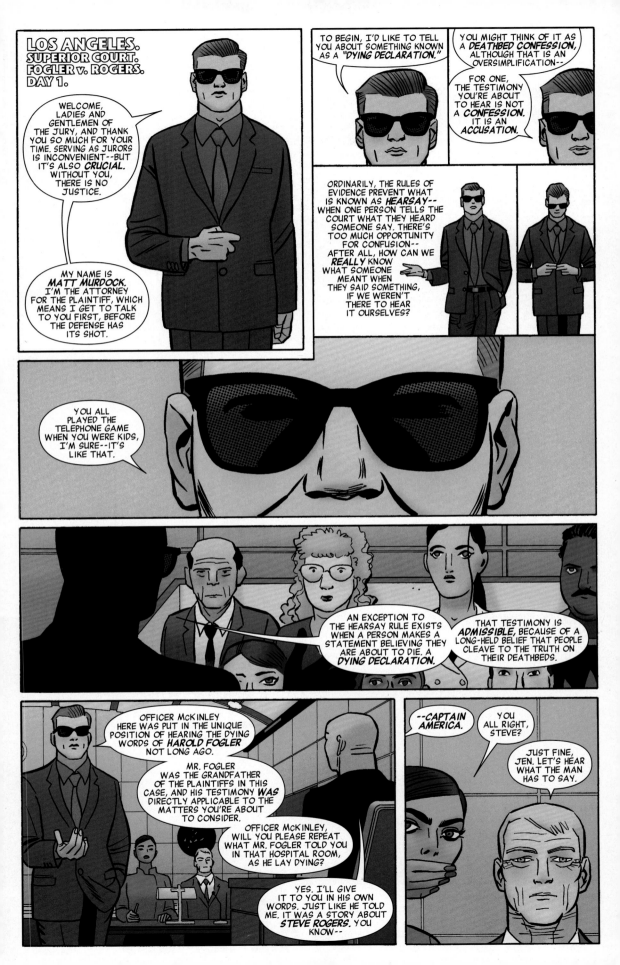

LOS ANGELES. SUPERIOR COURT. FOGLER v. ROGERS. DAY 1.

WELCOME, LADIES AND GENTLEMEN OF THE JURY, AND THANK YOU SO MUCH FOR YOUR TIME. SERVING AS JURORS IS INCONVENIENT--BUT IT'S ALSO *CRUCIAL*. WITHOUT YOU, THERE IS NO JUSTICE.

MY NAME IS *MATT MURDOCK.* I'M THE ATTORNEY FOR THE PLAINTIFF, WHICH MEANS I GET TO TALK TO YOU FIRST, BEFORE THE DEFENSE HAS ITS SHOT.

TO BEGIN, I'D LIKE TO TELL YOU ABOUT SOMETHING KNOWN AS A *"DYING DECLARATION."*

YOU MIGHT THINK OF IT AS A *DEATHBED CONFESSION,* ALTHOUGH THAT IS AN OVERSIMPLIFICATION--

FOR ONE, THE TESTIMONY YOU'RE ABOUT TO HEAR IS NOT A *CONFESSION.* IT IS AN *ACCUSATION.*

ORDINARILY, THE RULES OF EVIDENCE PREVENT WHAT IS KNOWN AS *HEARSAY*-- WHEN ONE PERSON TELLS THE COURT WHAT THEY HEARD SOMEONE SAY. THERE'S TOO MUCH OPPORTUNITY FOR CONFUSION-- AFTER ALL, HOW CAN WE *REALLY* KNOW WHAT SOMEONE MEANT WHEN THEY SAID SOMETHING, IF WE WEREN'T THERE TO HEAR IT OURSELVES?

YOU ALL PLAYED THE TELEPHONE GAME WHEN YOU WERE KIDS, I'M SURE--IT'S LIKE THAT.

AN EXCEPTION TO THE HEARSAY RULE EXISTS WHEN A PERSON MAKES A STATEMENT BELIEVING THEY ARE ABOUT TO DIE. A *DYING DECLARATION.*

THAT TESTIMONY IS *ADMISSIBLE,* BECAUSE OF A LONG-HELD BELIEF THAT PEOPLE CLEAVE TO THE TRUTH ON THEIR DEATHBEDS.

OFFICER McKINLEY HERE WAS PUT IN THE UNIQUE POSITION OF HEARING THE DYING WORDS OF *HAROLD FOGLER* NOT LONG AGO.

MR. FOGLER WAS THE GRANDFATHER OF THE PLAINTIFFS IN THIS CASE, AND HIS TESTIMONY *WAS* DIRECTLY APPLICABLE TO THE MATTERS YOU'RE ABOUT TO CONSIDER.

OFFICER McKINLEY, WILL YOU PLEASE REPEAT WHAT MR. FOGLER TOLD YOU IN THAT HOSPITAL ROOM, AS HE LAY DYING?

YES. I'LL GIVE IT TO YOU IN HIS OWN WORDS. JUST LIKE HE TOLD ME. IT WAS A STORY ABOUT *STEVE ROGERS.* YOU KNOW--

--*CAPTAIN AMERICA.*

YOU ALL RIGHT, STEVE?

JUST FINE, JEN. LET'S HEAR WHAT THE MAN HAS TO SAY.

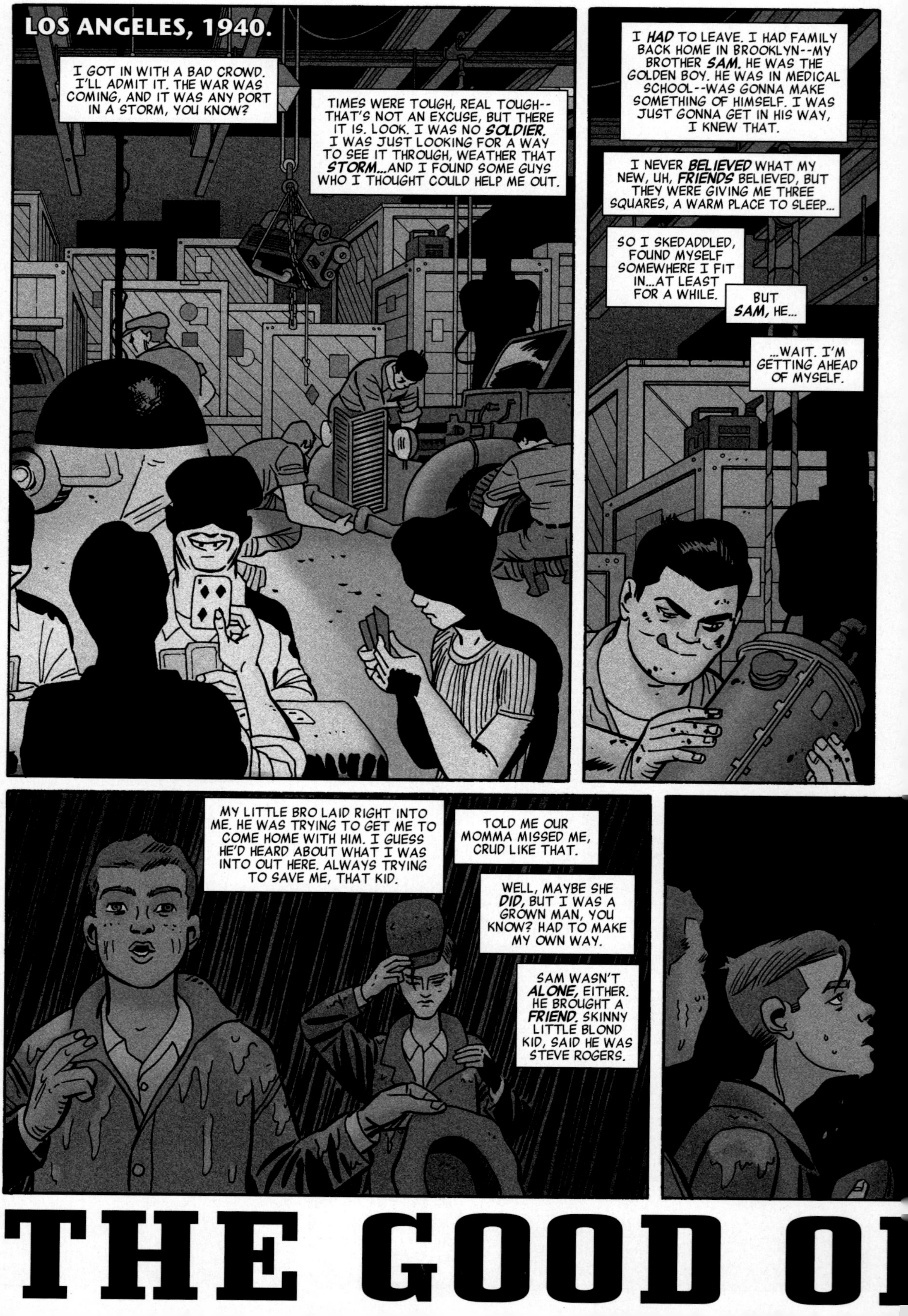
LOS ANGELES, 1940.
I GOT IN WITH A BAD CROWD. I'LL ADMIT IT. THE WAR WAS COMING, AND IT WAS ANY PORT IN A STORM, YOU KNOW?
TIMES WERE TOUGH, REAL TOUGH-- THAT'S NOT AN EXCUSE, BUT THERE IT IS. LOOK. I WAS NO SOLDIER. I WAS JUST LOOKING FOR A WAY TO SEE IT THROUGH, WEATHER THAT STORM... AND I FOUND SOME GUYS WHO I THOUGHT COULD HELP ME OUT.
I HAD TO LEAVE. I HAD FAMILY BACK HOME IN BROOKLYN--MY BROTHER SAM. HE WAS THE GOLDEN BOY. HE WAS IN MEDICAL SCHOOL--WAS GONNA MAKE SOMETHING OF HIMSELF. I WAS JUST GONNA GET IN HIS WAY, I KNEW THAT.
I NEVER BELIEVED WHAT MY NEW, UH, FRIENDS BELIEVED, BUT THEY WERE GIVING ME THREE SQUARES, A WARM PLACE TO SLEEP...
SO I SKEDADDLED, FOUND MYSELF SOMEWHERE I FIT IN... AT LEAST FOR A WHILE.
BUT SAM, HE...
...WAIT. I'M GETTING AHEAD OF MYSELF.
MY LITTLE BRO LAID RIGHT INTO ME. HE WAS TRYING TO GET ME TO COME HOME WITH HIM. I GUESS HE'D HEARD ABOUT WHAT I WAS INTO OUT HERE. ALWAYS TRYING TO SAVE ME, THAT KID.
TOLD ME OUR MOMMA MISSED ME, CRUD LIKE THAT.
WELL, MAYBE SHE DID, BUT I WAS A GROWN MAN, YOU KNOW? HAD TO MAKE MY OWN WAY.
SAM WASN'T ALONE, EITHER. HE BROUGHT A FRIEND. SKINNY LITTLE BLOND KID, SAID HE WAS STEVE ROGERS.
THE GOOD O

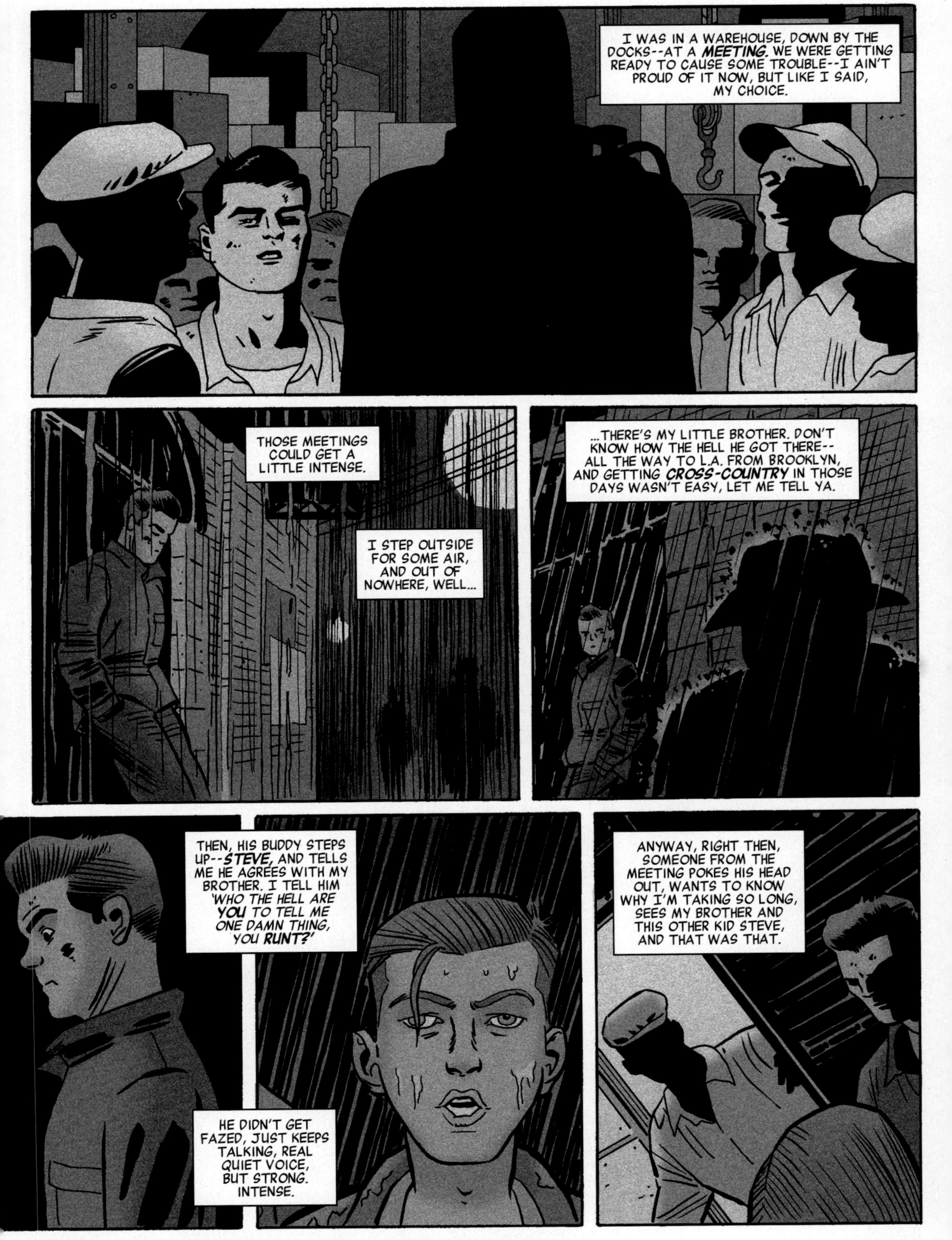
I WAS IN A WAREHOUSE, DOWN BY THE DOCKS--AT A MEETING. WE WERE GETTING READY TO CAUSE SOME TROUBLE--I AIN'T PROUD OF IT NOW, BUT LIKE I SAID, MY CHOICE.
THOSE MEETINGS COULD GET A LITTLE INTENSE.
I STEP OUTSIDE FOR SOME AIR, AND OUT OF NOWHERE, WELL...
...THERE'S MY LITTLE BROTHER. DON'T KNOW HOW THE HELL HE GOT THERE-- ALL THE WAY TO L.A. FROM BROOKLYN, AND GETTING CROSS-COUNTRY IN THOSE DAYS WASN'T EASY, LET ME TELL YA.
THEN, HIS BUDDY STEPS UP--STEVE, AND TELLS ME HE AGREES WITH MY BROTHER. I TELL HIM 'WHO THE HELL ARE YOU TO TELL ME ONE DAMN THING, YOU RUNT?'
HE DIDN'T GET FAZED, JUST KEEPS TALKING, REAL QUIET VOICE, BUT STRONG. INTENSE.
ANYWAY, RIGHT THEN, SOMEONE FROM THE MEETING POKES HIS HEAD OUT, WANTS TO KNOW WHY I'M TAKING SO LONG, SEES MY BROTHER AND THIS OTHER KID STEVE, AND THAT WAS THAT.

.D DAYS Part 2

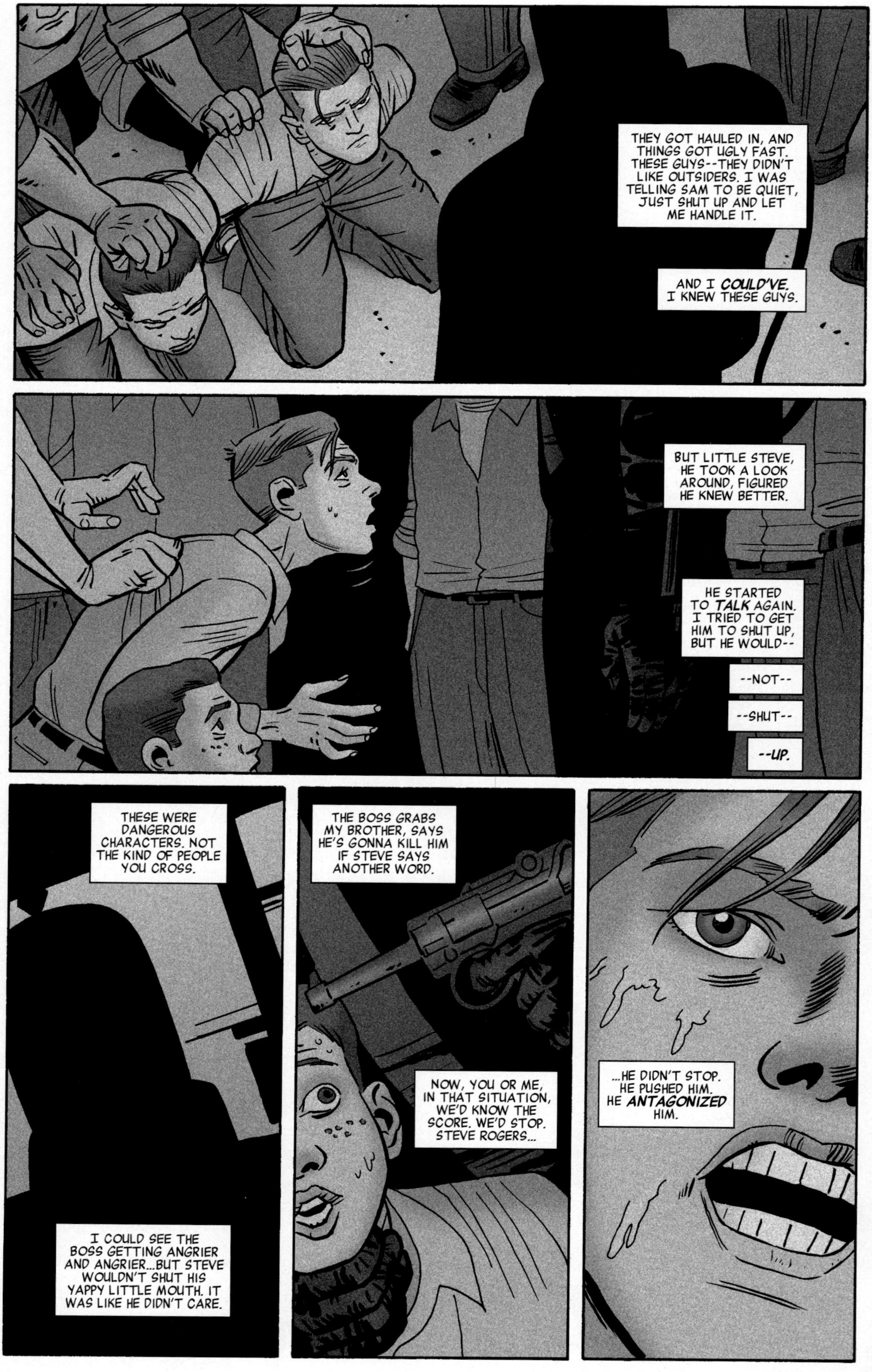
THEY GOT HAULED IN, AND THINGS GOT UGLY FAST. THESE GUYS--THEY DIDN'T LIKE OUTSIDERS. I WAS TELLING SAM TO BE QUIET, JUST SHUT UP AND LET ME HANDLE IT.
AND I ***COULD'VE.*** I KNEW THESE GUYS.
BUT LITTLE STEVE, HE TOOK A LOOK AROUND, FIGURED HE KNEW BETTER.
HE STARTED TO ***TALK*** AGAIN. I TRIED TO GET HIM TO SHUT UP, BUT HE WOULD--
--NOT--
--SHUT--
--UP.
THESE WERE DANGEROUS CHARACTERS. NOT THE KIND OF PEOPLE YOU CROSS.
I COULD SEE THE BOSS GETTING ANGRIER AND ANGRIER...BUT STEVE WOULDN'T SHUT HIS YAPPY LITTLE MOUTH. IT WAS LIKE HE DIDN'T CARE.
THE BOSS GRABS MY BROTHER, SAYS HE'S GONNA KILL HIM IF STEVE SAYS ANOTHER WORD.
NOW, YOU OR ME, IN THAT SITUATION, WE'D KNOW THE SCORE. WE'D STOP. STEVE ROGERS...
...HE DIDN'T STOP. HE PUSHED HIM. HE ***ANTAGONIZED*** HIM.

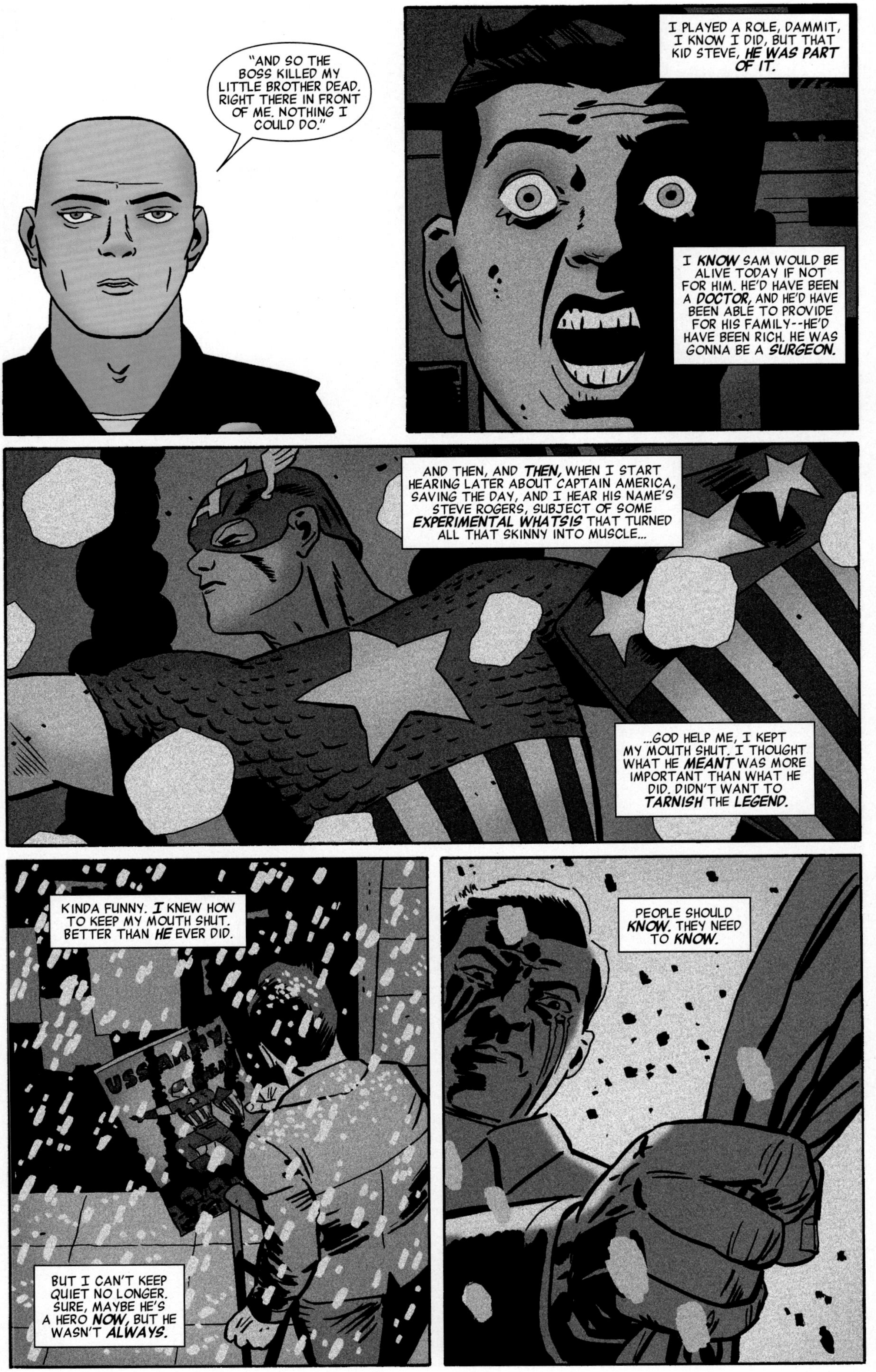
"AND SO THE BOSS KILLED MY LITTLE BROTHER DEAD. RIGHT THERE IN FRONT OF ME. NOTHING I COULD DO."
I PLAYED A ROLE, DAMMIT, I KNOW I DID, BUT THAT KID STEVE, HE WAS PART OF IT.
I KNOW SAM WOULD BE ALIVE TODAY IF NOT FOR HIM. HE'D HAVE BEEN A DOCTOR, AND HE'D HAVE BEEN ABLE TO PROVIDE FOR HIS FAMILY--HE'D HAVE BEEN RICH. HE WAS GONNA BE A SURGEON.
AND THEN, AND THEN, WHEN I START HEARING LATER ABOUT CAPTAIN AMERICA, SAVING THE DAY, AND I HEAR HIS NAME'S STEVE ROGERS, SUBJECT OF SOME EXPERIMENTAL WHATSIS THAT TURNED ALL THAT SKINNY INTO MUSCLE...
...GOD HELP ME, I KEPT MY MOUTH SHUT. I THOUGHT WHAT HE MEANT WAS MORE IMPORTANT THAN WHAT HE DID. DIDN'T WANT TO TARNISH THE LEGEND.
KINDA FUNNY. I KNEW HOW TO KEEP MY MOUTH SHUT. BETTER THAN HE EVER DID.
BUT I CAN'T KEEP QUIET NO LONGER. SURE, MAYBE HE'S A HERO NOW, BUT HE WASN'T ALWAYS.
PEOPLE SHOULD KNOW. THEY NEED TO KNOW.

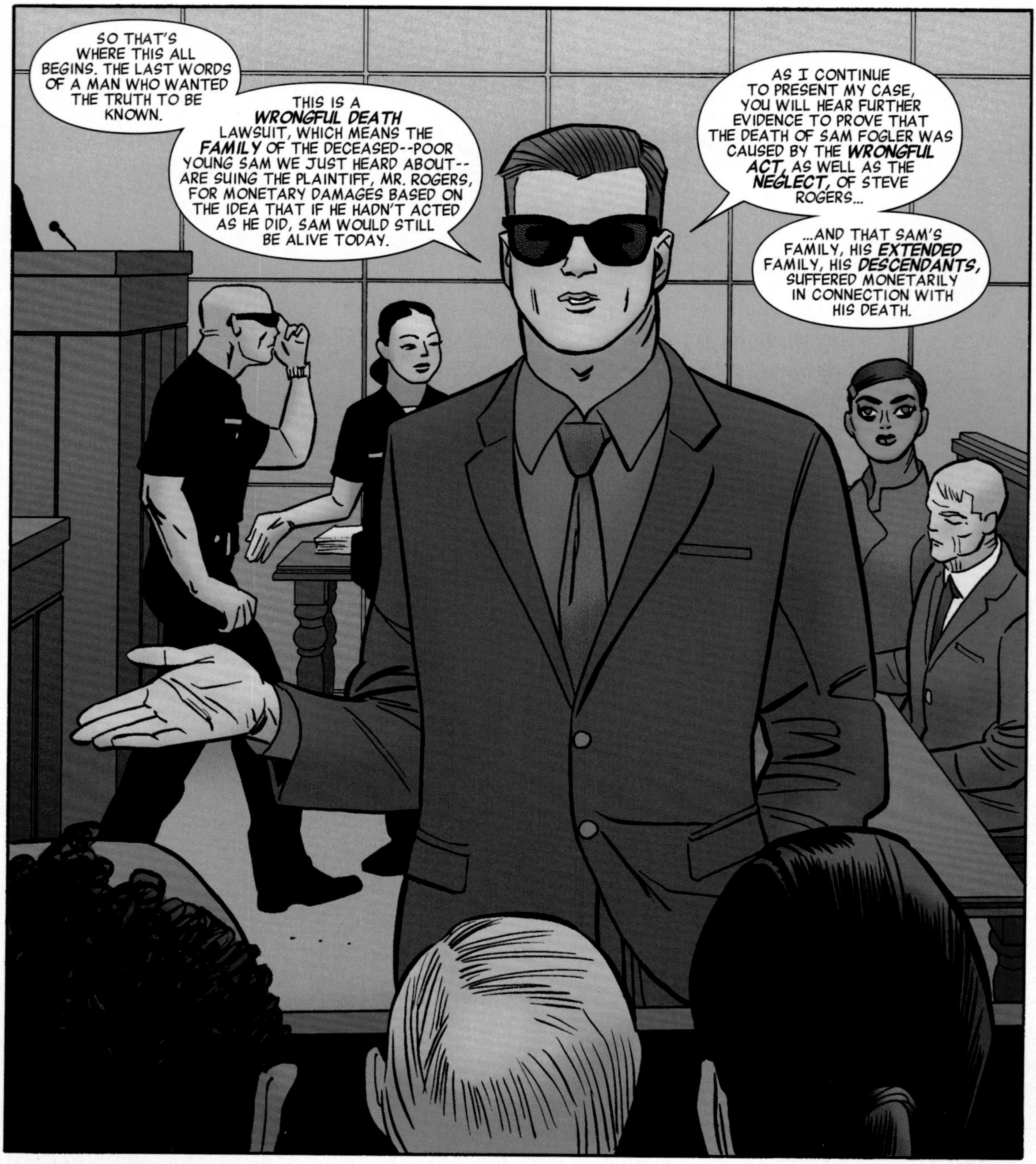
SO THAT'S WHERE THIS ALL BEGINS. THE LAST WORDS OF A MAN WHO WANTED THE TRUTH TO BE KNOWN.
THIS IS A WRONGFUL DEATH LAWSUIT, WHICH MEANS THE FAMILY OF THE DECEASED--POOR YOUNG SAM WE JUST HEARD ABOUT--ARE SUING THE PLAINTIFF, MR. ROGERS, FOR MONETARY DAMAGES BASED ON THE IDEA THAT IF HE HADN'T ACTED AS HE DID, SAM WOULD STILL BE ALIVE TODAY.
AS I CONTINUE TO PRESENT MY CASE, YOU WILL HEAR FURTHER EVIDENCE TO PROVE THAT THE DEATH OF SAM FOGLER WAS CAUSED BY THE WRONGFUL ACT, AS WELL AS THE NEGLECT, OF STEVE ROGERS...
...AND THAT SAM'S FAMILY, HIS EXTENDED FAMILY, HIS DESCENDANTS, SUFFERED MONETARILY IN CONNECTION WITH HIS DEATH.

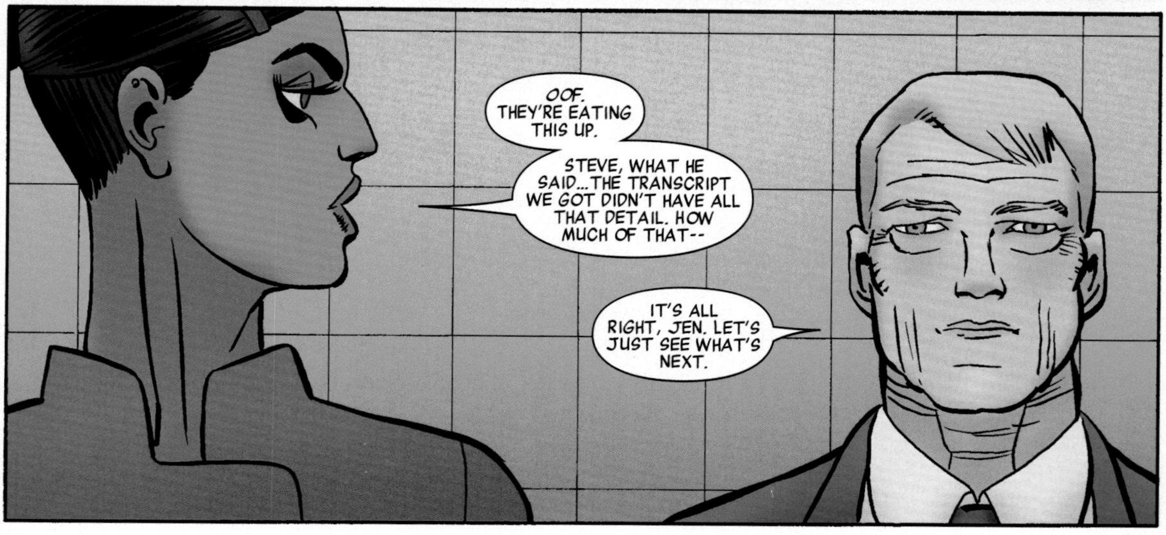
OOF. THEY'RE EATING THIS UP.
STEVE, WHAT HE SAID...THE TRANSCRIPT WE GOT DIDN'T HAVE ALL THAT DETAIL. HOW MUCH OF THAT--
IT'S ALL RIGHT, JEN. LET'S JUST SEE WHAT'S NEXT.

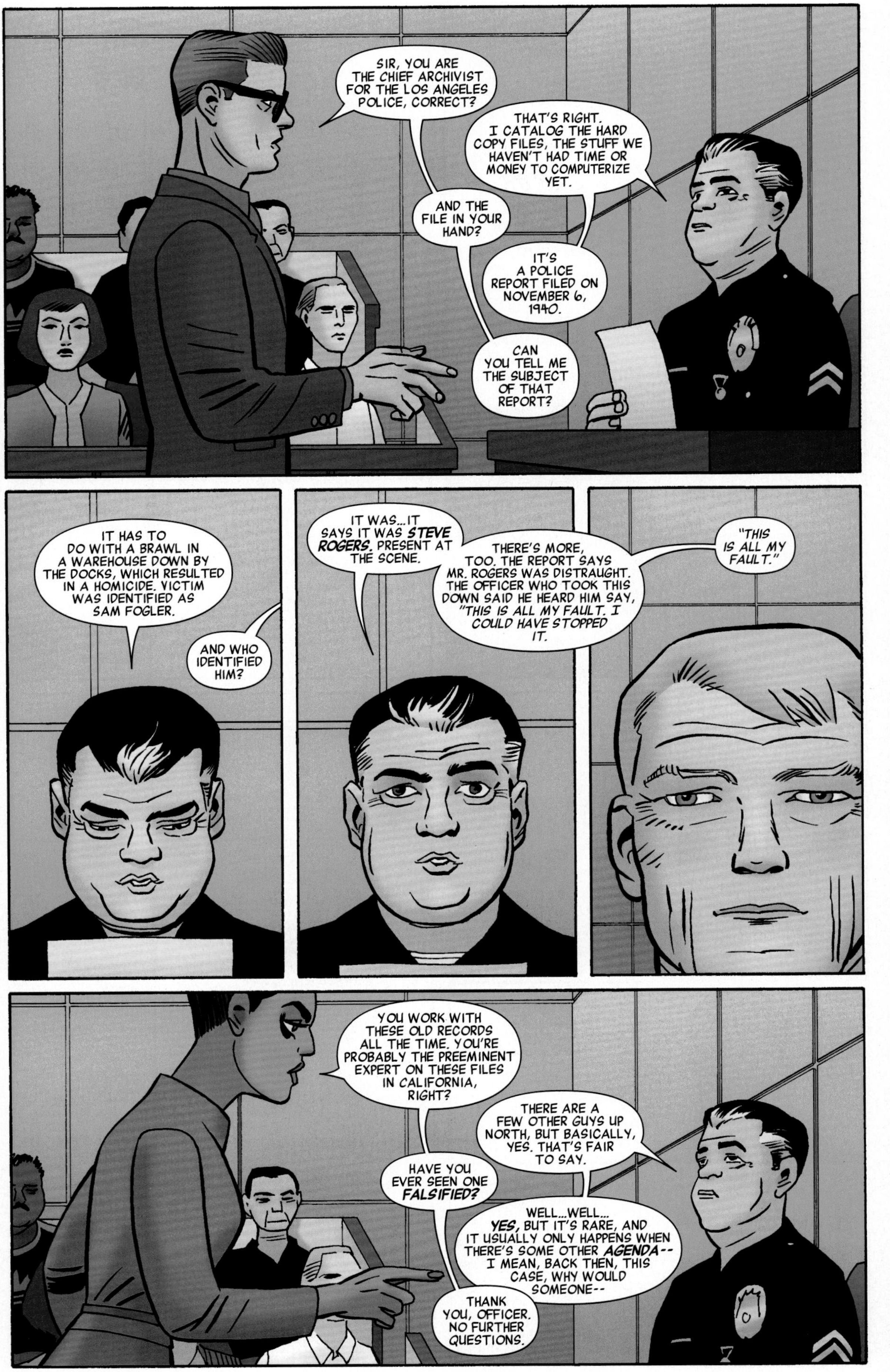
SIR, YOU ARE THE CHIEF ARCHIVIST FOR THE LOS ANGELES POLICE, CORRECT?
THAT'S RIGHT. I CATALOG THE HARD COPY FILES, THE STUFF WE HAVEN'T HAD TIME OR MONEY TO COMPUTERIZE YET.
AND THE FILE IN YOUR HAND?
IT'S A POLICE REPORT FILED ON NOVEMBER 6, 1940.
CAN YOU TELL ME THE SUBJECT OF THAT REPORT?
IT HAS TO DO WITH A BRAWL IN A WAREHOUSE DOWN BY THE DOCKS, WHICH RESULTED IN A HOMICIDE. VICTIM WAS IDENTIFIED AS SAM FOGLER.
AND WHO IDENTIFIED HIM?
IT WAS...IT SAYS IT WAS STEVE ROGERS. PRESENT AT THE SCENE.
THERE'S MORE, TOO. THE REPORT SAYS MR. ROGERS WAS DISTRAUGHT. THE OFFICER WHO TOOK THIS DOWN SAID HE HEARD HIM SAY, "THIS IS ALL MY FAULT. I COULD HAVE STOPPED IT.
"THIS IS ALL MY FAULT."
YOU WORK WITH THESE OLD RECORDS ALL THE TIME. YOU'RE PROBABLY THE PREEMINENT EXPERT ON THESE FILES IN CALIFORNIA, RIGHT?
THERE ARE A FEW OTHER GUYS UP NORTH, BUT BASICALLY, YES. THAT'S FAIR TO SAY.
HAVE YOU EVER SEEN ONE FALSIFIED?
WELL...WELL... YES, BUT IT'S RARE, AND IT USUALLY ONLY HAPPENS WHEN THERE'S SOME OTHER AGENDA-- I MEAN, BACK THEN, THIS CASE, WHY WOULD SOMEONE--
THANK YOU, OFFICER. NO FURTHER QUESTIONS.

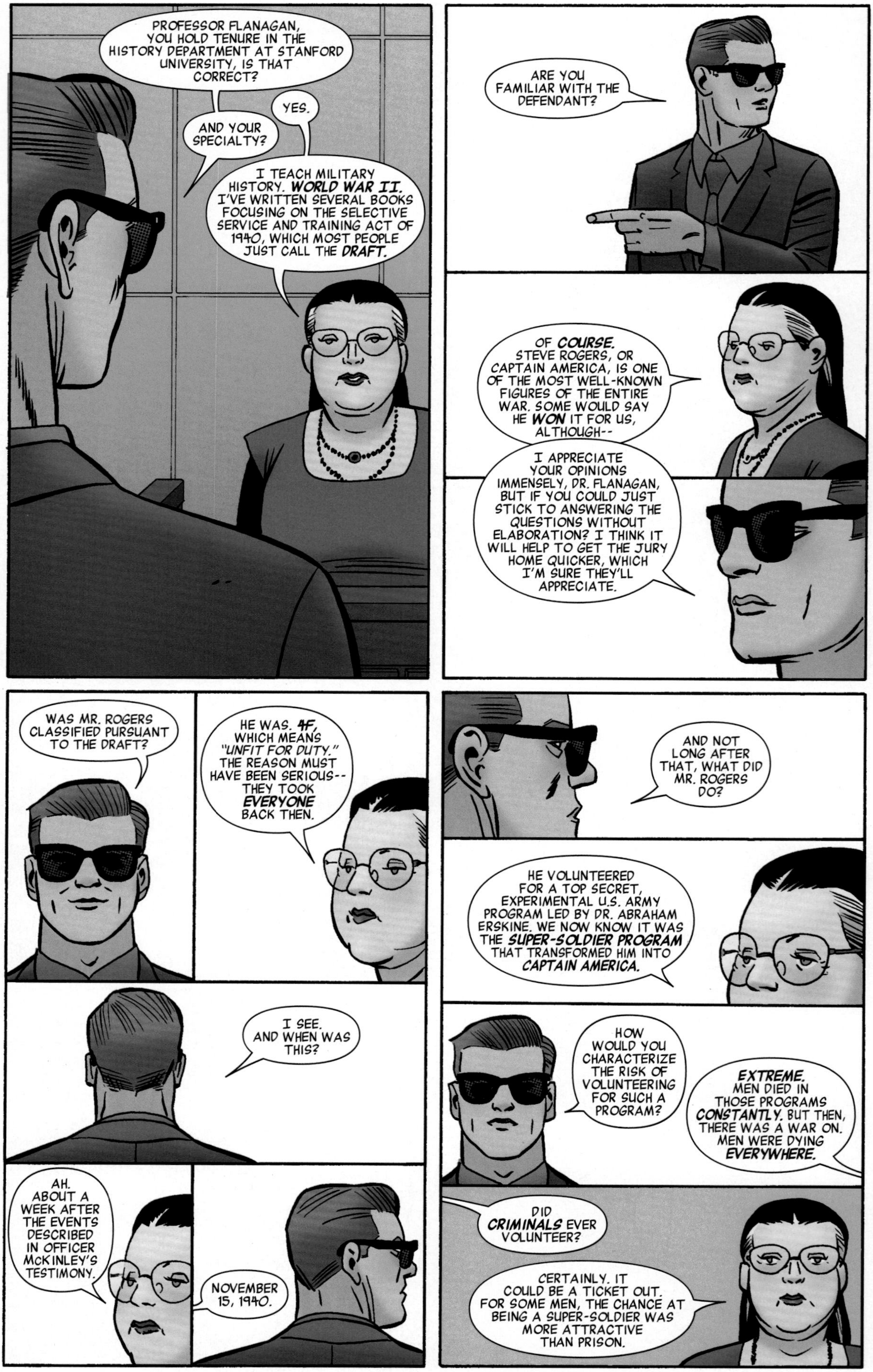
PROFESSOR FLANAGAN, YOU HOLD TENURE IN THE HISTORY DEPARTMENT AT STANFORD UNIVERSITY, IS THAT CORRECT?
YES.
AND YOUR SPECIALTY?
I TEACH MILITARY HISTORY. WORLD WAR II. I'VE WRITTEN SEVERAL BOOKS FOCUSING ON THE SELECTIVE SERVICE AND TRAINING ACT OF 1940, WHICH MOST PEOPLE JUST CALL THE DRAFT.
ARE YOU FAMILIAR WITH THE DEFENDANT?
OF COURSE. STEVE ROGERS, OR CAPTAIN AMERICA, IS ONE OF THE MOST WELL-KNOWN FIGURES OF THE ENTIRE WAR. SOME WOULD SAY HE WON IT FOR US, ALTHOUGH--
I APPRECIATE YOUR OPINIONS IMMENSELY, DR. FLANAGAN, BUT IF YOU COULD JUST STICK TO ANSWERING THE QUESTIONS WITHOUT ELABORATION? I THINK IT WILL HELP TO GET THE JURY HOME QUICKER, WHICH I'M SURE THEY'LL APPRECIATE.
WAS MR. ROGERS CLASSIFIED PURSUANT TO THE DRAFT?
HE WAS. 4F, WHICH MEANS "UNFIT FOR DUTY." THE REASON MUST HAVE BEEN SERIOUS-- THEY TOOK EVERYONE BACK THEN.
I SEE. AND WHEN WAS THIS?
AH. ABOUT A WEEK AFTER THE EVENTS DESCRIBED IN OFFICER McKINLEY'S TESTIMONY.
NOVEMBER 15, 1940.
AND NOT LONG AFTER THAT, WHAT DID MR. ROGERS DO?
HE VOLUNTEERED FOR A TOP SECRET, EXPERIMENTAL U.S. ARMY PROGRAM LED BY DR. ABRAHAM ERSKINE. WE NOW KNOW IT WAS THE SUPER-SOLDIER PROGRAM THAT TRANSFORMED HIM INTO CAPTAIN AMERICA.
HOW WOULD YOU CHARACTERIZE THE RISK OF VOLUNTEERING FOR SUCH A PROGRAM?
EXTREME. MEN DIED IN THOSE PROGRAMS CONSTANTLY. BUT THEN, THERE WAS A WAR ON. MEN WERE DYING EVERYWHERE.
DID CRIMINALS EVER VOLUNTEER?
CERTAINLY. IT COULD BE A TICKET OUT. FOR SOME MEN, THE CHANCE AT BEING A SUPER-SOLDIER WAS MORE ATTRACTIVE THAN PRISON.

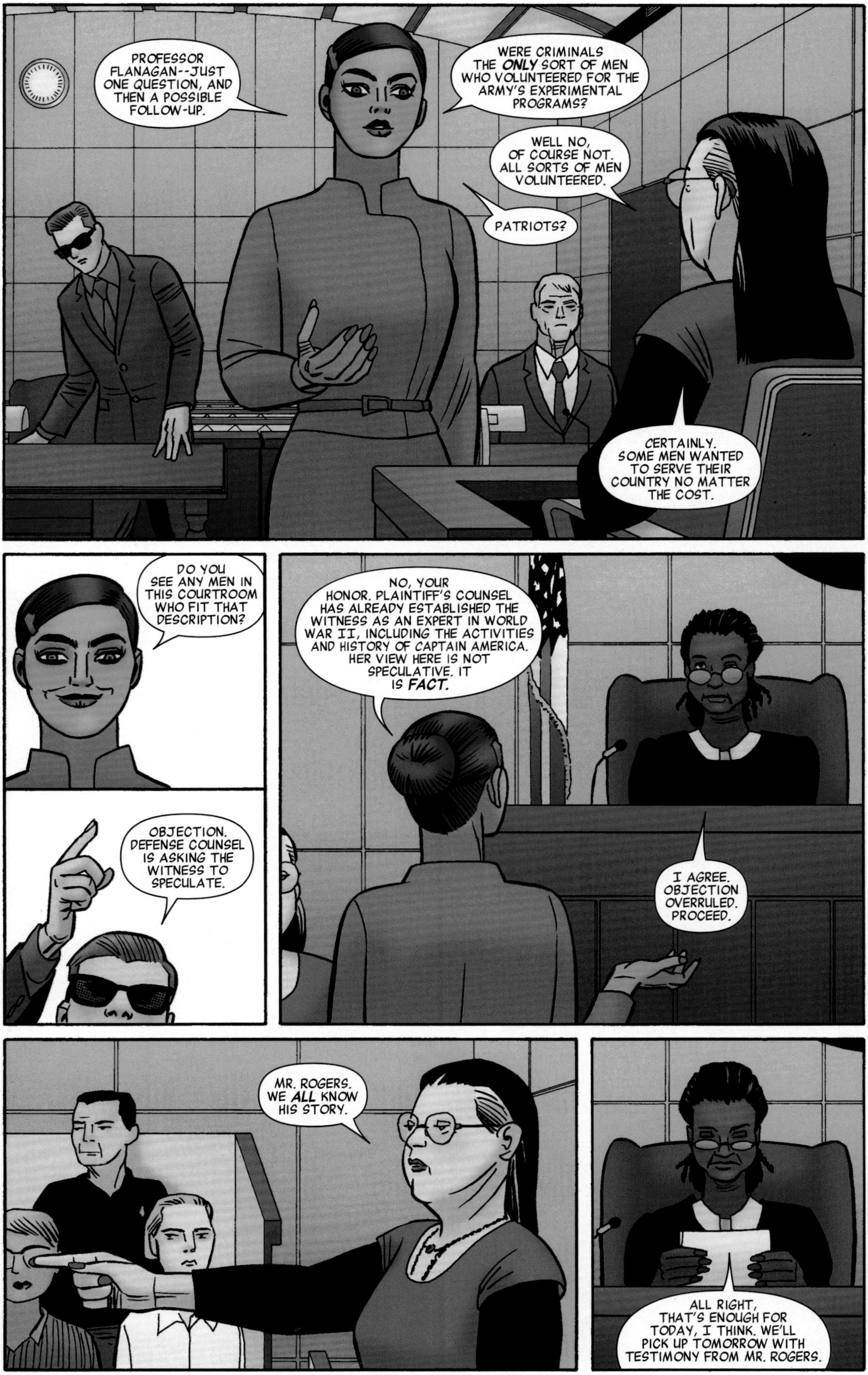
PROFESSOR FLANAGAN--JUST ONE QUESTION, AND THEN A POSSIBLE FOLLOW-UP.
WERE CRIMINALS THE ONLY SORT OF MEN WHO VOLUNTEERED FOR THE ARMY'S EXPERIMENTAL PROGRAMS?
WELL NO, OF COURSE NOT. ALL SORTS OF MEN VOLUNTEERED.
PATRIOTS?
CERTAINLY. SOME MEN WANTED TO SERVE THEIR COUNTRY NO MATTER THE COST.
DO YOU SEE ANY MEN IN THIS COURTROOM WHO FIT THAT DESCRIPTION?
OBJECTION. DEFENSE COUNSEL IS ASKING THE WITNESS TO SPECULATE.
NO, YOUR HONOR. PLAINTIFF'S COUNSEL HAS ALREADY ESTABLISHED THE WITNESS AS AN EXPERT IN WORLD WAR II, INCLUDING THE ACTIVITIES AND HISTORY OF CAPTAIN AMERICA. HER VIEW HERE IS NOT SPECULATIVE. IT IS FACT.
I AGREE. OBJECTION OVERRULED. PROCEED.
MR. ROGERS. WE ALL KNOW HIS STORY.
ALL RIGHT, THAT'S ENOUGH FOR TODAY, I THINK. WE'LL PICK UP TOMORROW WITH TESTIMONY FROM MR. ROGERS.

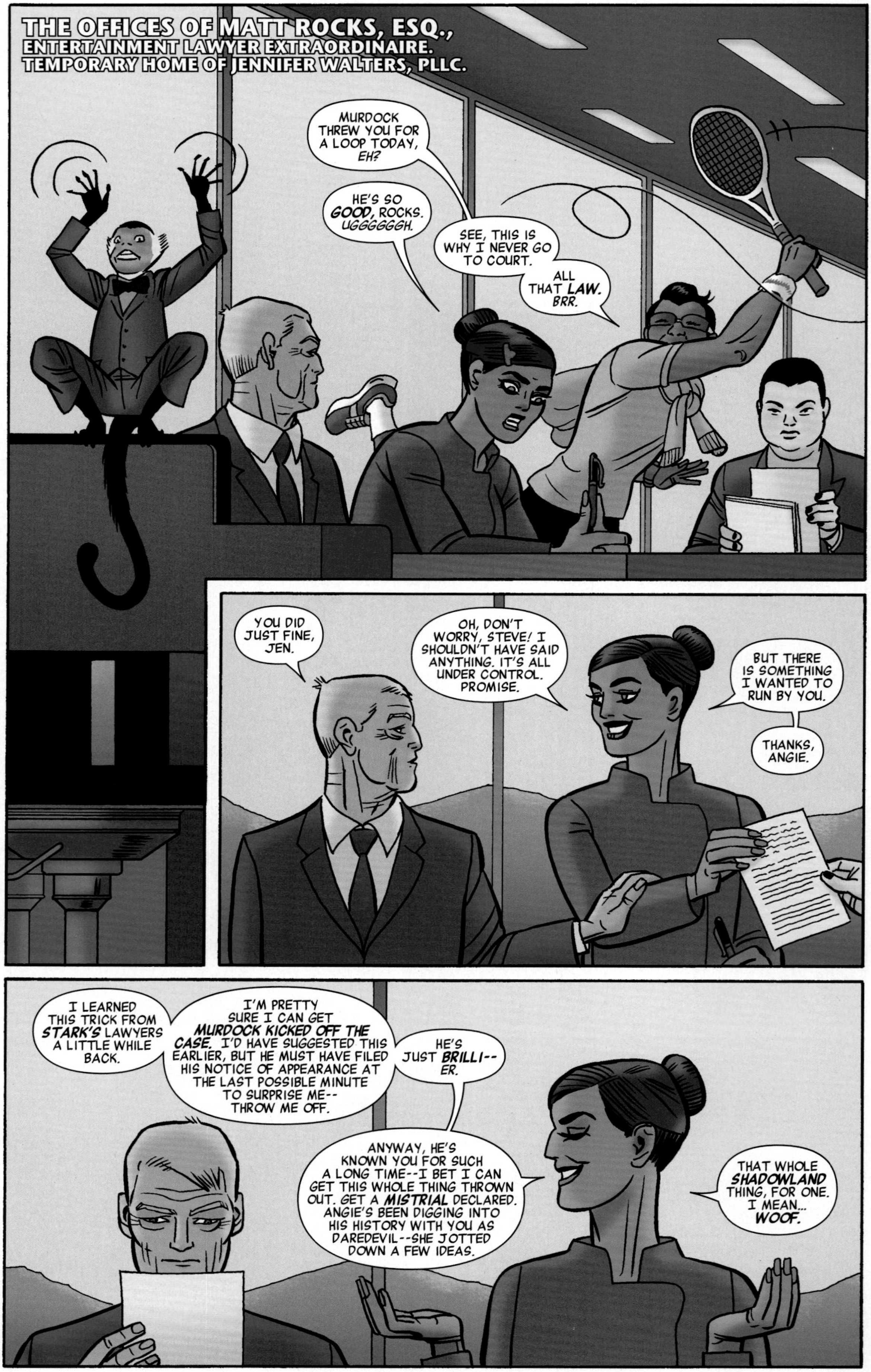
THE OFFICES OF MATT ROCKS, ESQ.,
ENTERTAINMENT LAWYER EXTRAORDINAIRE.
TEMPORARY HOME OF JENNIFER WALTERS, PLLC.
MURDOCK THREW YOU FOR A LOOP TODAY, EH?
HE'S SO GOOD, ROCKS. UGGGGGGH.
SEE, THIS IS WHY I NEVER GO TO COURT.
ALL THAT LAW. BRR.
YOU DID JUST FINE, JEN.
OH, DON'T WORRY, STEVE! I SHOULDN'T HAVE SAID ANYTHING. IT'S ALL UNDER CONTROL. PROMISE.
BUT THERE IS SOMETHING I WANTED TO RUN BY YOU.
THANKS, ANGIE.
I LEARNED THIS TRICK FROM STARK'S LAWYERS A LITTLE WHILE BACK.
I'M PRETTY SURE I CAN GET MURDOCK KICKED OFF THE CASE. I'D HAVE SUGGESTED THIS EARLIER, BUT HE MUST HAVE FILED HIS NOTICE OF APPEARANCE AT THE LAST POSSIBLE MINUTE TO SURPRISE ME-- THROW ME OFF.
HE'S JUST BRILLI-- ER.
ANYWAY, HE'S KNOWN YOU FOR SUCH A LONG TIME--I BET I CAN GET THIS WHOLE THING THROWN OUT. GET A MISTRIAL DECLARED. ANGIE'S BEEN DIGGING INTO HIS HISTORY WITH YOU AS DAREDEVIL--SHE JOTTED DOWN A FEW IDEAS.
THAT WHOLE SHADOWLAND THING, FOR ONE. I MEAN... WOOF.

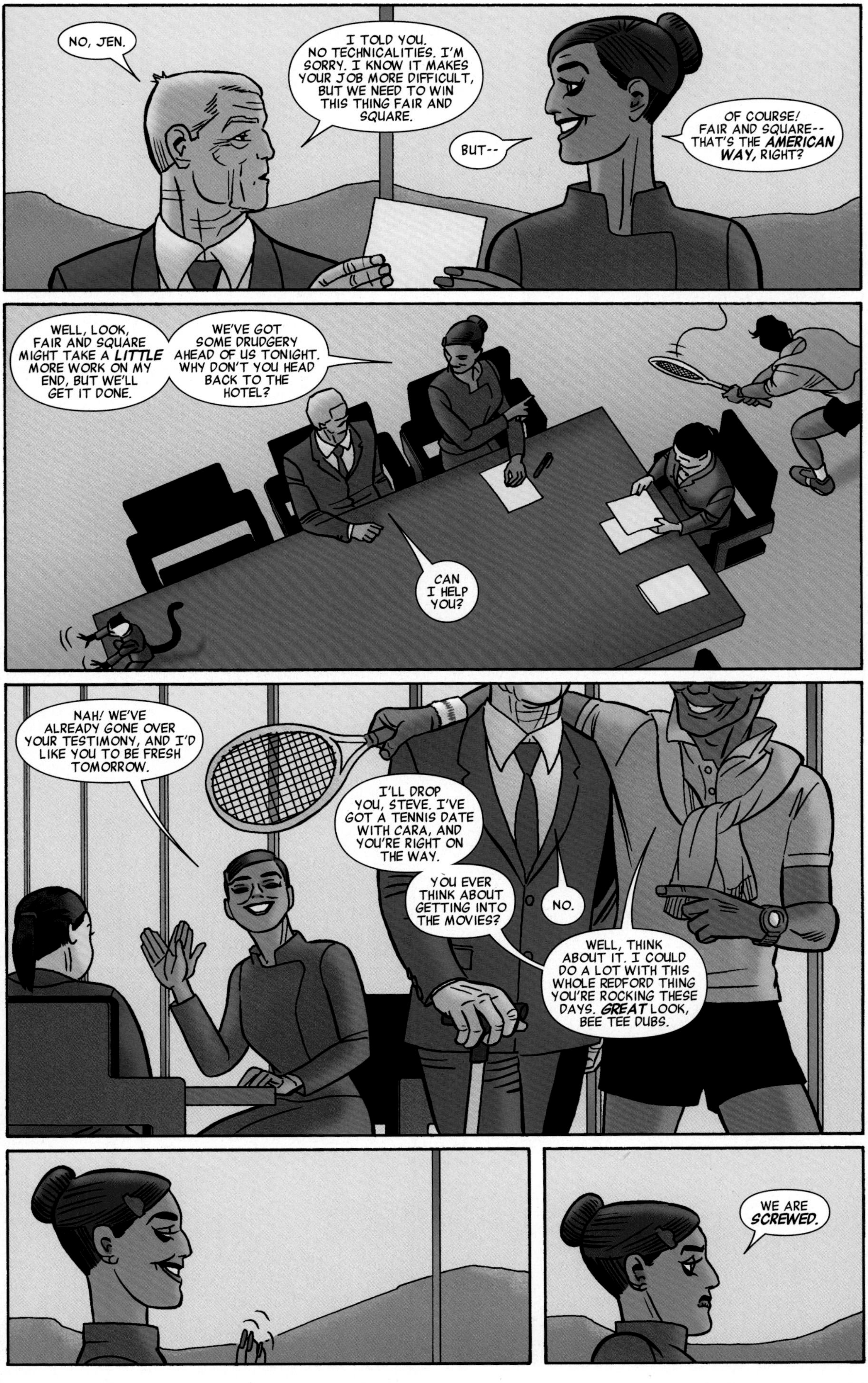
NO, JEN.
I TOLD YOU. NO TECHNICALITIES. I'M SORRY. I KNOW IT MAKES YOUR JOB MORE DIFFICULT, BUT WE NEED TO WIN THIS THING FAIR AND SQUARE.
BUT--
OF COURSE! FAIR AND SQUARE-- THAT'S THE *AMERICAN WAY,* RIGHT?
WELL, LOOK, FAIR AND SQUARE MIGHT TAKE A *LITTLE* MORE WORK ON MY END, BUT WE'LL GET IT DONE.
WE'VE GOT SOME DRUDGERY AHEAD OF US TONIGHT. WHY DON'T YOU HEAD BACK TO THE HOTEL?
CAN I HELP YOU?
NAH! WE'VE ALREADY GONE OVER YOUR TESTIMONY, AND I'D LIKE YOU TO BE FRESH TOMORROW.
I'LL DROP YOU, STEVE. I'VE GOT A TENNIS DATE WITH CARA, AND YOU'RE RIGHT ON THE WAY.
YOU EVER THINK ABOUT GETTING INTO THE MOVIES?
NO.
WELL, THINK ABOUT IT. I COULD DO A LOT WITH THIS WHOLE REDFORD THING YOU'RE ROCKING THESE DAYS. *GREAT* LOOK, BEE TEE DUBS.
WE ARE *SCREWED.*

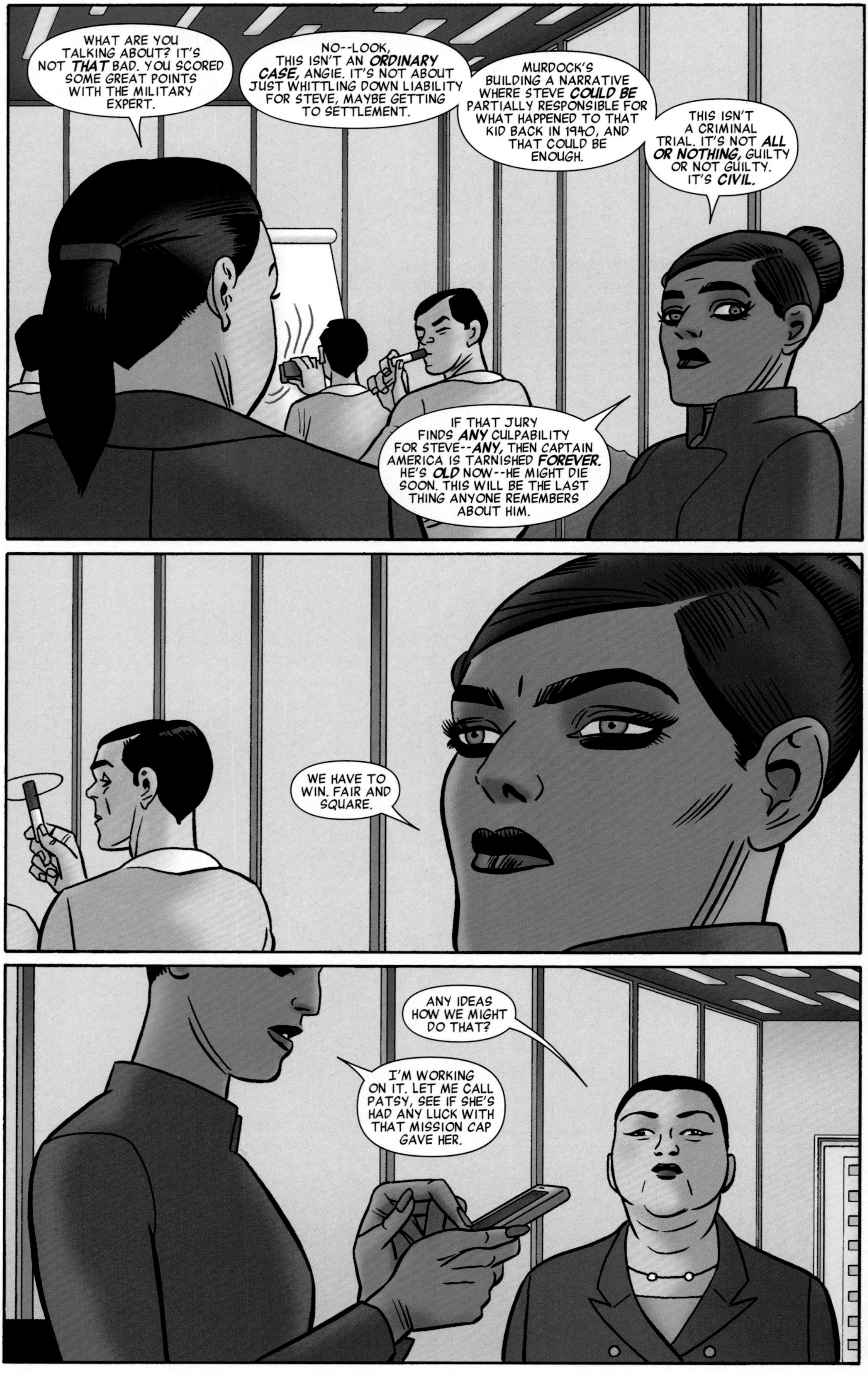
WHAT ARE YOU TALKING ABOUT? IT'S NOT **THAT** BAD. YOU SCORED SOME GREAT POINTS WITH THE MILITARY EXPERT.
NO--LOOK, THIS ISN'T AN **ORDINARY CASE,** ANGIE. IT'S NOT ABOUT JUST WHITTLING DOWN LIABILITY FOR STEVE, MAYBE GETTING TO SETTLEMENT.
MURDOCK'S BUILDING A NARRATIVE WHERE STEVE **COULD BE** PARTIALLY RESPONSIBLE FOR WHAT HAPPENED TO THAT KID BACK IN 1940, AND THAT COULD BE ENOUGH.
THIS ISN'T A CRIMINAL TRIAL. IT'S NOT **ALL OR NOTHING,** GUILTY OR NOT GUILTY. IT'S **CIVIL.**
IF THAT JURY FINDS **ANY** CULPABILITY FOR STEVE--**ANY,** THEN CAPTAIN AMERICA IS TARNISHED **FOREVER.** HE'S **OLD** NOW--HE MIGHT DIE SOON. THIS WILL BE THE LAST THING ANYONE REMEMBERS ABOUT HIM.
WE HAVE TO WIN. FAIR AND SQUARE.
ANY IDEAS HOW WE MIGHT DO THAT?
I'M WORKING ON IT. LET ME CALL PATSY, SEE IF SHE'S HAD ANY LUCK WITH THAT MISSION CAP GAVE HER.

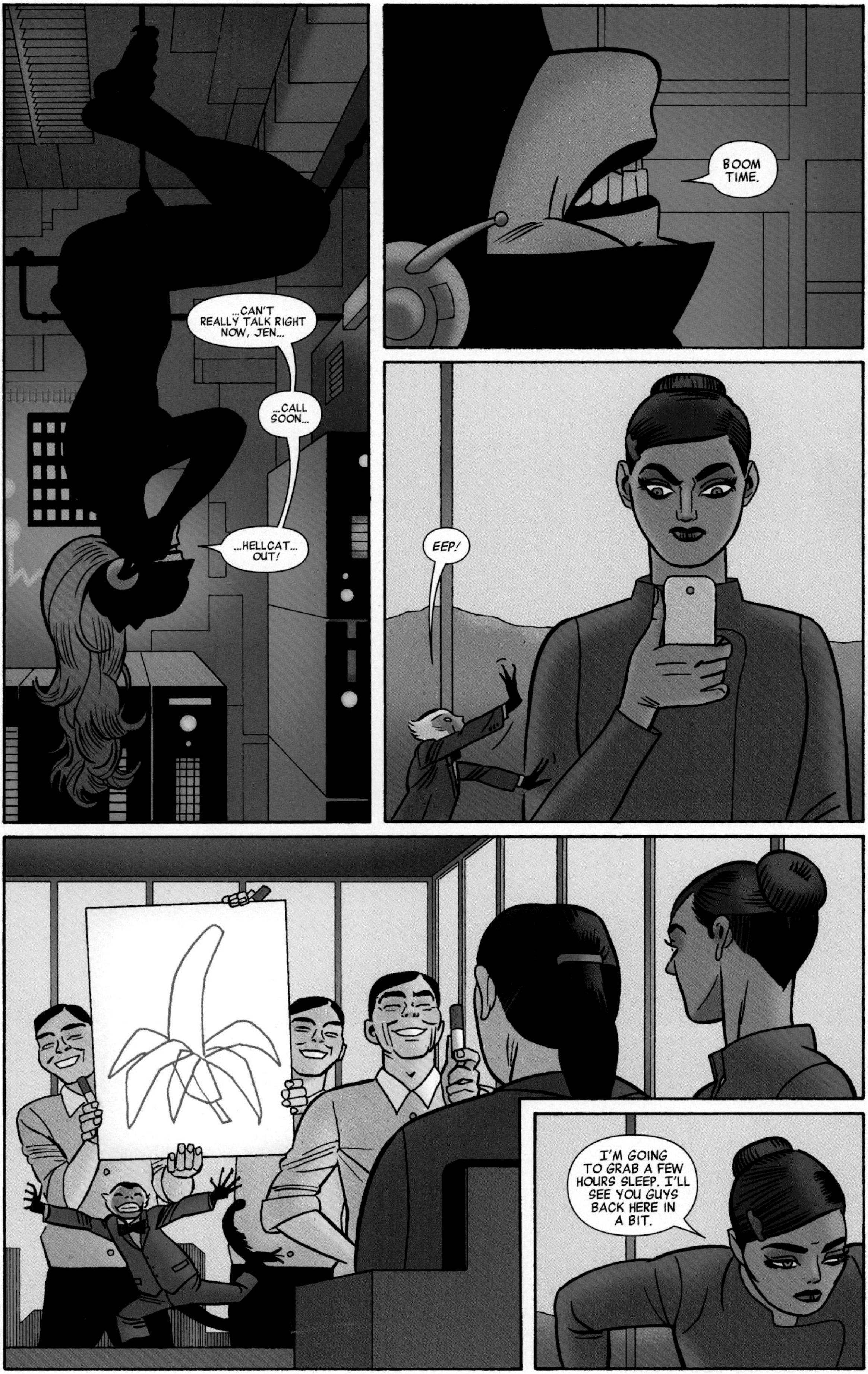
...CAN'T REALLY TALK RIGHT NOW, JEN...
...CALL SOON...
...HELLCAT... OUT!
BOOM TIME.
EEP!
I'M GOING TO GRAB A FEW HOURS SLEEP. I'LL SEE YOU GUYS BACK HERE IN A BIT.

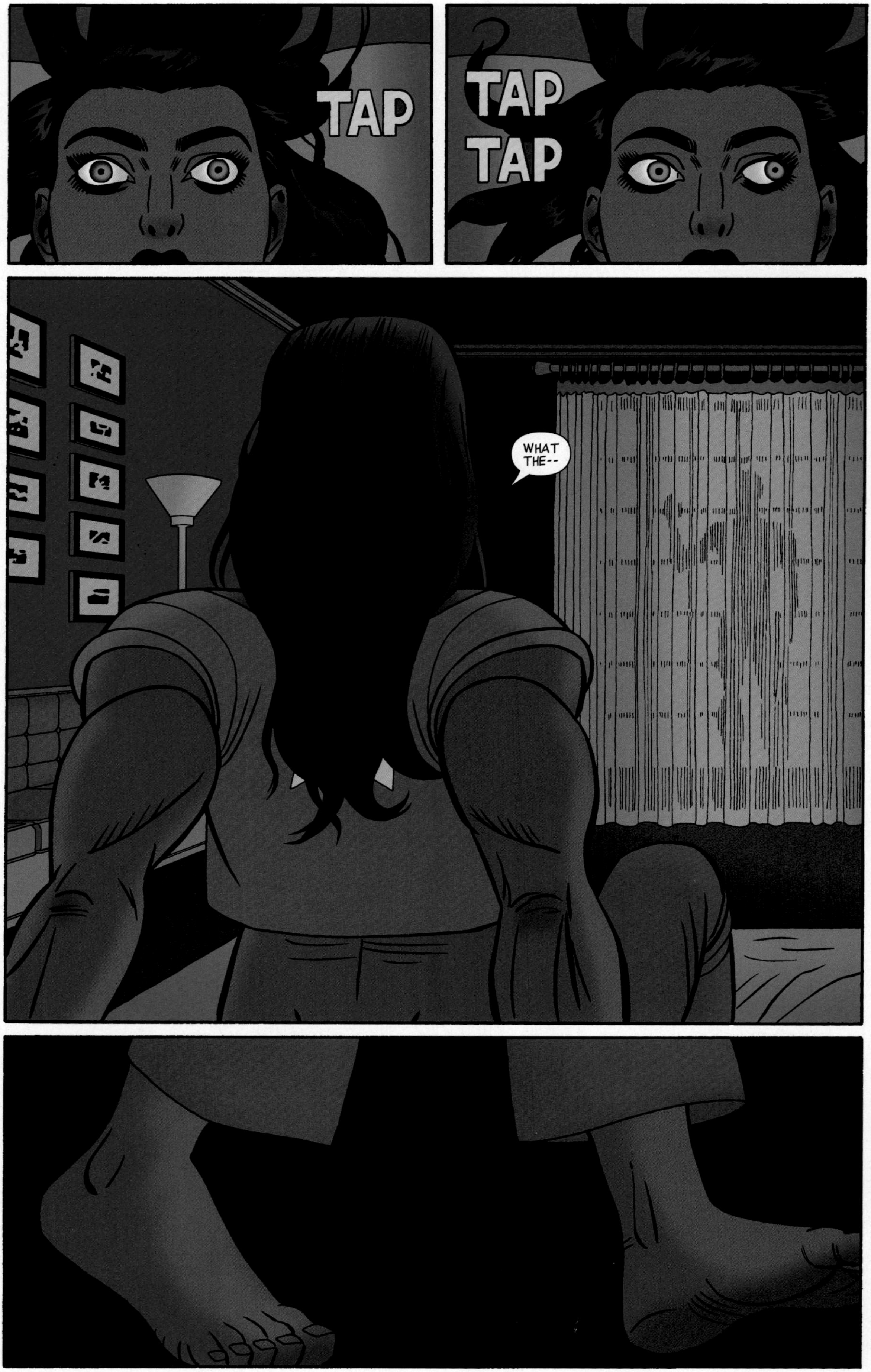
TAP
TAP
TAP
WHAT THE--

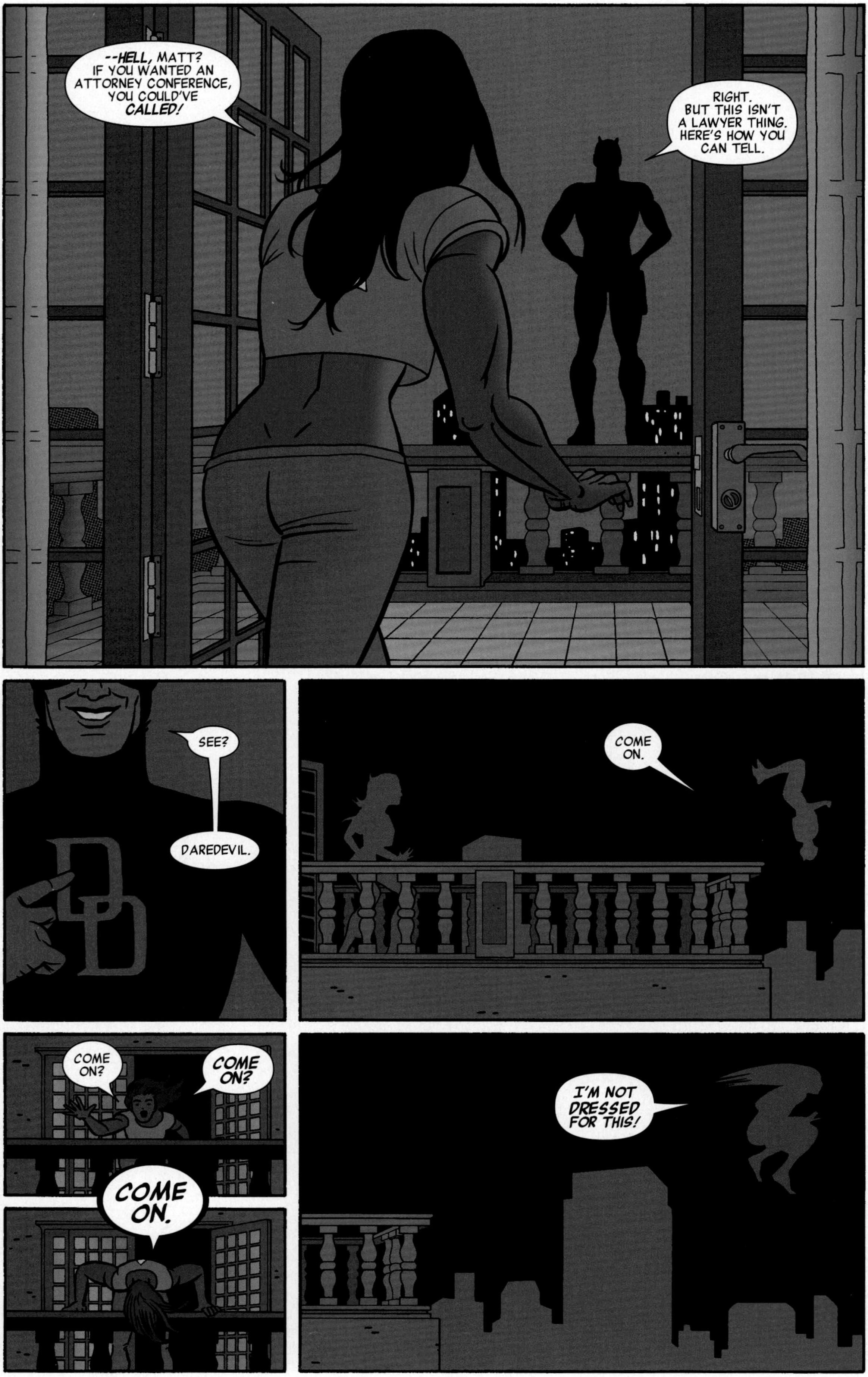
--HELL, MATT? IF YOU WANTED AN ATTORNEY CONFERENCE, YOU COULD'VE CALLED!
RIGHT. BUT THIS ISN'T A LAWYER THING. HERE'S HOW YOU CAN TELL.
SEE?
DAREDEVIL.
COME ON.
COME ON?
COME ON?
COME ON.
I'M NOT DRESSED FOR THIS!

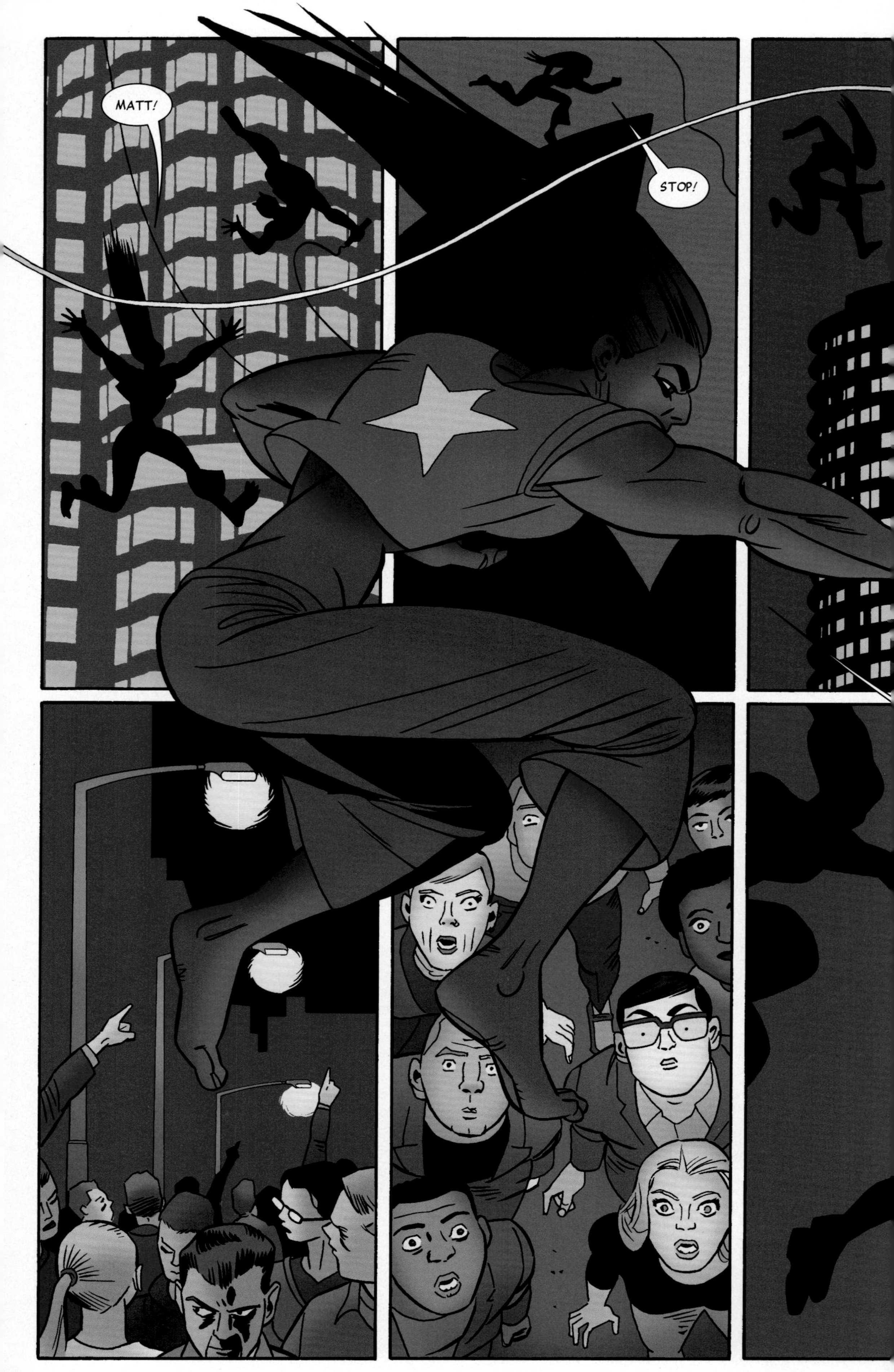
MATT!
STOP!

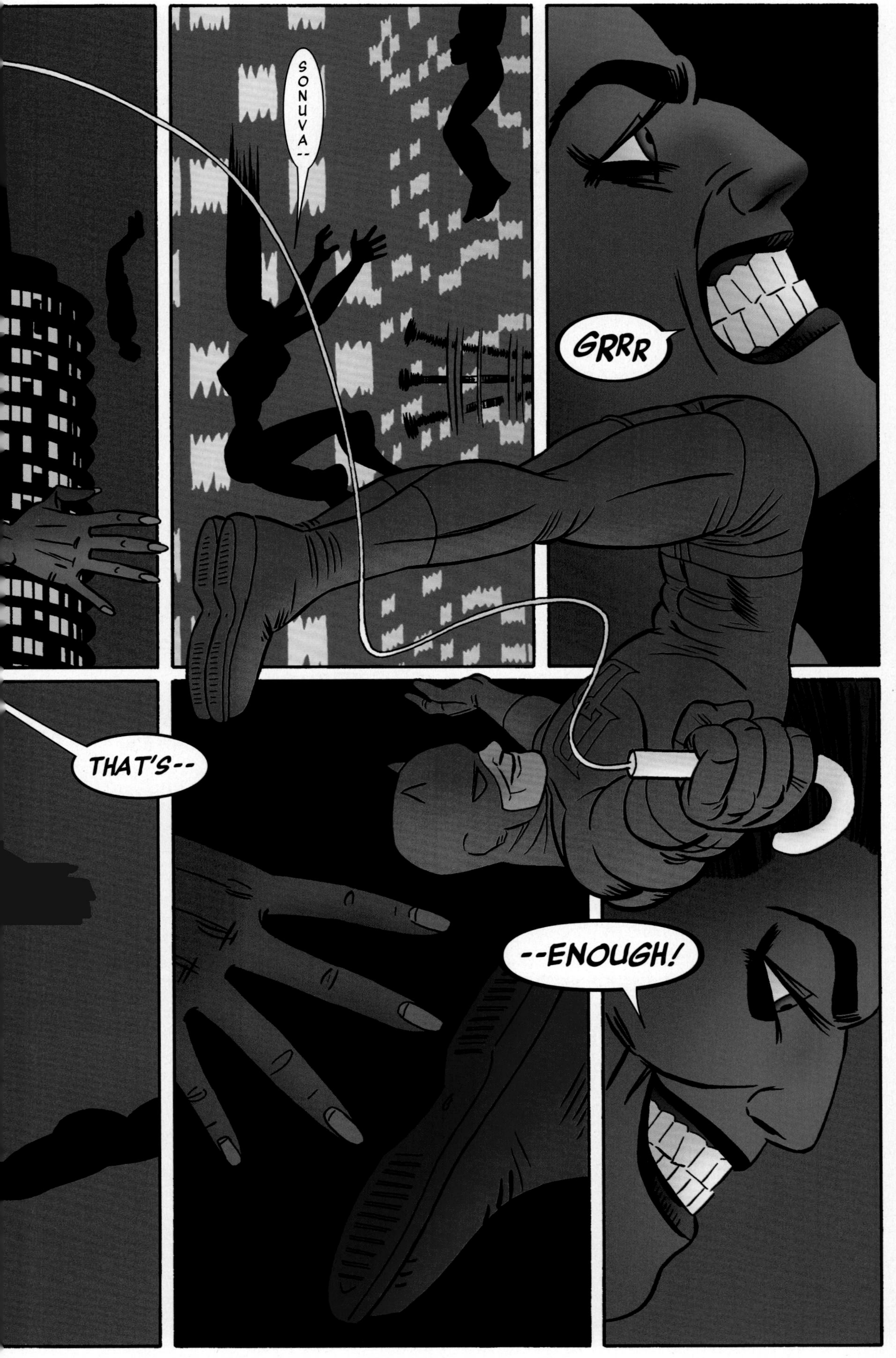
SONUVA--
GRRR
THAT'S--
--ENOUGH!

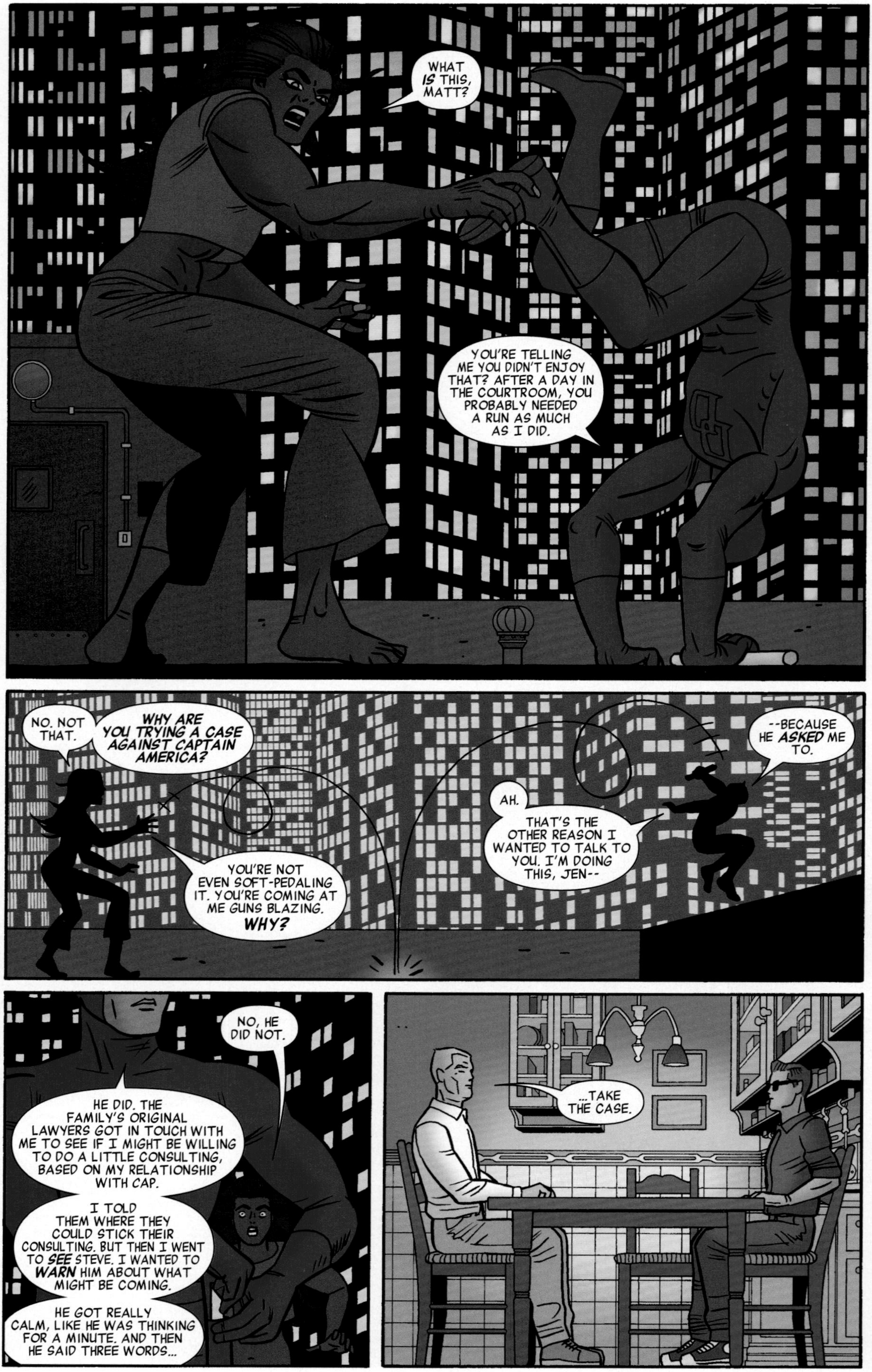
WHAT *IS* THIS, MATT?
YOU'RE TELLING ME YOU DIDN'T ENJOY THAT? AFTER A DAY IN THE COURTROOM, YOU PROBABLY NEEDED A RUN AS MUCH AS I DID.
NO. NOT THAT.
WHY ARE YOU TRYING A CASE AGAINST CAPTAIN AMERICA?
YOU'RE NOT EVEN SOFT-PEDALING IT. YOU'RE COMING AT ME GUNS BLAZING. *WHY?*
AH.
THAT'S THE OTHER REASON I WANTED TO TALK TO YOU. I'M DOING THIS, JEN--
--BECAUSE HE *ASKED* ME TO.
NO, HE DID NOT.
HE DID. THE FAMILY'S ORIGINAL LAWYERS GOT IN TOUCH WITH ME TO SEE IF I MIGHT BE WILLING TO DO A LITTLE CONSULTING, BASED ON MY RELATIONSHIP WITH CAP.
I TOLD THEM WHERE THEY COULD STICK THEIR CONSULTING. BUT THEN I WENT TO *SEE* STEVE. I WANTED TO *WARN* HIM ABOUT WHAT MIGHT BE COMING.
HE GOT REALLY CALM, LIKE HE WAS THINKING FOR A MINUTE. AND THEN HE SAID THREE WORDS...
...TAKE THE CASE.

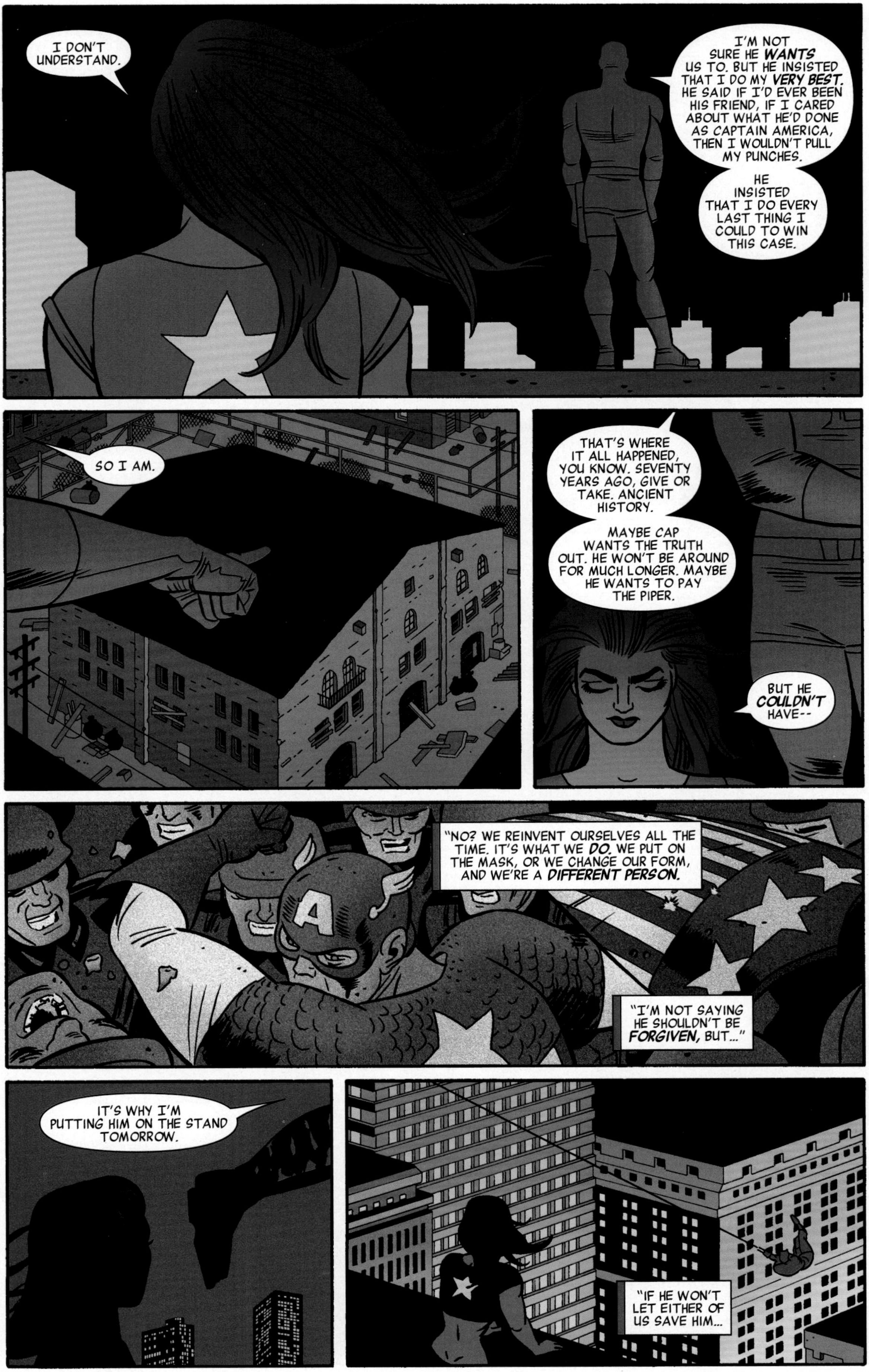
I DON'T UNDERSTAND.
I'M NOT SURE HE **WANTS** US TO. BUT HE INSISTED THAT I DO MY **VERY BEST.** HE SAID IF I'D EVER BEEN HIS FRIEND, IF I CARED ABOUT WHAT HE'D DONE AS CAPTAIN AMERICA, THEN I WOULDN'T PULL MY PUNCHES.
HE INSISTED THAT I DO EVERY LAST THING I COULD TO WIN THIS CASE.
SO I AM.
THAT'S WHERE IT ALL HAPPENED, YOU KNOW. SEVENTY YEARS AGO, GIVE OR TAKE. ANCIENT HISTORY.
MAYBE CAP WANTS THE TRUTH OUT. HE WON'T BE AROUND FOR MUCH LONGER. MAYBE HE WANTS TO PAY THE PIPER.
BUT HE **COULDN'T** HAVE--
"NO? WE REINVENT OURSELVES ALL THE TIME. IT'S WHAT WE **DO.** WE PUT ON THE MASK, OR WE CHANGE OUR FORM, AND WE'RE A **DIFFERENT PERSON.**
"I'M NOT SAYING HE SHOULDN'T BE **FORGIVEN,** BUT..."
IT'S WHY I'M PUTTING HIM ON THE STAND TOMORROW.
"IF HE WON'T LET EITHER OF US SAVE HIM...

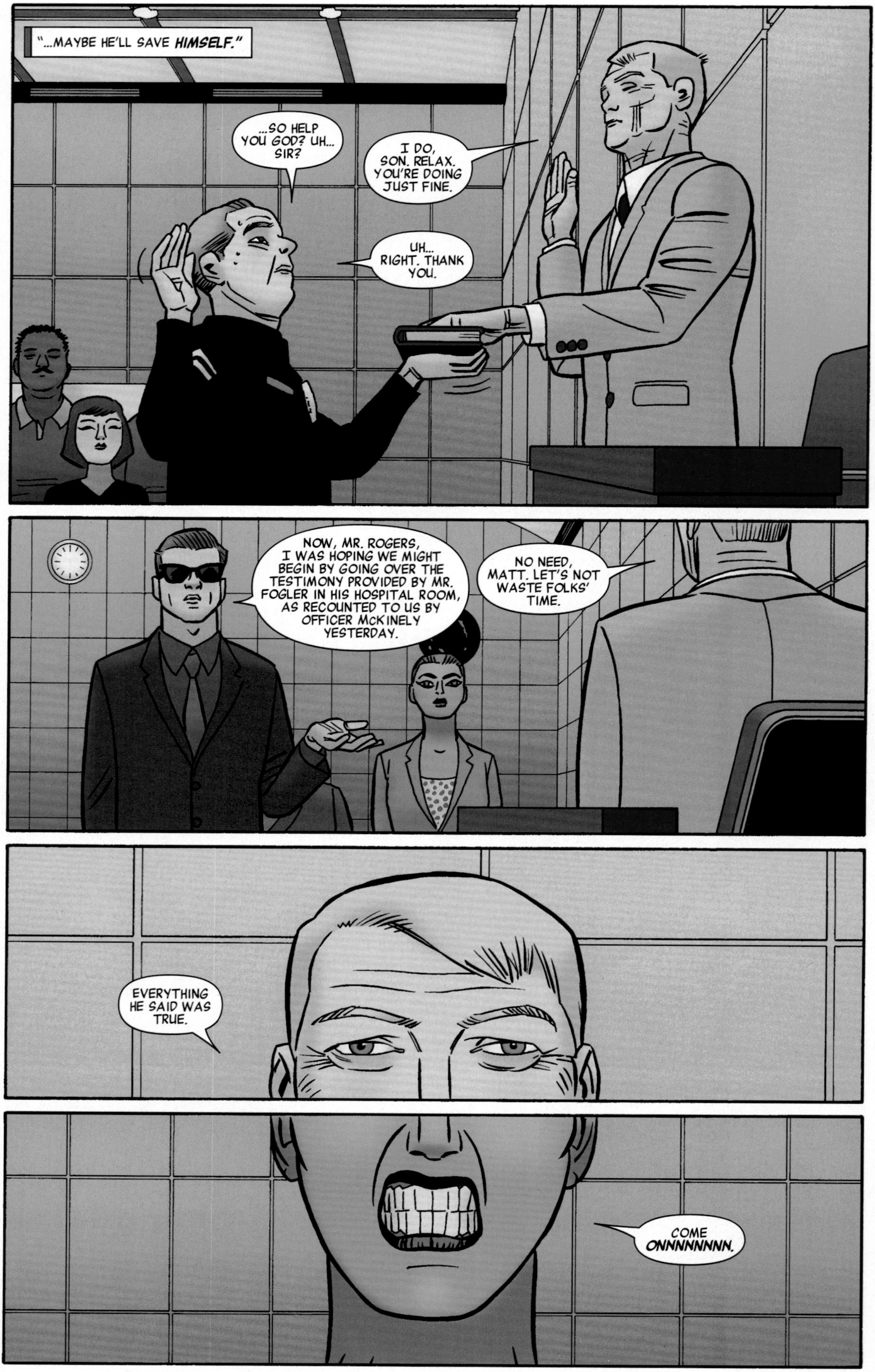
"...MAYBE HE'LL SAVE HIMSELF."
...SO HELP YOU GOD? UH... SIR?
I DO, SON. RELAX. YOU'RE DOING JUST FINE.
UH... RIGHT. THANK YOU.
NOW, MR. ROGERS, I WAS HOPING WE MIGHT BEGIN BY GOING OVER THE TESTIMONY PROVIDED BY MR. FOGLER IN HIS HOSPITAL ROOM, AS RECOUNTED TO US BY OFFICER MCKINELY YESTERDAY.
NO NEED, MATT. LET'S NOT WASTE FOLKS' TIME.
EVERYTHING HE SAID WAS TRUE.
COME ONNNNNNNN.

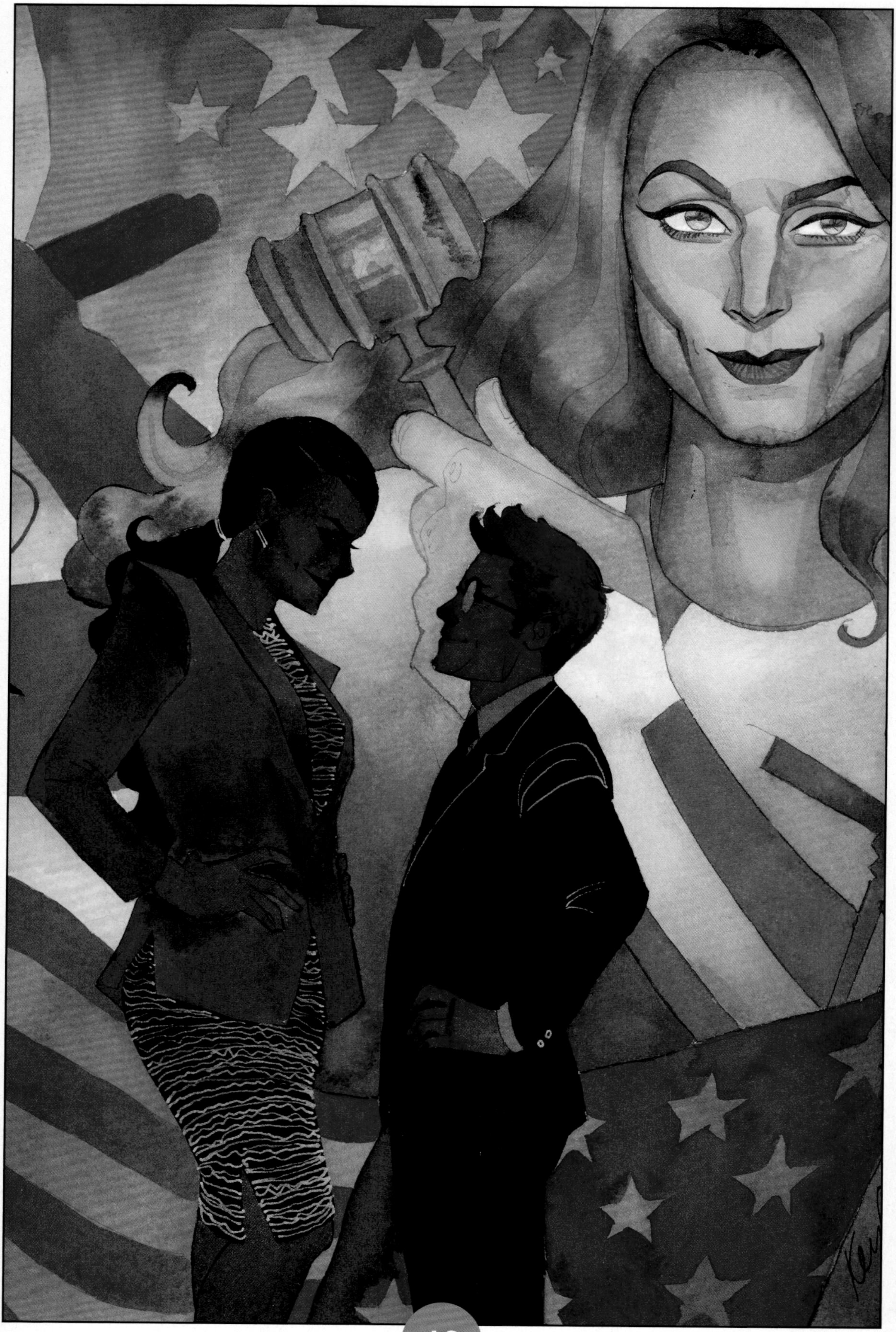

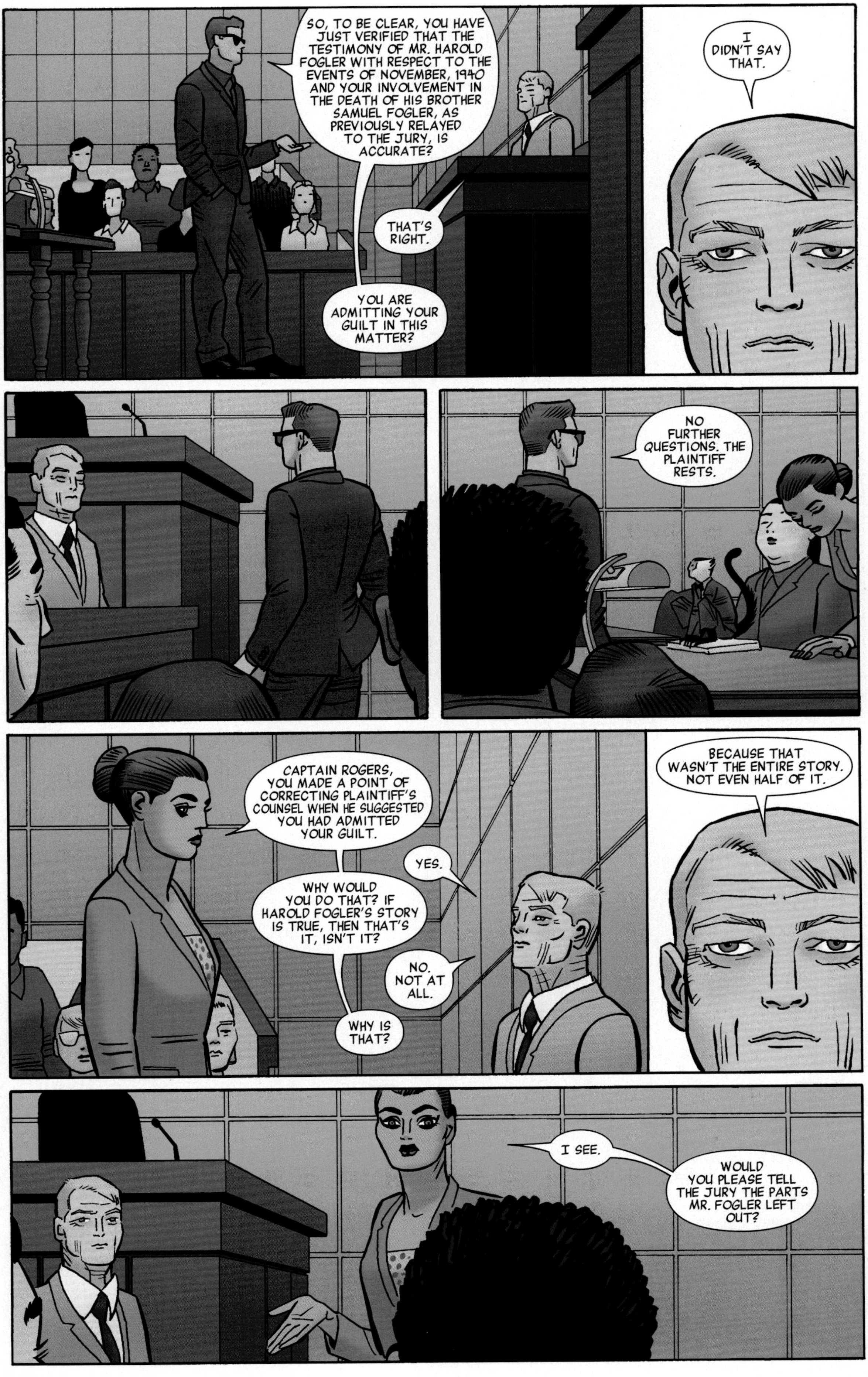
SO, TO BE CLEAR, YOU HAVE JUST VERIFIED THAT THE TESTIMONY OF MR. HAROLD FOGLER WITH RESPECT TO THE EVENTS OF NOVEMBER, 1940 AND YOUR INVOLVEMENT IN THE DEATH OF HIS BROTHER SAMUEL FOGLER, AS PREVIOUSLY RELAYED TO THE JURY, IS ACCURATE?
THAT'S RIGHT.
YOU ARE ADMITTING YOUR GUILT IN THIS MATTER?
I DIDN'T SAY THAT.
NO FURTHER QUESTIONS. THE PLAINTIFF RESTS.
CAPTAIN ROGERS, YOU MADE A POINT OF CORRECTING PLAINTIFF'S COUNSEL WHEN HE SUGGESTED YOU HAD ADMITTED YOUR GUILT.
YES.
WHY WOULD YOU DO THAT? IF HAROLD FOGLER'S STORY IS TRUE, THEN THAT'S IT, ISN'T IT?
NO. NOT AT ALL.
WHY IS THAT?
BECAUSE THAT WASN'T THE ENTIRE STORY. NOT EVEN HALF OF IT.
I SEE.
WOULD YOU PLEASE TELL THE JURY THE PARTS MR. FOGLER LEFT OUT?

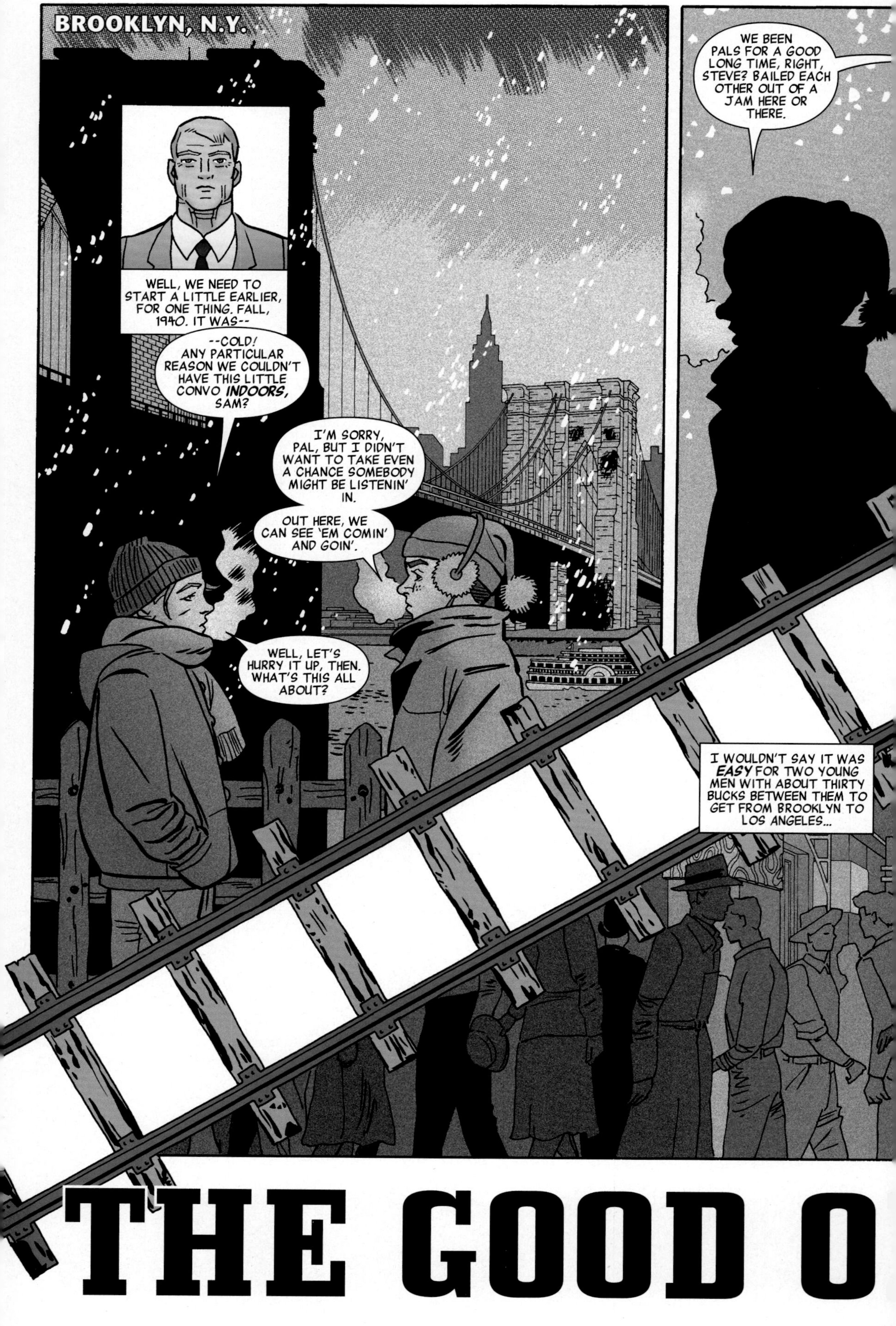
BROOKLYN, N.Y.
WELL, WE NEED TO START A LITTLE EARLIER, FOR ONE THING. FALL, 1940. IT WAS--
--COLD! ANY PARTICULAR REASON WE COULDN'T HAVE THIS LITTLE CONVO INDOORS, SAM?
I'M SORRY, PAL, BUT I DIDN'T WANT TO TAKE EVEN A CHANCE SOMEBODY MIGHT BE LISTENIN' IN.
OUT HERE, WE CAN SEE 'EM COMIN' AND GOIN'.
WELL, LET'S HURRY IT UP, THEN. WHAT'S THIS ALL ABOUT?
WE BEEN PALS FOR A GOOD LONG TIME, RIGHT, STEVE? BAILED EACH OTHER OUT OF A JAM HERE OR THERE.
I WOULDN'T SAY IT WAS EASY FOR TWO YOUNG MEN WITH ABOUT THIRTY BUCKS BETWEEN THEM TO GET FROM BROOKLYN TO LOS ANGELES...
THE GOOD O

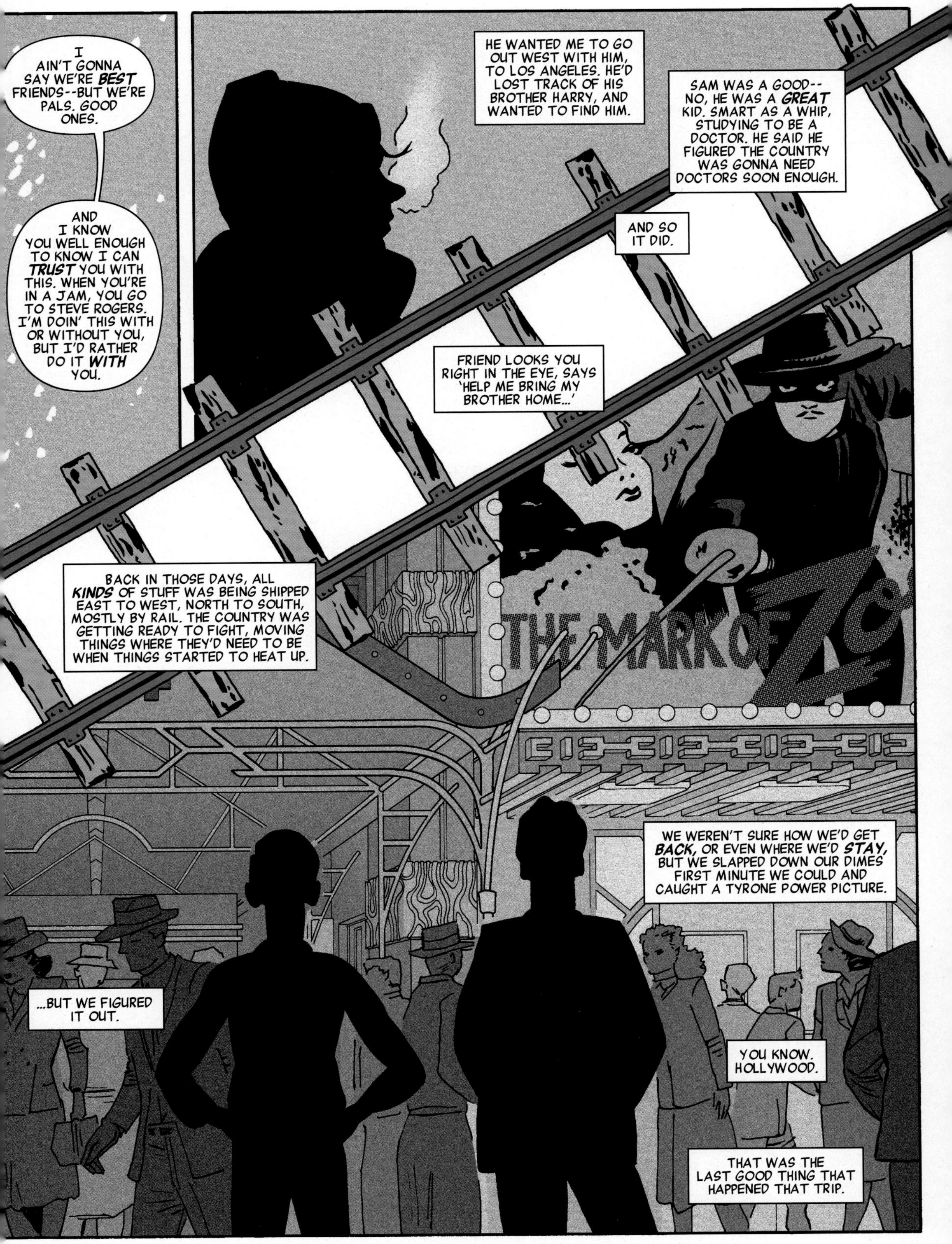
I AIN'T GONNA SAY WE'RE BEST FRIENDS--BUT WE'RE PALS. GOOD ONES.
AND I KNOW YOU WELL ENOUGH TO KNOW I CAN TRUST YOU WITH THIS. WHEN YOU'RE IN A JAM, YOU GO TO STEVE ROGERS. I'M DOIN' THIS WITH OR WITHOUT YOU, BUT I'D RATHER DO IT WITH YOU.
HE WANTED ME TO GO OUT WEST WITH HIM, TO LOS ANGELES. HE'D LOST TRACK OF HIS BROTHER HARRY, AND WANTED TO FIND HIM.
SAM WAS A GOOD-- NO, HE WAS A GREAT KID. SMART AS A WHIP, STUDYING TO BE A DOCTOR. HE SAID HE FIGURED THE COUNTRY WAS GONNA NEED DOCTORS SOON ENOUGH.
AND SO IT DID.
FRIEND LOOKS YOU RIGHT IN THE EYE, SAYS 'HELP ME BRING MY BROTHER HOME...'
BACK IN THOSE DAYS, ALL KINDS OF STUFF WAS BEING SHIPPED EAST TO WEST, NORTH TO SOUTH, MOSTLY BY RAIL. THE COUNTRY WAS GETTING READY TO FIGHT, MOVING THINGS WHERE THEY'D NEED TO BE WHEN THINGS STARTED TO HEAT UP.
THE MARK OF Z
WE WEREN'T SURE HOW WE'D GET BACK, OR EVEN WHERE WE'D STAY, BUT WE SLAPPED DOWN OUR DIMES FIRST MINUTE WE COULD AND CAUGHT A TYRONE POWER PICTURE.
...BUT WE FIGURED IT OUT.
YOU KNOW. HOLLYWOOD.
THAT WAS THE LAST GOOD THING THAT HAPPENED THAT TRIP.

D DAYS CONCLUSION

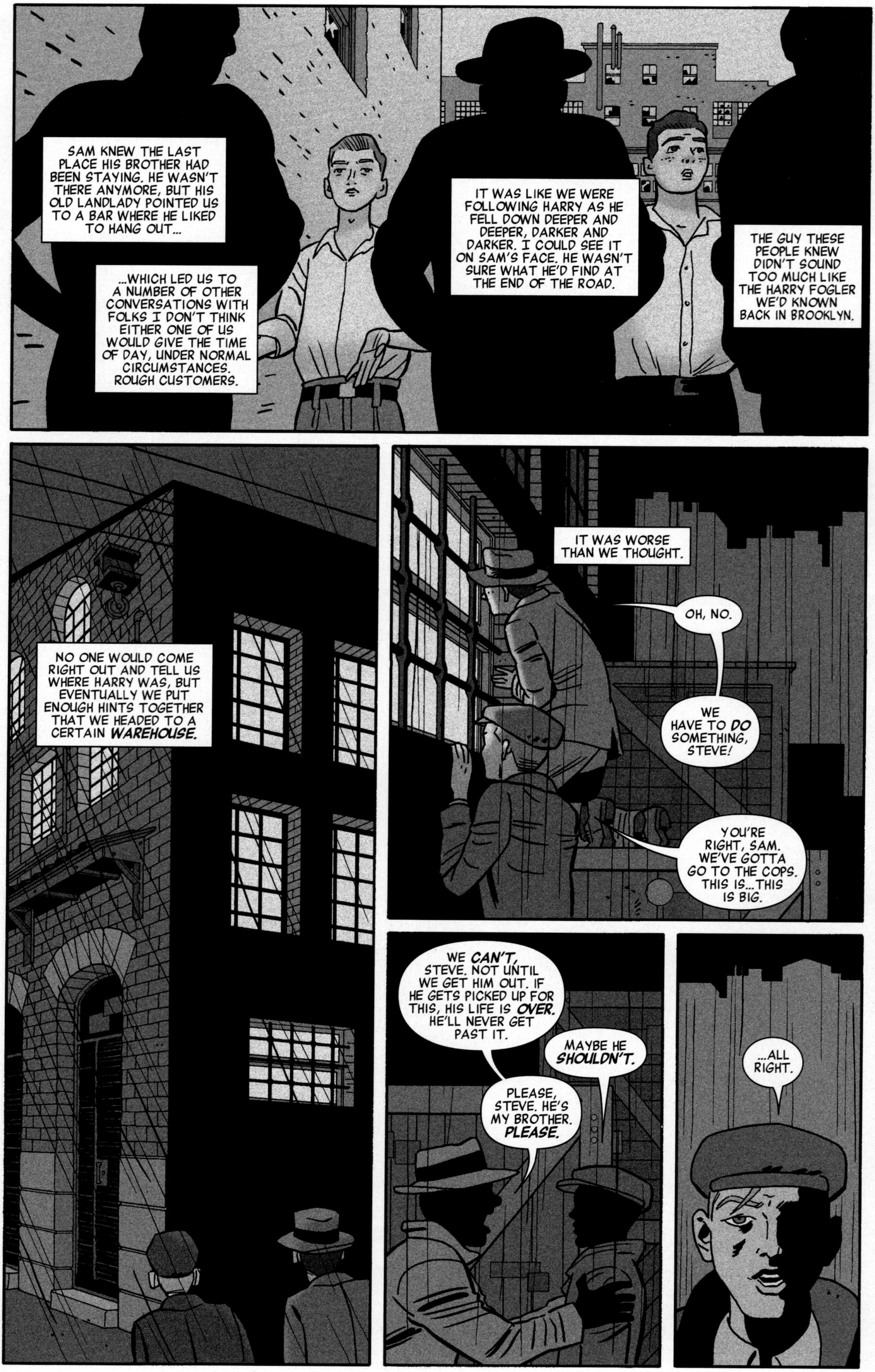
SAM KNEW THE LAST PLACE HIS BROTHER HAD BEEN STAYING. HE WASN'T THERE ANYMORE, BUT HIS OLD LANDLADY POINTED US TO A BAR WHERE HE LIKED TO HANG OUT...
...WHICH LED US TO A NUMBER OF OTHER CONVERSATIONS WITH FOLKS I DON'T THINK EITHER ONE OF US WOULD GIVE THE TIME OF DAY, UNDER NORMAL CIRCUMSTANCES. ROUGH CUSTOMERS.
IT WAS LIKE WE WERE FOLLOWING HARRY AS HE FELL DOWN DEEPER AND DEEPER, DARKER AND DARKER. I COULD SEE IT ON SAM'S FACE. HE WASN'T SURE WHAT HE'D FIND AT THE END OF THE ROAD.
THE GUY THESE PEOPLE KNEW DIDN'T SOUND TOO MUCH LIKE THE HARRY FOGLER WE'D KNOWN BACK IN BROOKLYN.
NO ONE WOULD COME RIGHT OUT AND TELL US WHERE HARRY WAS, BUT EVENTUALLY WE PUT ENOUGH HINTS TOGETHER THAT WE HEADED TO A CERTAIN ***WAREHOUSE.***
IT WAS WORSE THAN WE THOUGHT.
OH, NO.
WE HAVE TO ***DO*** SOMETHING, STEVE!
YOU'RE RIGHT, SAM. WE'VE GOTTA GO TO THE COPS. THIS IS...THIS IS BIG.
WE ***CAN'T,*** STEVE. NOT UNTIL WE GET HIM OUT. IF HE GETS PICKED UP FOR THIS, HIS LIFE IS ***OVER.*** HE'LL NEVER GET PAST IT.
MAYBE HE ***SHOULDN'T.***
PLEASE, STEVE. HE'S MY BROTHER. ***PLEASE.***
...ALL RIGHT.

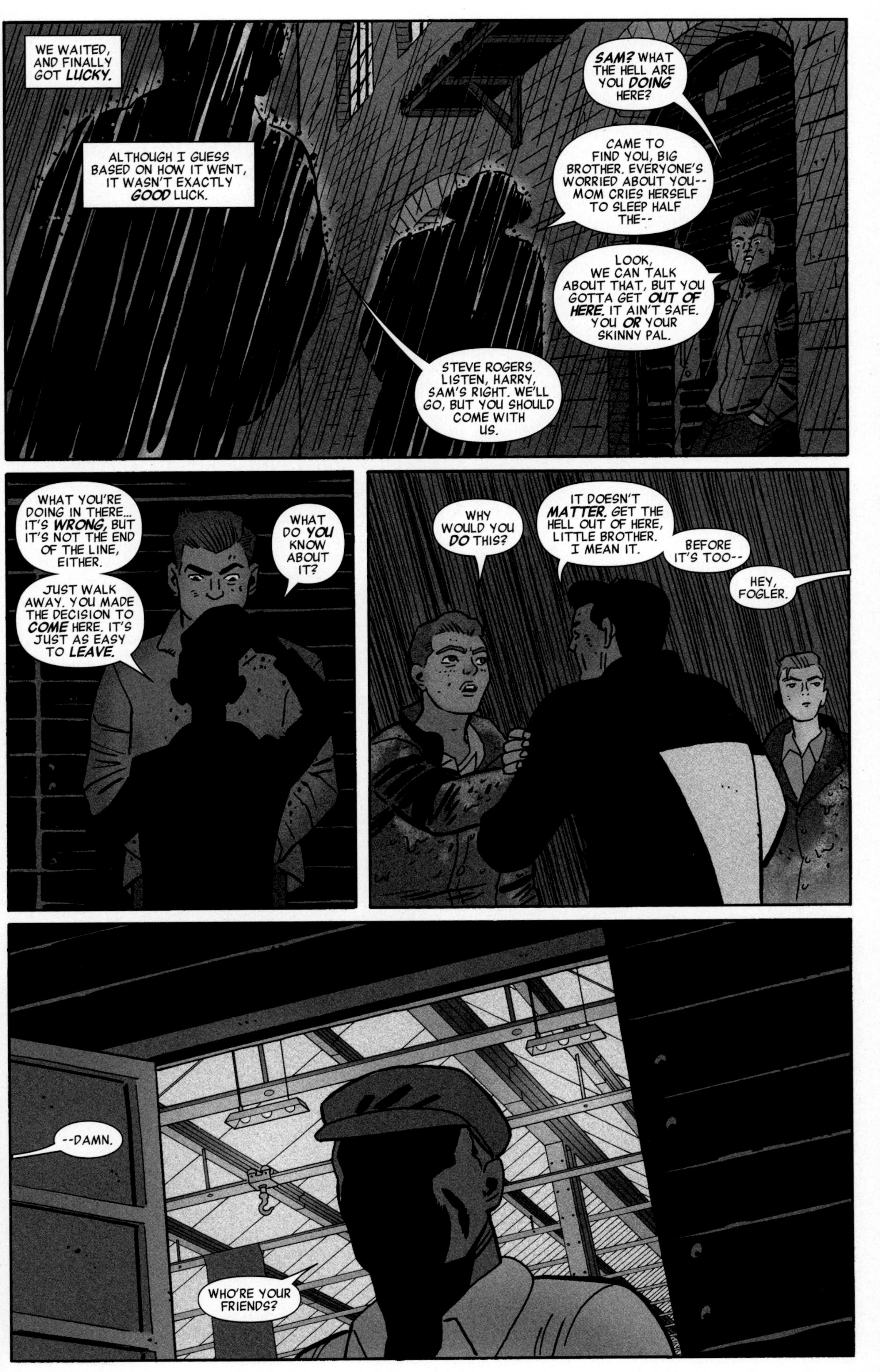
WE WAITED, AND FINALLY GOT LUCKY.
ALTHOUGH I GUESS BASED ON HOW IT WENT, IT WASN'T EXACTLY GOOD LUCK.
SAM? WHAT THE HELL ARE YOU DOING HERE?
CAME TO FIND YOU, BIG BROTHER. EVERYONE'S WORRIED ABOUT YOU-- MOM CRIES HERSELF TO SLEEP HALF THE--
LOOK, WE CAN TALK ABOUT THAT, BUT YOU GOTTA GET OUT OF HERE. IT AIN'T SAFE. YOU OR YOUR SKINNY PAL.
STEVE ROGERS. LISTEN, HARRY, SAM'S RIGHT. WE'LL GO, BUT YOU SHOULD COME WITH US.
WHAT YOU'RE DOING IN THERE... IT'S WRONG, BUT IT'S NOT THE END OF THE LINE, EITHER.
JUST WALK AWAY. YOU MADE THE DECISION TO COME HERE. IT'S JUST AS EASY TO LEAVE.
WHAT DO YOU KNOW ABOUT IT?
WHY WOULD YOU DO THIS?
IT DOESN'T MATTER. GET THE HELL OUT OF HERE, LITTLE BROTHER. I MEAN IT.
BEFORE IT'S TOO--
HEY, FOGLER.
--DAMN.
WHO'RE YOUR FRIENDS?

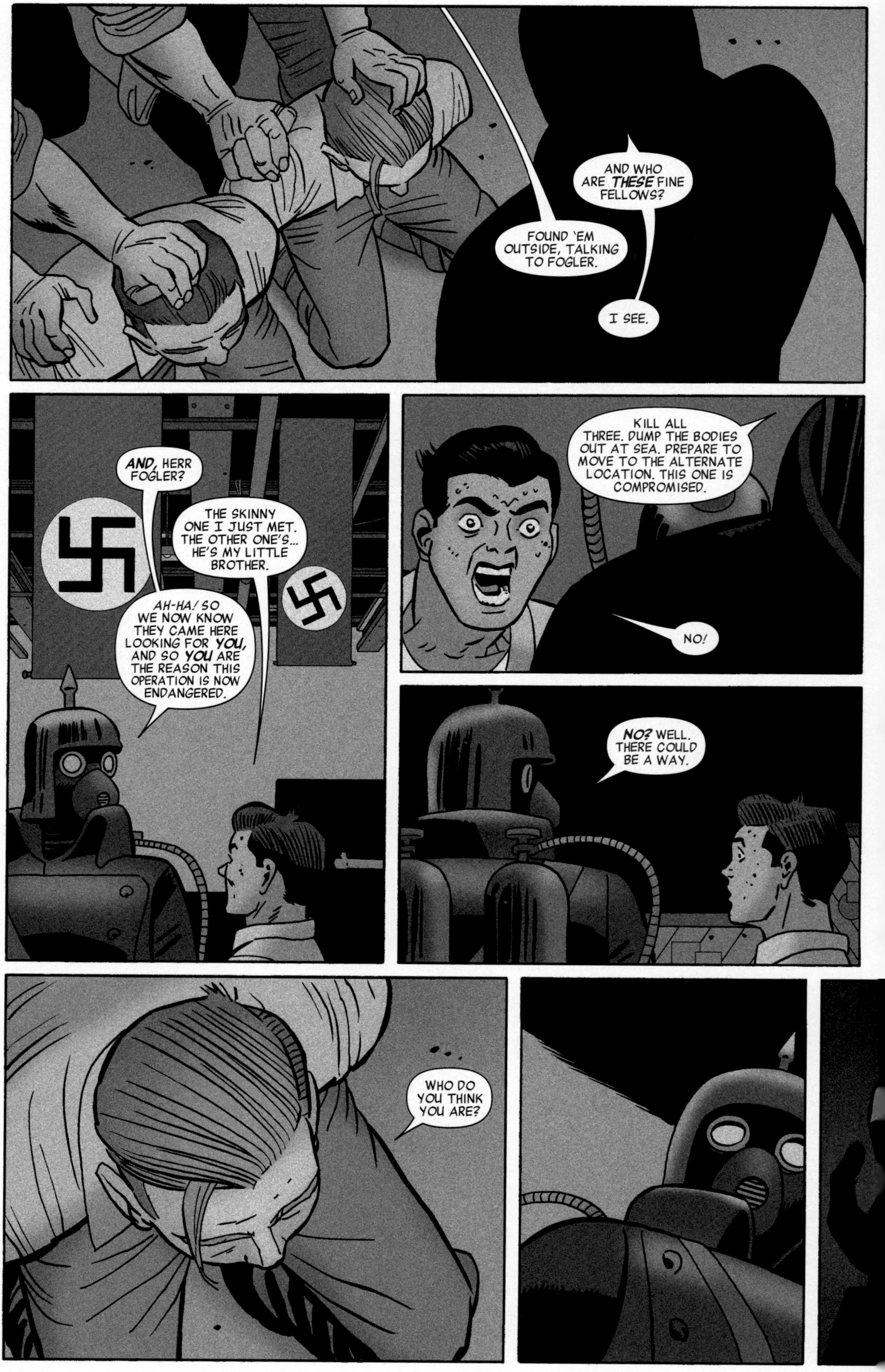
AND WHO ARE THESE FINE FELLOWS?
FOUND 'EM OUTSIDE, TALKING TO FOGLER.
I SEE.
AND, HERR FOGLER?
THE SKINNY ONE I JUST MET. THE OTHER ONE'S... HE'S MY LITTLE BROTHER.
AH-HA! SO WE NOW KNOW THEY CAME HERE LOOKING FOR YOU, AND SO YOU ARE THE REASON THIS OPERATION IS NOW ENDANGERED.
KILL ALL THREE. DUMP THE BODIES OUT AT SEA. PREPARE TO MOVE TO THE ALTERNATE LOCATION. THIS ONE IS COMPROMISED.
NO!
NO? WELL. THERE COULD BE A WAY.
WHO DO YOU THINK YOU ARE?

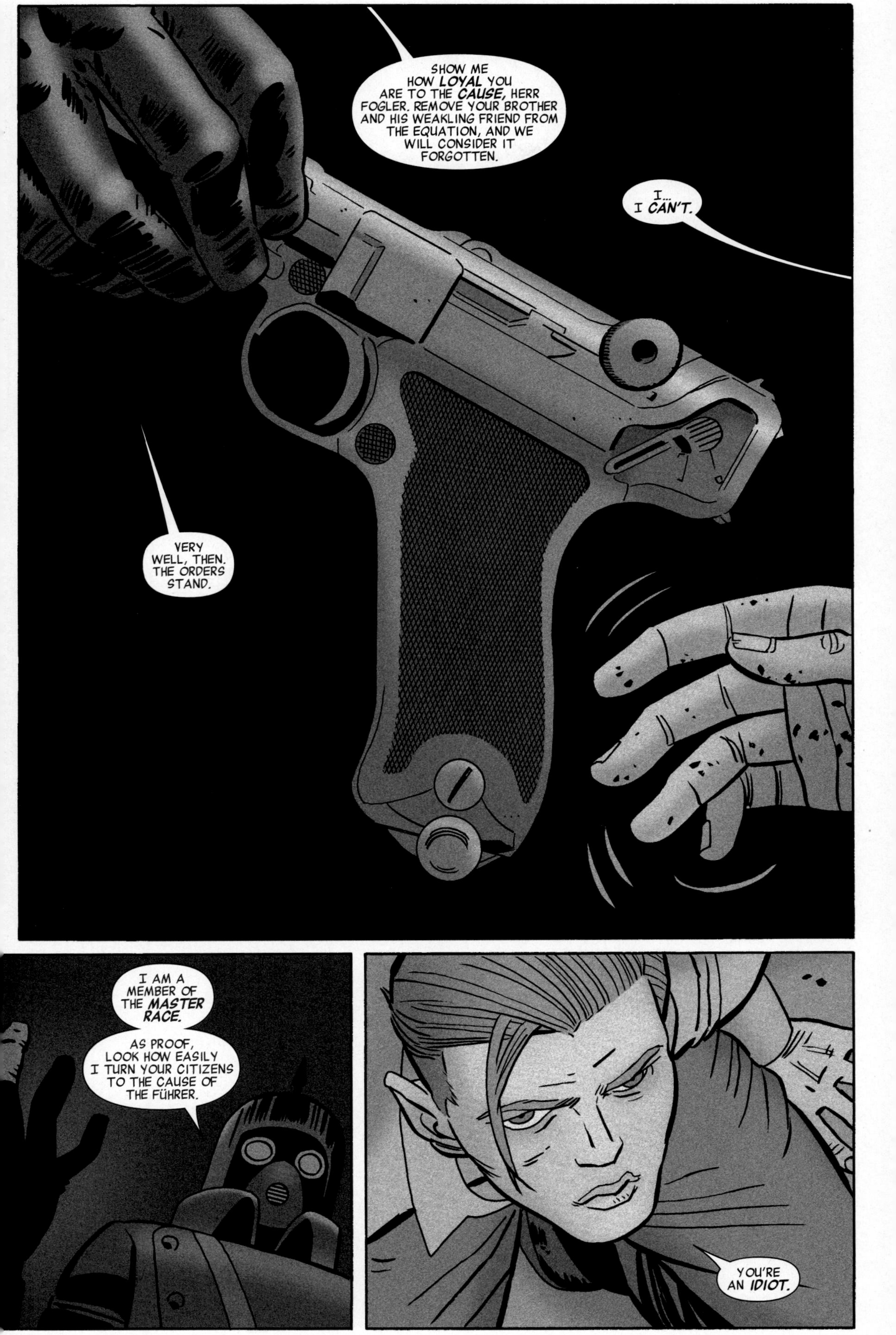
SHOW ME HOW **LOYAL** YOU ARE TO THE **CAUSE,** HERR FOGLER. REMOVE YOUR BROTHER AND HIS WEAKLING FRIEND FROM THE EQUATION, AND WE WILL CONSIDER IT FORGOTTEN.
I... I **CAN'T.**
VERY WELL, THEN. THE ORDERS STAND.
I AM A MEMBER OF THE **MASTER RACE.**
AS PROOF, LOOK HOW EASILY I TURN YOUR CITIZENS TO THE CAUSE OF THE FÜHRER.
YOU'RE AN **IDIOT.**

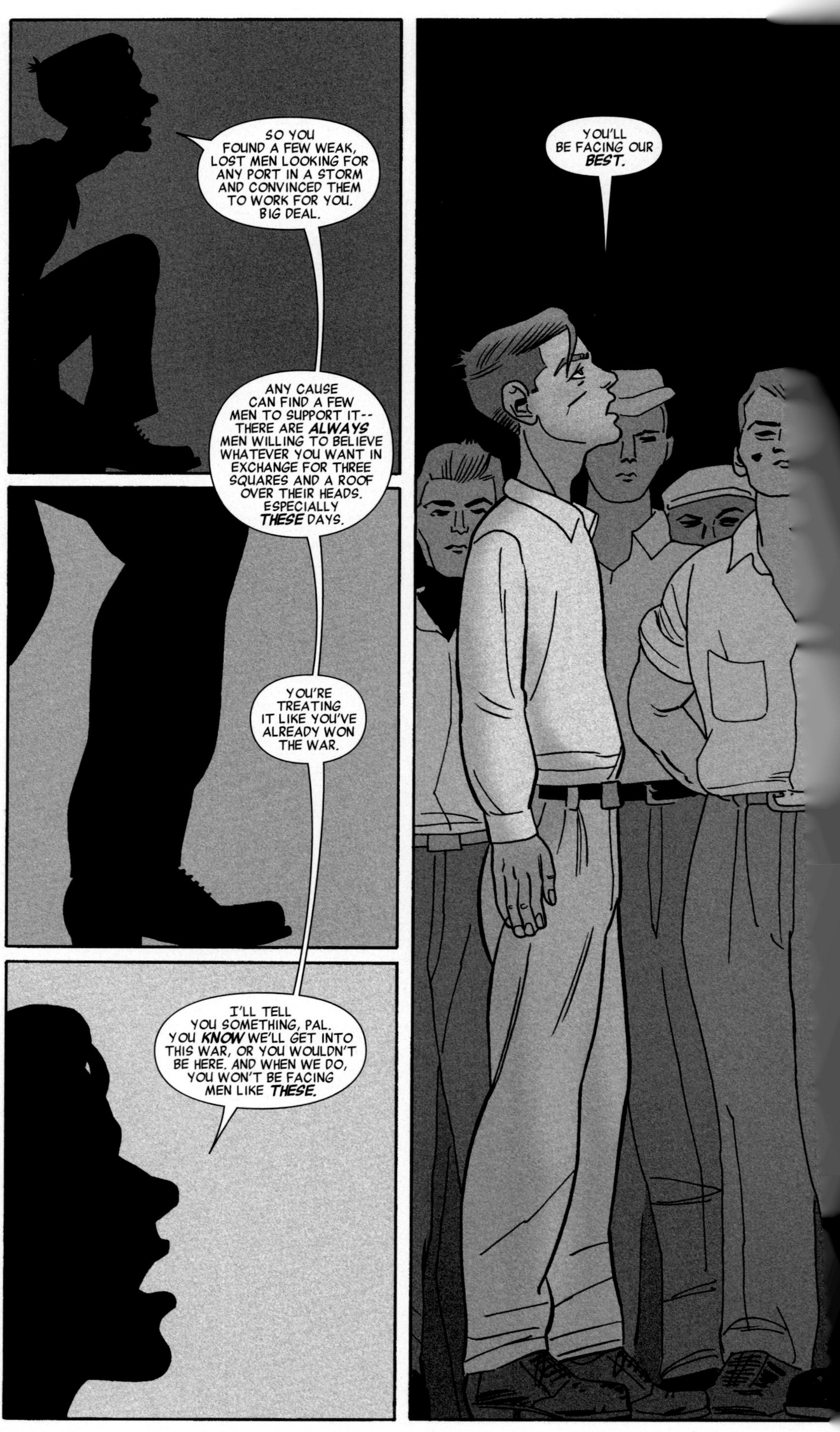
SO YOU FOUND A FEW WEAK, LOST MEN LOOKING FOR ANY PORT IN A STORM AND CONVINCED THEM TO WORK FOR YOU. BIG DEAL.
ANY CAUSE CAN FIND A FEW MEN TO SUPPORT IT-- THERE ARE ALWAYS MEN WILLING TO BELIEVE WHATEVER YOU WANT IN EXCHANGE FOR THREE SQUARES AND A ROOF OVER THEIR HEADS. ESPECIALLY THESE DAYS.
YOU'RE TREATING IT LIKE YOU'VE ALREADY WON THE WAR.
I'LL TELL YOU SOMETHING, PAL. YOU KNOW WE'LL GET INTO THIS WAR, OR YOU WOULDN'T BE HERE. AND WHEN WE DO, YOU WON'T BE FACING MEN LIKE THESE.
YOU'LL BE FACING OUR BEST.

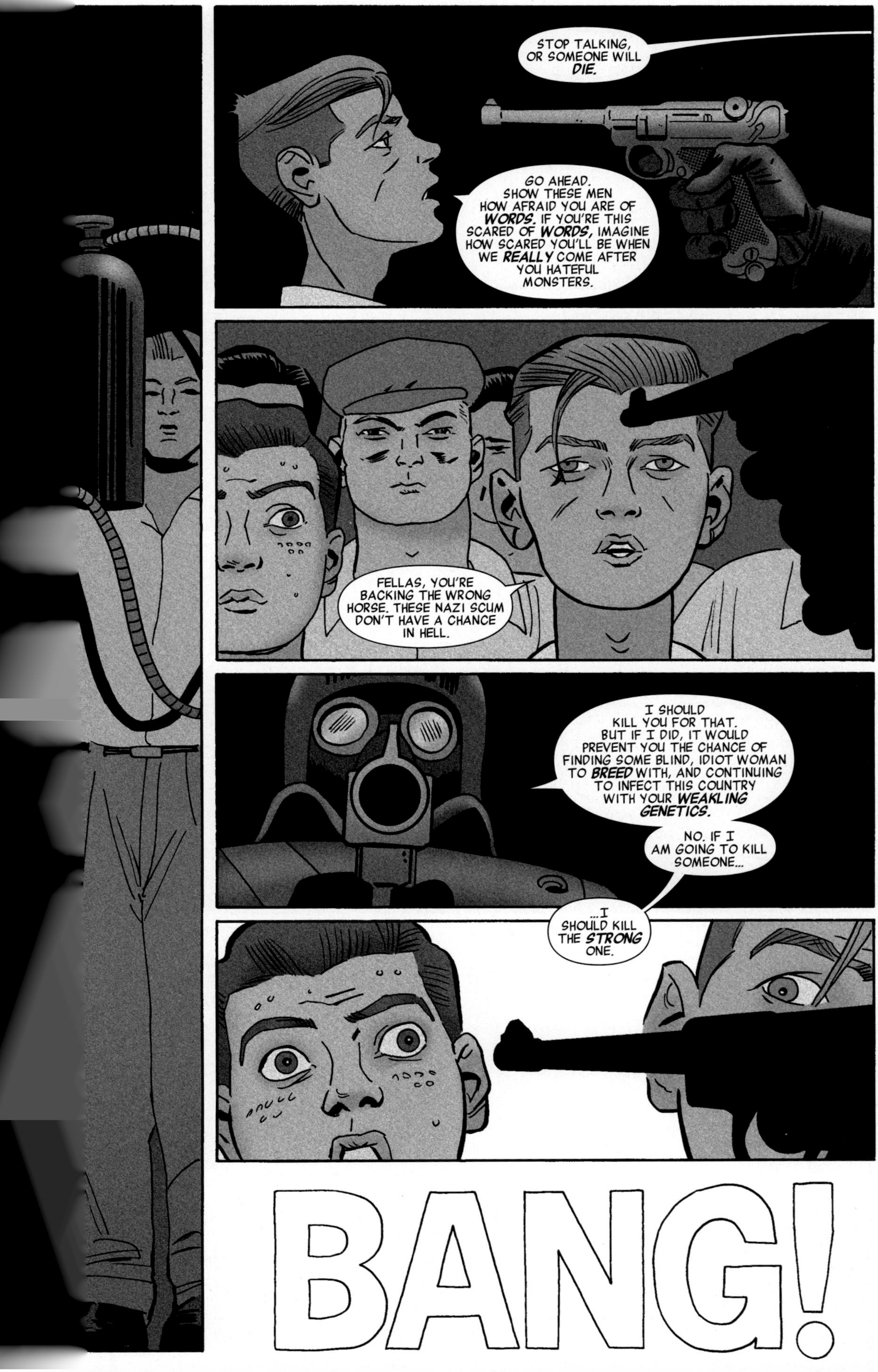

STOP TALKING, OR SOMEONE WILL DIE.
GO AHEAD. SHOW THESE MEN HOW AFRAID YOU ARE OF WORDS. IF YOU'RE THIS SCARED OF WORDS, IMAGINE HOW SCARED YOU'LL BE WHEN WE REALLY COME AFTER YOU HATEFUL MONSTERS.
FELLAS, YOU'RE BACKING THE WRONG HORSE. THESE NAZI SCUM DON'T HAVE A CHANCE IN HELL.
I SHOULD KILL YOU FOR THAT. BUT IF I DID, IT WOULD PREVENT YOU THE CHANCE OF FINDING SOME BLIND, IDIOT WOMAN TO BREED WITH, AND CONTINUING TO INFECT THIS COUNTRY WITH YOUR WEAKLING GENETICS.
NO. IF I AM GOING TO KILL SOMEONE...
...I SHOULD KILL THE STRONG ONE.
BANG!

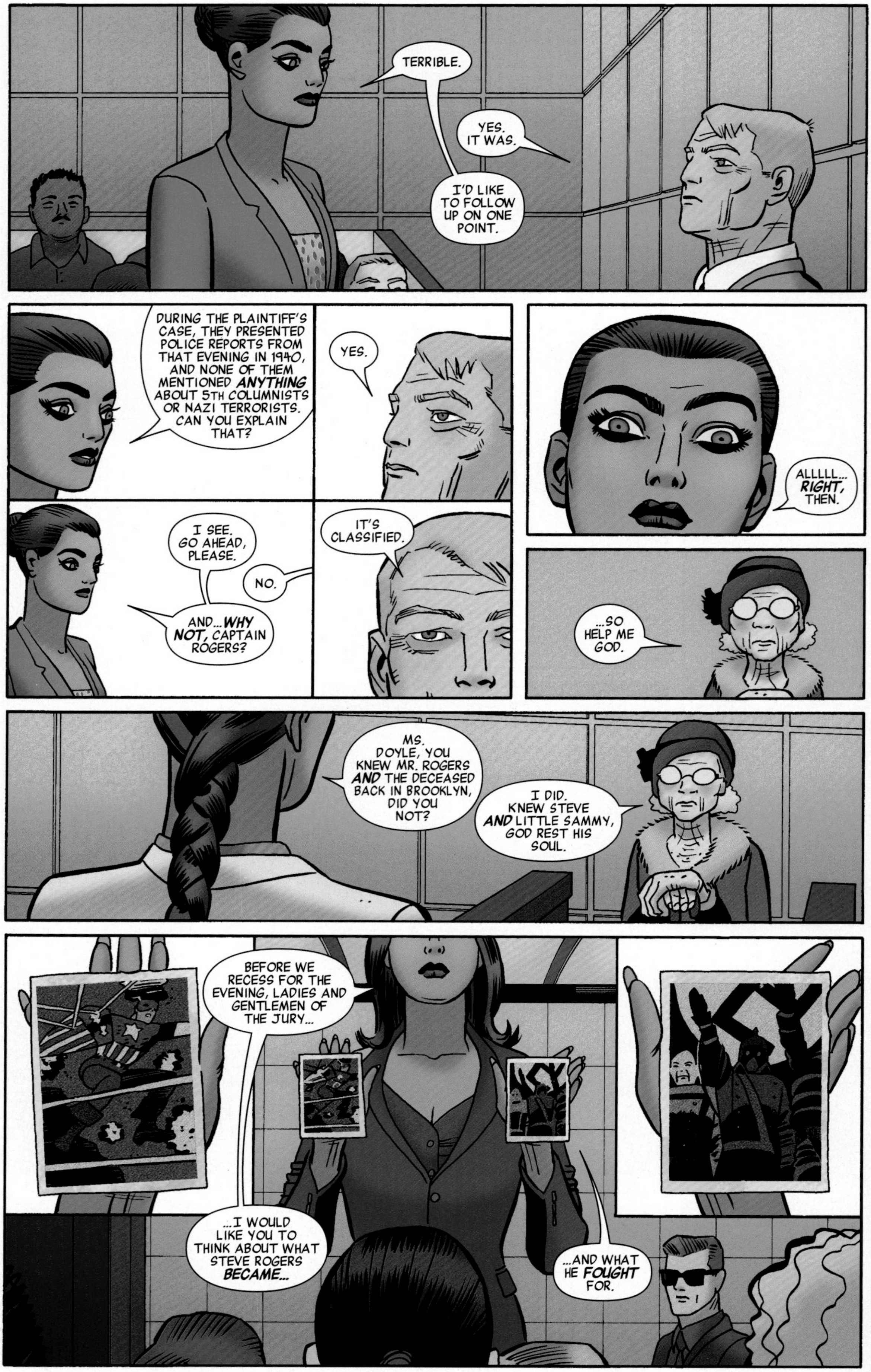
TERRIBLE.
YES. IT WAS.
I'D LIKE TO FOLLOW UP ON ONE POINT.
DURING THE PLAINTIFF'S CASE, THEY PRESENTED POLICE REPORTS FROM THAT EVENING IN 1940, AND NONE OF THEM MENTIONED **ANYTHING** ABOUT 5TH COLUMNISTS OR NAZI TERRORISTS. CAN YOU EXPLAIN THAT?
YES.
I SEE. GO AHEAD, PLEASE.
IT'S CLASSIFIED.
NO.
AND... **WHY NOT,** CAPTAIN ROGERS?
ALLLLL... **RIGHT,** THEN.
...SO HELP ME GOD.
MS. DOYLE, YOU KNEW MR. ROGERS **AND** THE DECEASED BACK IN BROOKLYN, DID YOU NOT?
I DID. KNEW STEVE **AND** LITTLE SAMMY, GOD REST HIS SOUL.
BEFORE WE RECESS FOR THE EVENING, LADIES AND GENTLEMEN OF THE JURY...
...I WOULD LIKE YOU TO THINK ABOUT WHAT STEVE ROGERS **BECAME...**
...AND WHAT HE **FOUGHT** FOR.

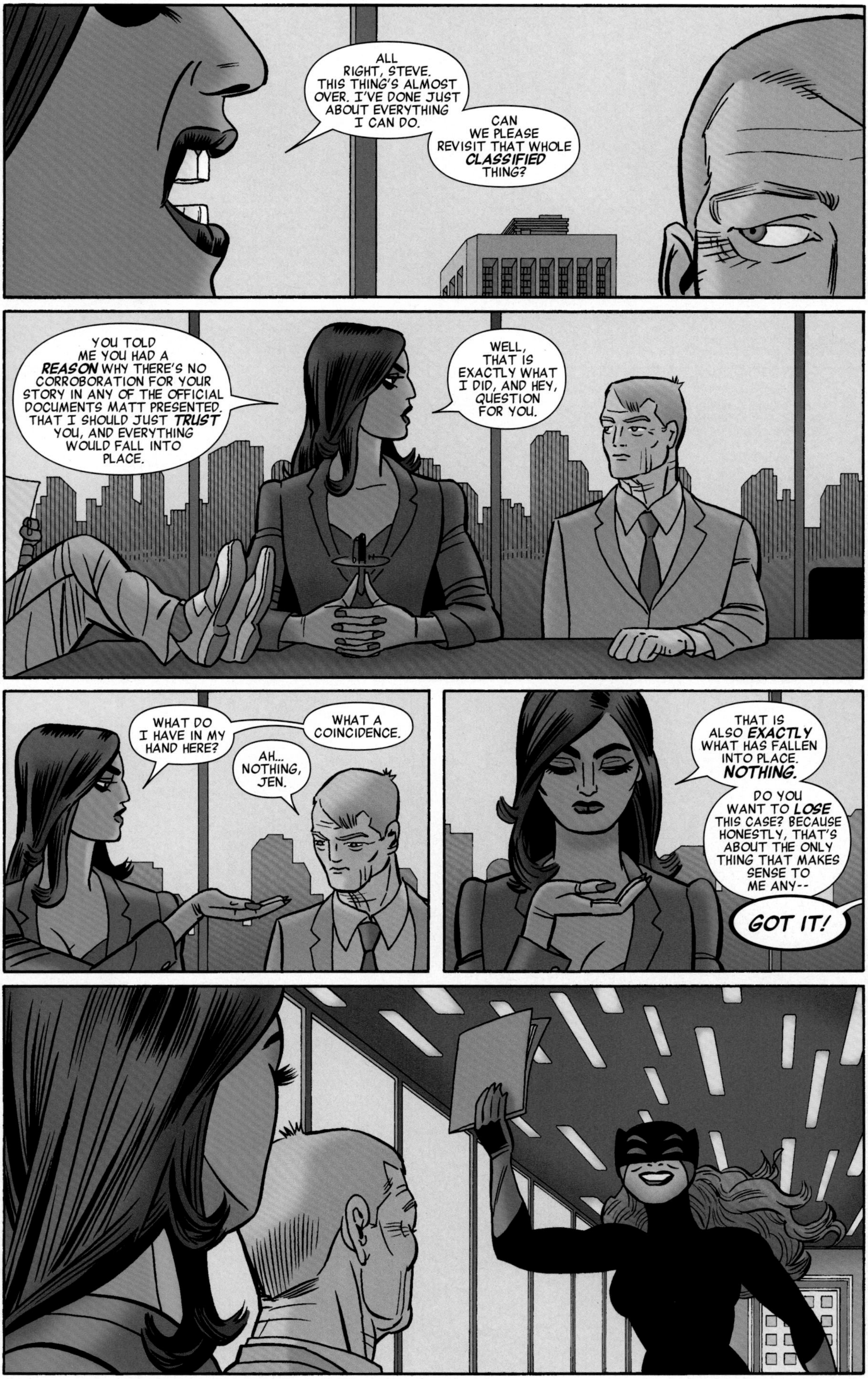
ALL RIGHT, STEVE. THIS THING'S ALMOST OVER. I'VE DONE JUST ABOUT EVERYTHING I CAN DO.
CAN WE PLEASE REVISIT THAT WHOLE CLASSIFIED THING?
YOU TOLD ME YOU HAD A REASON WHY THERE'S NO CORROBORATION FOR YOUR STORY IN ANY OF THE OFFICIAL DOCUMENTS MATT PRESENTED. THAT I SHOULD JUST TRUST YOU, AND EVERYTHING WOULD FALL INTO PLACE.
WELL, THAT IS EXACTLY WHAT I DID, AND HEY, QUESTION FOR YOU.
WHAT DO I HAVE IN MY HAND HERE?
AH... NOTHING, JEN.
WHAT A COINCIDENCE.
THAT IS ALSO EXACTLY WHAT HAS FALLEN INTO PLACE. NOTHING.
DO YOU WANT TO LOSE THIS CASE? BECAUSE HONESTLY, THAT'S ABOUT THE ONLY THING THAT MAKES SENSE TO ME ANY--
GOT IT!

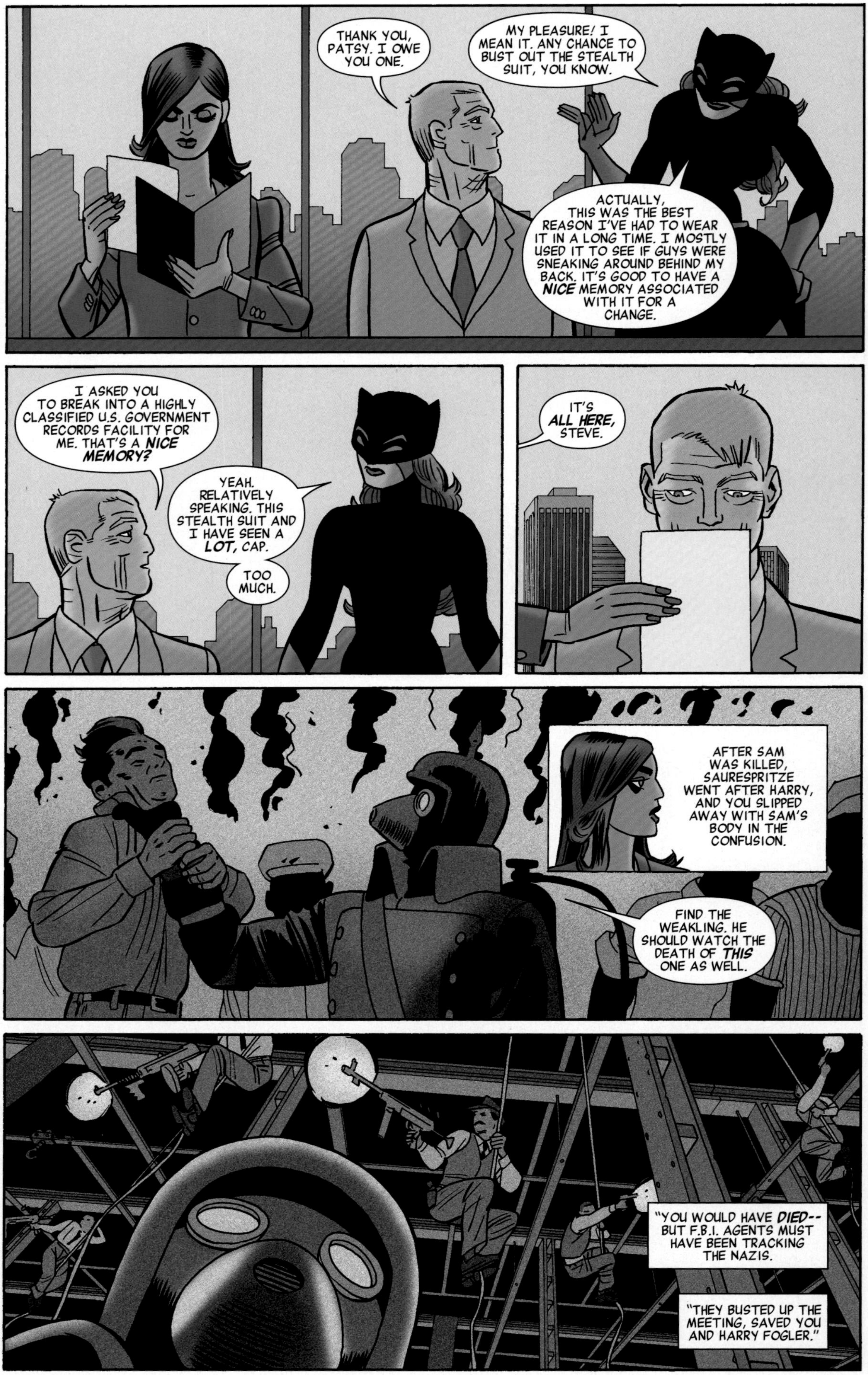
THANK YOU, PATSY. I OWE YOU ONE.
MY PLEASURE! I MEAN IT. ANY CHANCE TO BUST OUT THE STEALTH SUIT, YOU KNOW.
ACTUALLY, THIS WAS THE BEST REASON I'VE HAD TO WEAR IT IN A LONG TIME. I MOSTLY USED IT TO SEE IF GUYS WERE SNEAKING AROUND BEHIND MY BACK. IT'S GOOD TO HAVE A NICE MEMORY ASSOCIATED WITH IT FOR A CHANGE.
I ASKED YOU TO BREAK INTO A HIGHLY CLASSIFIED U.S. GOVERNMENT RECORDS FACILITY FOR ME. THAT'S A NICE MEMORY?
YEAH. RELATIVELY SPEAKING. THIS STEALTH SUIT AND I HAVE SEEN A LOT, CAP.
TOO MUCH.
IT'S ALL HERE, STEVE.
AFTER SAM WAS KILLED, SAURESPRITZE WENT AFTER HARRY, AND YOU SLIPPED AWAY WITH SAM'S BODY IN THE CONFUSION.
FIND THE WEAKLING. HE SHOULD WATCH THE DEATH OF THIS ONE AS WELL.
"YOU WOULD HAVE DIED--BUT F.B.I. AGENTS MUST HAVE BEEN TRACKING THE NAZIS.
"THEY BUSTED UP THE MEETING, SAVED YOU AND HARRY FOGLER."

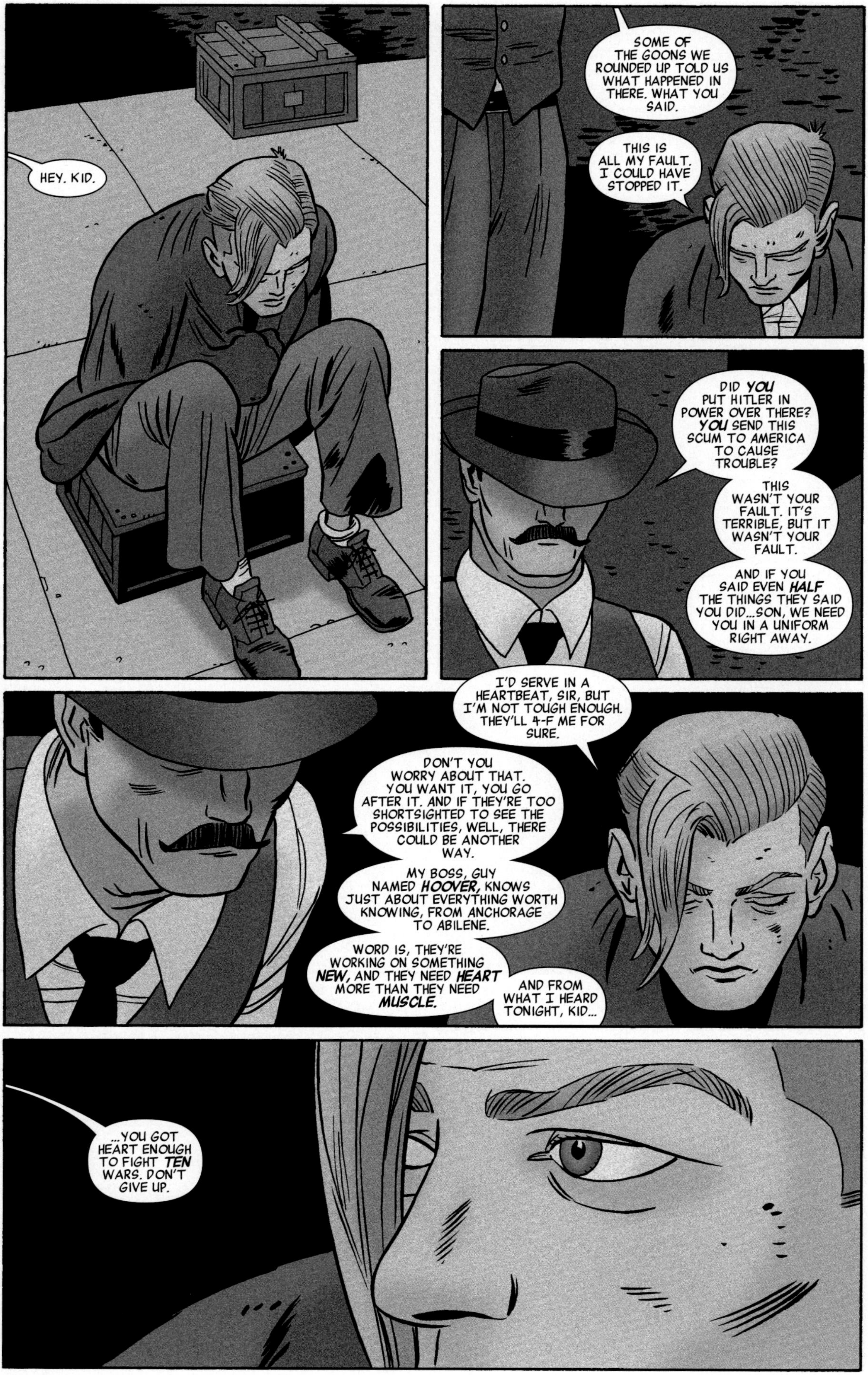
HEY. KID.
SOME OF THE GOONS WE ROUNDED UP TOLD US WHAT HAPPENED IN THERE. WHAT YOU SAID.
THIS IS ALL MY FAULT. I COULD HAVE STOPPED IT.
DID YOU PUT HITLER IN POWER OVER THERE? YOU SEND THIS SCUM TO AMERICA TO CAUSE TROUBLE?
THIS WASN'T YOUR FAULT. IT'S TERRIBLE, BUT IT WASN'T YOUR FAULT.
AND IF YOU SAID EVEN HALF THE THINGS THEY SAID YOU DID...SON, WE NEED YOU IN A UNIFORM RIGHT AWAY.
I'D SERVE IN A HEARTBEAT, SIR, BUT I'M NOT TOUGH ENOUGH. THEY'LL 4-F ME FOR SURE.
DON'T YOU WORRY ABOUT THAT. YOU WANT IT, YOU GO AFTER IT. AND IF THEY'RE TOO SHORTSIGHTED TO SEE THE POSSIBILITIES, WELL, THERE COULD BE ANOTHER WAY.
MY BOSS, GUY NAMED HOOVER, KNOWS JUST ABOUT EVERYTHING WORTH KNOWING, FROM ANCHORAGE TO ABILENE.
WORD IS, THEY'RE WORKING ON SOMETHING NEW, AND THEY NEED HEART MORE THAN THEY NEED MUSCLE.
AND FROM WHAT I HEARD TONIGHT, KID...
...YOU GOT HEART ENOUGH TO FIGHT TEN WARS. DON'T GIVE UP.

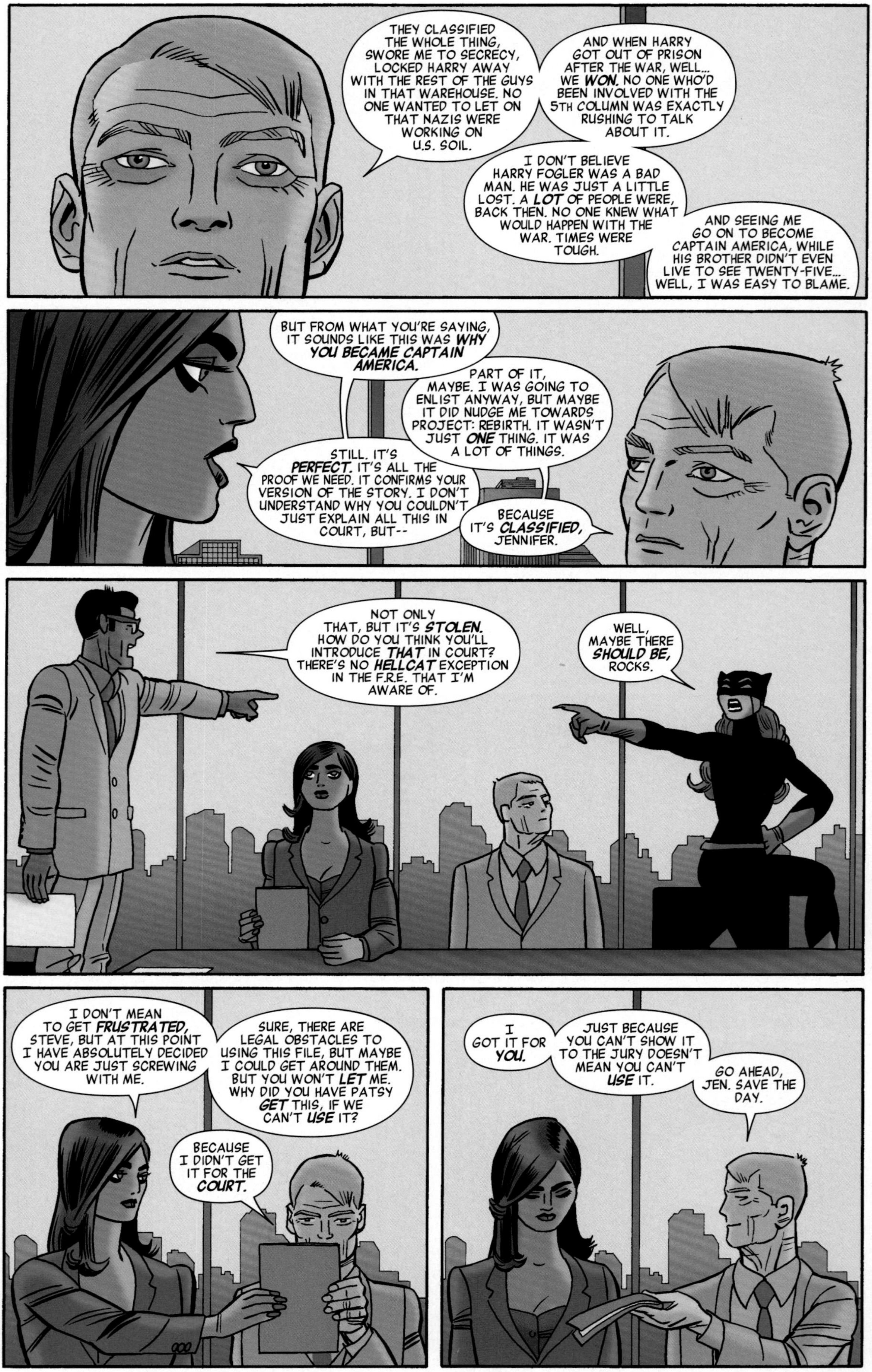
THEY CLASSIFIED THE WHOLE THING, SWORE ME TO SECRECY, LOCKED HARRY AWAY WITH THE REST OF THE GUYS IN THAT WAREHOUSE. NO ONE WANTED TO LET ON THAT NAZIS WERE WORKING ON U.S. SOIL.
AND WHEN HARRY GOT OUT OF PRISON AFTER THE WAR, WELL... WE WON. NO ONE WHO'D BEEN INVOLVED WITH THE 5TH COLUMN WAS EXACTLY RUSHING TO TALK ABOUT IT.
I DON'T BELIEVE HARRY FOGLER WAS A BAD MAN. HE WAS JUST A LITTLE LOST. A LOT OF PEOPLE WERE, BACK THEN. NO ONE KNEW WHAT WOULD HAPPEN WITH THE WAR. TIMES WERE TOUGH.
AND SEEING ME GO ON TO BECOME CAPTAIN AMERICA, WHILE HIS BROTHER DIDN'T EVEN LIVE TO SEE TWENTY-FIVE... WELL, I WAS EASY TO BLAME.
BUT FROM WHAT YOU'RE SAYING, IT SOUNDS LIKE THIS WAS WHY YOU BECAME CAPTAIN AMERICA.
PART OF IT, MAYBE. I WAS GOING TO ENLIST ANYWAY, BUT MAYBE IT DID NUDGE ME TOWARDS PROJECT: REBIRTH. IT WASN'T JUST ONE THING. IT WAS A LOT OF THINGS.
STILL. IT'S PERFECT. IT'S ALL THE PROOF WE NEED. IT CONFIRMS YOUR VERSION OF THE STORY. I DON'T UNDERSTAND WHY YOU COULDN'T JUST EXPLAIN ALL THIS IN COURT, BUT--
BECAUSE IT'S CLASSIFIED, JENNIFER.
NOT ONLY THAT, BUT IT'S STOLEN. HOW DO YOU THINK YOU'LL INTRODUCE THAT IN COURT? THERE'S NO HELLCAT EXCEPTION IN THE F.R.E. THAT I'M AWARE OF.
WELL, MAYBE THERE SHOULD BE, ROCKS.
I DON'T MEAN TO GET FRUSTRATED, STEVE, BUT AT THIS POINT I HAVE ABSOLUTELY DECIDED YOU ARE JUST SCREWING WITH ME.
SURE, THERE ARE LEGAL OBSTACLES TO USING THIS FILE, BUT MAYBE I COULD GET AROUND THEM. BUT YOU WON'T LET ME. WHY DID YOU HAVE PATSY GET THIS, IF WE CAN'T USE IT?
BECAUSE I DIDN'T GET IT FOR THE COURT.
I GOT IT FOR YOU.
JUST BECAUSE YOU CAN'T SHOW IT TO THE JURY DOESN'T MEAN YOU CAN'T USE IT.
GO AHEAD, JEN. SAVE THE DAY.

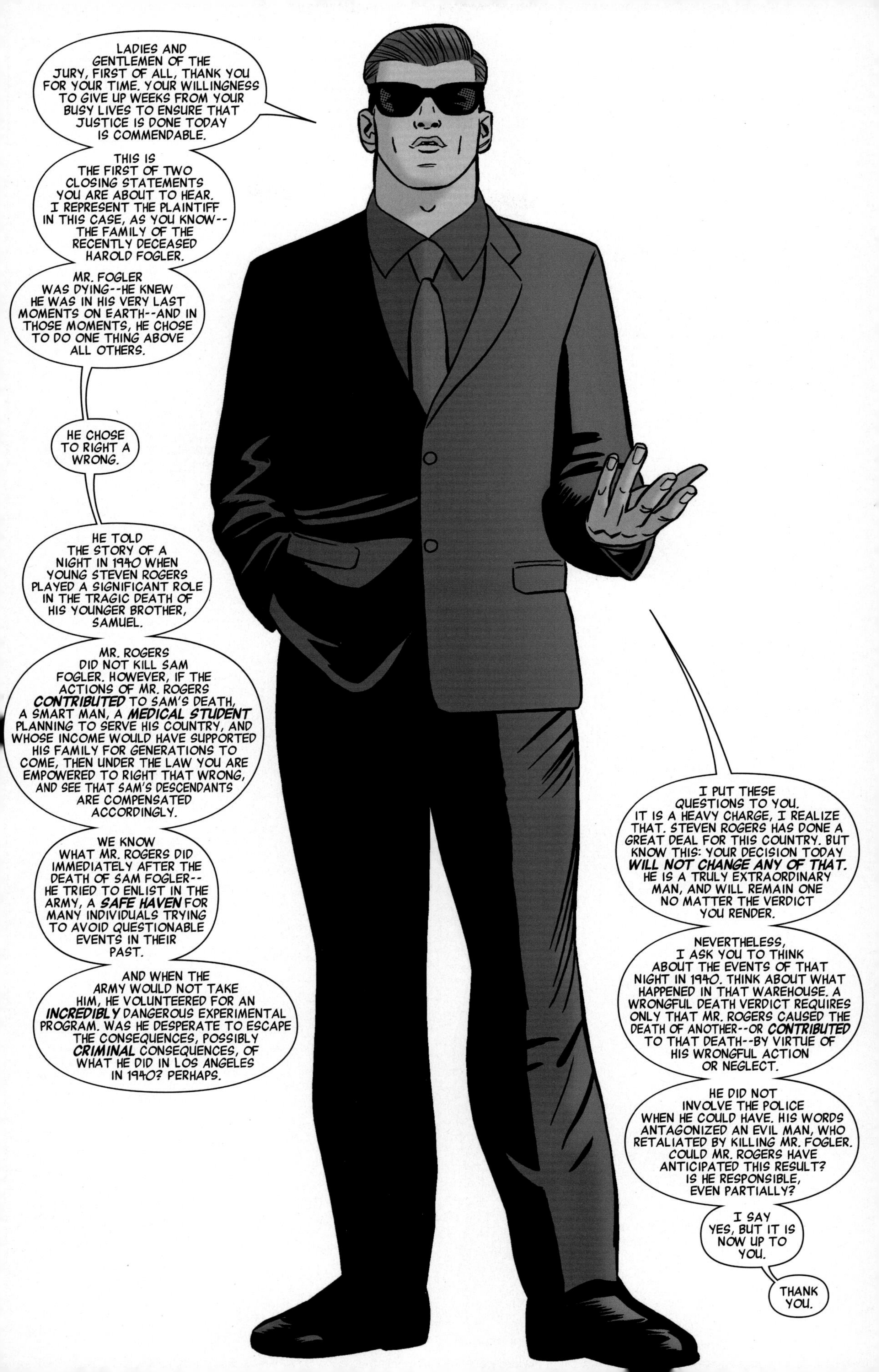
LADIES AND GENTLEMEN OF THE JURY, FIRST OF ALL, THANK YOU FOR YOUR TIME. YOUR WILLINGNESS TO GIVE UP WEEKS FROM YOUR BUSY LIVES TO ENSURE THAT JUSTICE IS DONE TODAY IS COMMENDABLE.
THIS IS THE FIRST OF TWO CLOSING STATEMENTS YOU ARE ABOUT TO HEAR. I REPRESENT THE PLAINTIFF IN THIS CASE, AS YOU KNOW-- THE FAMILY OF THE RECENTLY DECEASED HAROLD FOGLER.
MR. FOGLER WAS DYING--HE KNEW HE WAS IN HIS VERY LAST MOMENTS ON EARTH--AND IN THOSE MOMENTS, HE CHOSE TO DO ONE THING ABOVE ALL OTHERS.
HE CHOSE TO RIGHT A WRONG.
HE TOLD THE STORY OF A NIGHT IN 1940 WHEN YOUNG STEVEN ROGERS PLAYED A SIGNIFICANT ROLE IN THE TRAGIC DEATH OF HIS YOUNGER BROTHER, SAMUEL.
MR. ROGERS DID NOT KILL SAM FOGLER. HOWEVER, IF THE ACTIONS OF MR. ROGERS ***CONTRIBUTED*** TO SAM'S DEATH, A SMART MAN, A ***MEDICAL STUDENT*** PLANNING TO SERVE HIS COUNTRY, AND WHOSE INCOME WOULD HAVE SUPPORTED HIS FAMILY FOR GENERATIONS TO COME, THEN UNDER THE LAW YOU ARE EMPOWERED TO RIGHT THAT WRONG, AND SEE THAT SAM'S DESCENDANTS ARE COMPENSATED ACCORDINGLY.
WE KNOW WHAT MR. ROGERS DID IMMEDIATELY AFTER THE DEATH OF SAM FOGLER-- HE TRIED TO ENLIST IN THE ARMY, A ***SAFE HAVEN*** FOR MANY INDIVIDUALS TRYING TO AVOID QUESTIONABLE EVENTS IN THEIR PAST.
AND WHEN THE ARMY WOULD NOT TAKE HIM, HE VOLUNTEERED FOR AN ***INCREDIBLY*** DANGEROUS EXPERIMENTAL PROGRAM. WAS HE DESPERATE TO ESCAPE THE CONSEQUENCES, POSSIBLY ***CRIMINAL*** CONSEQUENCES, OF WHAT HE DID IN LOS ANGELES IN 1940? PERHAPS.
I PUT THESE QUESTIONS TO YOU. IT IS A HEAVY CHARGE, I REALIZE THAT. STEVEN ROGERS HAS DONE A GREAT DEAL FOR THIS COUNTRY. BUT KNOW THIS: YOUR DECISION TODAY ***WILL NOT CHANGE ANY OF THAT.*** HE IS A TRULY EXTRAORDINARY MAN, AND WILL REMAIN ONE NO MATTER THE VERDICT YOU RENDER.
NEVERTHELESS, I ASK YOU TO THINK ABOUT THE EVENTS OF THAT NIGHT IN 1940. THINK ABOUT WHAT HAPPENED IN THAT WAREHOUSE. A WRONGFUL DEATH VERDICT REQUIRES ONLY THAT MR. ROGERS CAUSED THE DEATH OF ANOTHER--OR ***CONTRIBUTED*** TO THAT DEATH--BY VIRTUE OF HIS WRONGFUL ACTION OR NEGLECT.
HE DID NOT INVOLVE THE POLICE WHEN HE COULD HAVE. HIS WORDS ANTAGONIZED AN EVIL MAN, WHO RETALIATED BY KILLING MR. FOGLER. COULD MR. ROGERS HAVE ANTICIPATED THIS RESULT? IS HE RESPONSIBLE, EVEN PARTIALLY?
I SAY YES, BUT IT IS NOW UP TO YOU.
THANK YOU.

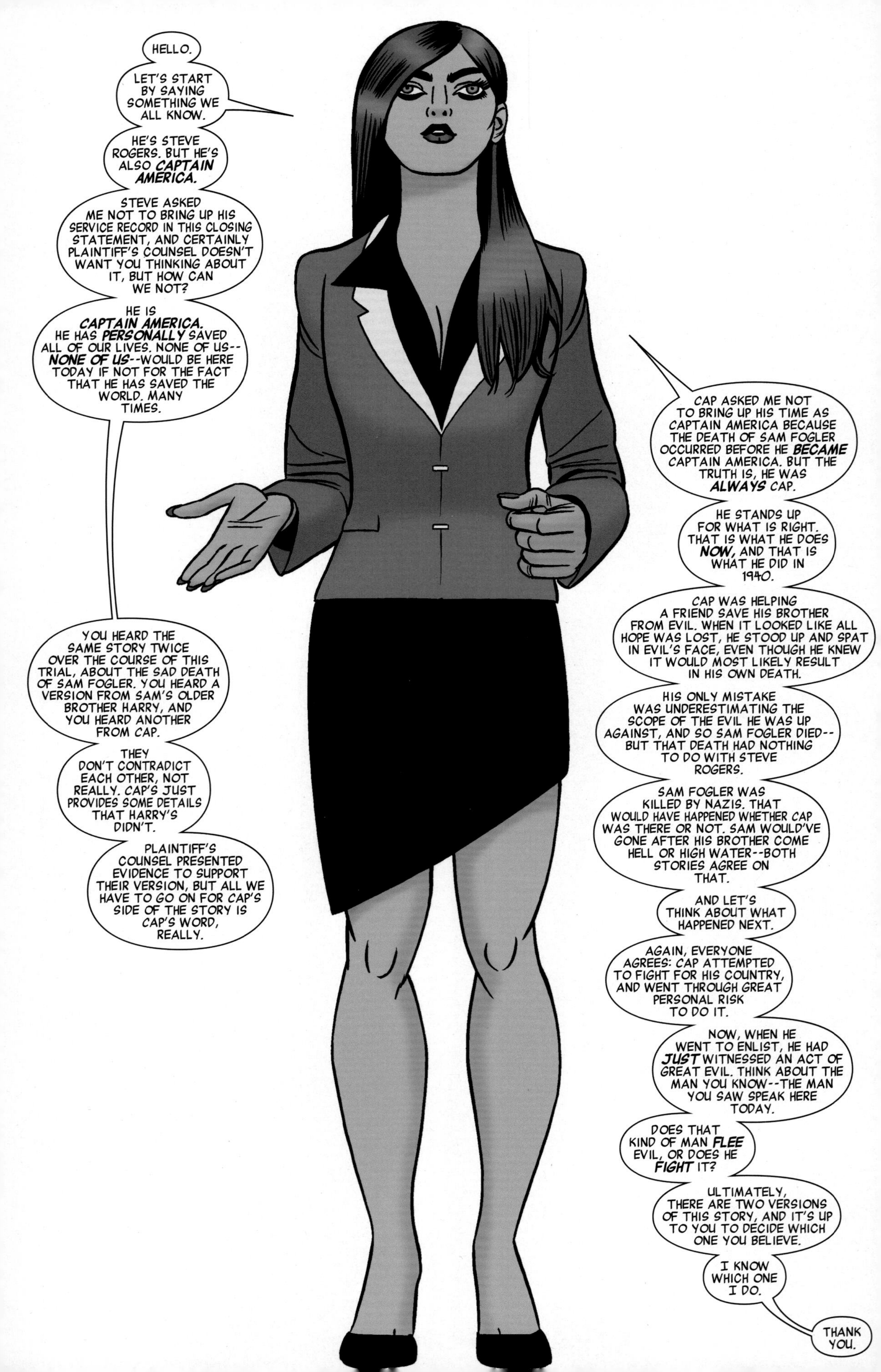
HELLO.
LET'S START BY SAYING SOMETHING WE ALL KNOW.
HE'S STEVE ROGERS. BUT HE'S ALSO CAPTAIN AMERICA.
STEVE ASKED ME NOT TO BRING UP HIS SERVICE RECORD IN THIS CLOSING STATEMENT, AND CERTAINLY PLAINTIFF'S COUNSEL DOESN'T WANT YOU THINKING ABOUT IT, BUT HOW CAN WE NOT?
HE IS CAPTAIN AMERICA. HE HAS PERSONALLY SAVED ALL OF OUR LIVES. NONE OF US--NONE OF US--WOULD BE HERE TODAY IF NOT FOR THE FACT THAT HE HAS SAVED THE WORLD. MANY TIMES.
YOU HEARD THE SAME STORY TWICE OVER THE COURSE OF THIS TRIAL, ABOUT THE SAD DEATH OF SAM FOGLER. YOU HEARD A VERSION FROM SAM'S OLDER BROTHER HARRY, AND YOU HEARD ANOTHER FROM CAP.
THEY DON'T CONTRADICT EACH OTHER, NOT REALLY. CAP'S JUST PROVIDES SOME DETAILS THAT HARRY'S DIDN'T.
PLAINTIFF'S COUNSEL PRESENTED EVIDENCE TO SUPPORT THEIR VERSION, BUT ALL WE HAVE TO GO ON FOR CAP'S SIDE OF THE STORY IS CAP'S WORD, REALLY.
CAP ASKED ME NOT TO BRING UP HIS TIME AS CAPTAIN AMERICA BECAUSE THE DEATH OF SAM FOGLER OCCURRED BEFORE HE BECAME CAPTAIN AMERICA. BUT THE TRUTH IS, HE WAS ALWAYS CAP.
HE STANDS UP FOR WHAT IS RIGHT. THAT IS WHAT HE DOES NOW, AND THAT IS WHAT HE DID IN 1940.
CAP WAS HELPING A FRIEND SAVE HIS BROTHER FROM EVIL. WHEN IT LOOKED LIKE ALL HOPE WAS LOST, HE STOOD UP AND SPAT IN EVIL'S FACE, EVEN THOUGH HE KNEW IT WOULD MOST LIKELY RESULT IN HIS OWN DEATH.
HIS ONLY MISTAKE WAS UNDERESTIMATING THE SCOPE OF THE EVIL HE WAS UP AGAINST, AND SO SAM FOGLER DIED--BUT THAT DEATH HAD NOTHING TO DO WITH STEVE ROGERS.
SAM FOGLER WAS KILLED BY NAZIS. THAT WOULD HAVE HAPPENED WHETHER CAP WAS THERE OR NOT. SAM WOULD'VE GONE AFTER HIS BROTHER COME HELL OR HIGH WATER--BOTH STORIES AGREE ON THAT.
AND LET'S THINK ABOUT WHAT HAPPENED NEXT.
AGAIN, EVERYONE AGREES: CAP ATTEMPTED TO FIGHT FOR HIS COUNTRY, AND WENT THROUGH GREAT PERSONAL RISK TO DO IT.
NOW, WHEN HE WENT TO ENLIST, HE HAD JUST WITNESSED AN ACT OF GREAT EVIL. THINK ABOUT THE MAN YOU KNOW--THE MAN YOU SAW SPEAK HERE TODAY.
DOES THAT KIND OF MAN FLEE EVIL, OR DOES HE FIGHT IT?
ULTIMATELY, THERE ARE TWO VERSIONS OF THIS STORY, AND IT'S UP TO YOU TO DECIDE WHICH ONE YOU BELIEVE.
I KNOW WHICH ONE I DO.
THANK YOU.

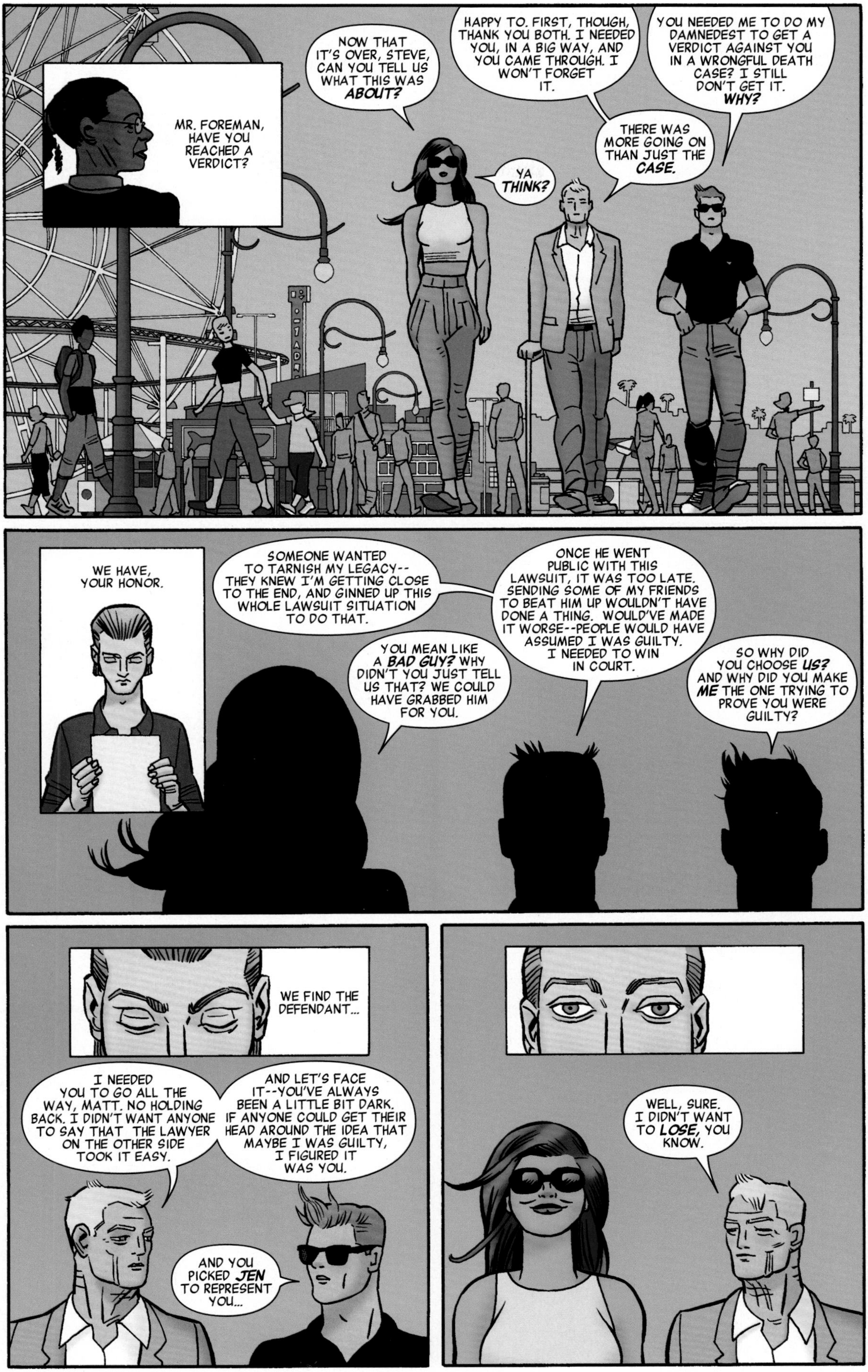

MR. FOREMAN, HAVE YOU REACHED A VERDICT?
NOW THAT IT'S OVER, STEVE, CAN YOU TELL US WHAT THIS WAS ABOUT?
YA THINK?
HAPPY TO. FIRST, THOUGH, THANK YOU BOTH. I NEEDED YOU, IN A BIG WAY, AND YOU CAME THROUGH. I WON'T FORGET IT.
THERE WAS MORE GOING ON THAN JUST THE CASE.
YOU NEEDED ME TO DO MY DAMNEDEST TO GET A VERDICT AGAINST YOU IN A WRONGFUL DEATH CASE? I STILL DON'T GET IT. WHY?
WE HAVE, YOUR HONOR.
SOMEONE WANTED TO TARNISH MY LEGACY-- THEY KNEW I'M GETTING CLOSE TO THE END, AND GINNED UP THIS WHOLE LAWSUIT SITUATION TO DO THAT.
YOU MEAN LIKE A BAD GUY? WHY DIDN'T YOU JUST TELL US THAT? WE COULD HAVE GRABBED HIM FOR YOU.
ONCE HE WENT PUBLIC WITH THIS LAWSUIT, IT WAS TOO LATE. SENDING SOME OF MY FRIENDS TO BEAT HIM UP WOULDN'T HAVE DONE A THING. WOULD'VE MADE IT WORSE--PEOPLE WOULD HAVE ASSUMED I WAS GUILTY. I NEEDED TO WIN IN COURT.
SO WHY DID YOU CHOOSE US? AND WHY DID YOU MAKE ME THE ONE TRYING TO PROVE YOU WERE GUILTY?
WE FIND THE DEFENDANT...
I NEEDED YOU TO GO ALL THE WAY, MATT. NO HOLDING BACK. I DIDN'T WANT ANYONE TO SAY THAT THE LAWYER ON THE OTHER SIDE TOOK IT EASY.
AND LET'S FACE IT--YOU'VE ALWAYS BEEN A LITTLE BIT DARK. IF ANYONE COULD GET THEIR HEAD AROUND THE IDEA THAT MAYBE I WAS GUILTY, I FIGURED IT WAS YOU.
AND YOU PICKED JEN TO REPRESENT YOU...
WELL, SURE. I DIDN'T WANT TO LOSE, YOU KNOW.

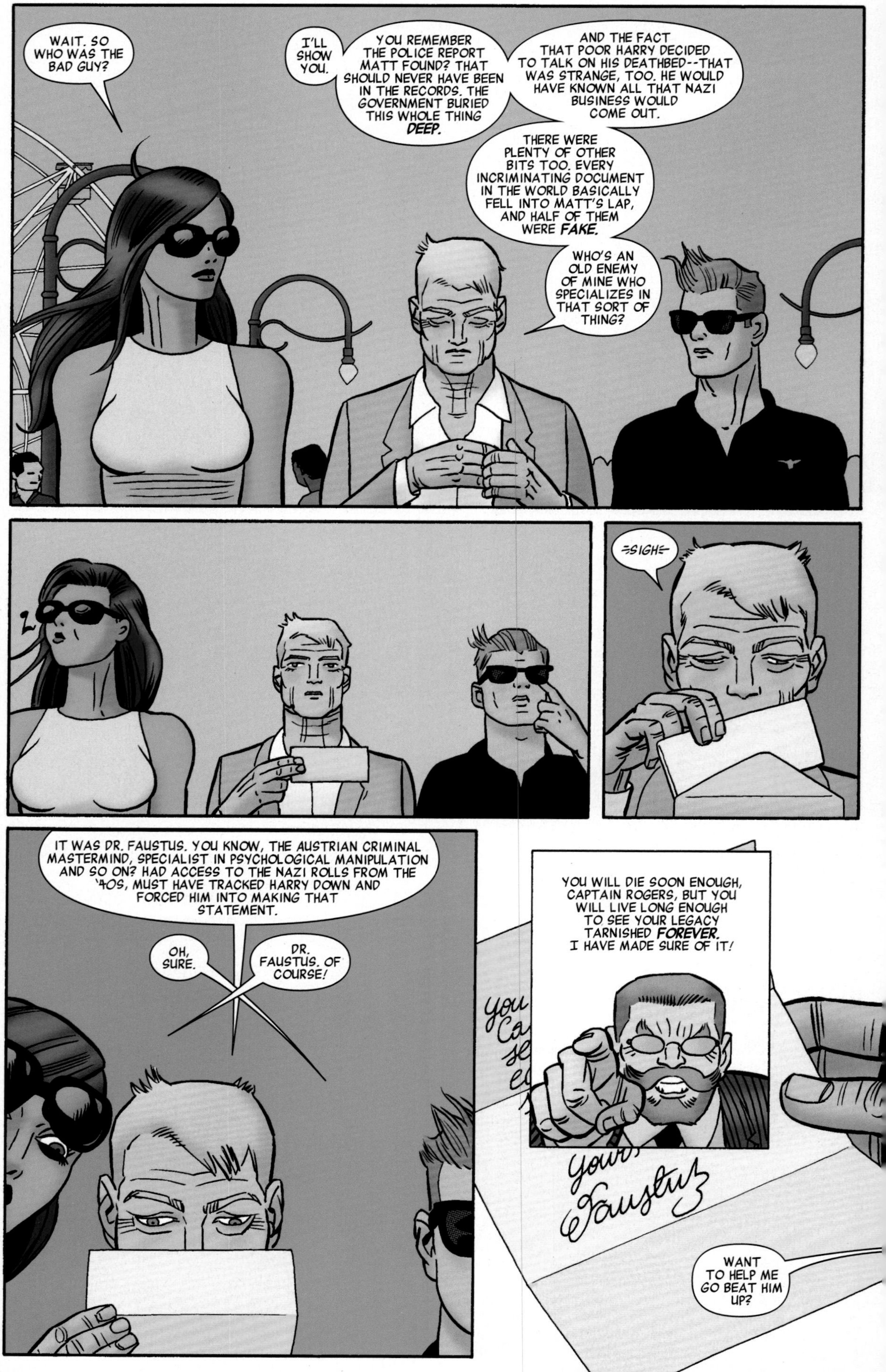

WAIT. SO WHO WAS THE BAD GUY?
I'LL SHOW YOU.
YOU REMEMBER THE POLICE REPORT MATT FOUND? THAT SHOULD NEVER HAVE BEEN IN THE RECORDS. THE GOVERNMENT BURIED THIS WHOLE THING DEEP.
AND THE FACT THAT POOR HARRY DECIDED TO TALK ON HIS DEATHBED--THAT WAS STRANGE, TOO. HE WOULD HAVE KNOWN ALL THAT NAZI BUSINESS WOULD COME OUT.
THERE WERE PLENTY OF OTHER BITS TOO. EVERY INCRIMINATING DOCUMENT IN THE WORLD BASICALLY FELL INTO MATT'S LAP, AND HALF OF THEM WERE FAKE.
WHO'S AN OLD ENEMY OF MINE WHO SPECIALIZES IN THAT SORT OF THING?
Z
=SIGH=
IT WAS DR. FAUSTUS. YOU KNOW, THE AUSTRIAN CRIMINAL MASTERMIND, SPECIALIST IN PSYCHOLOGICAL MANIPULATION AND SO ON? HAD ACCESS TO THE NAZI ROLLS FROM THE '40S, MUST HAVE TRACKED HARRY DOWN AND FORCED HIM INTO MAKING THAT STATEMENT.
OH, SURE.
DR. FAUSTUS. OF COURSE!
YOU WILL DIE SOON ENOUGH, CAPTAIN ROGERS, BUT YOU WILL LIVE LONG ENOUGH TO SEE YOUR LEGACY TARNISHED FOREVER. I HAVE MADE SURE OF IT!
Yours, Faustus
WANT TO HELP ME GO BEAT HIM UP?

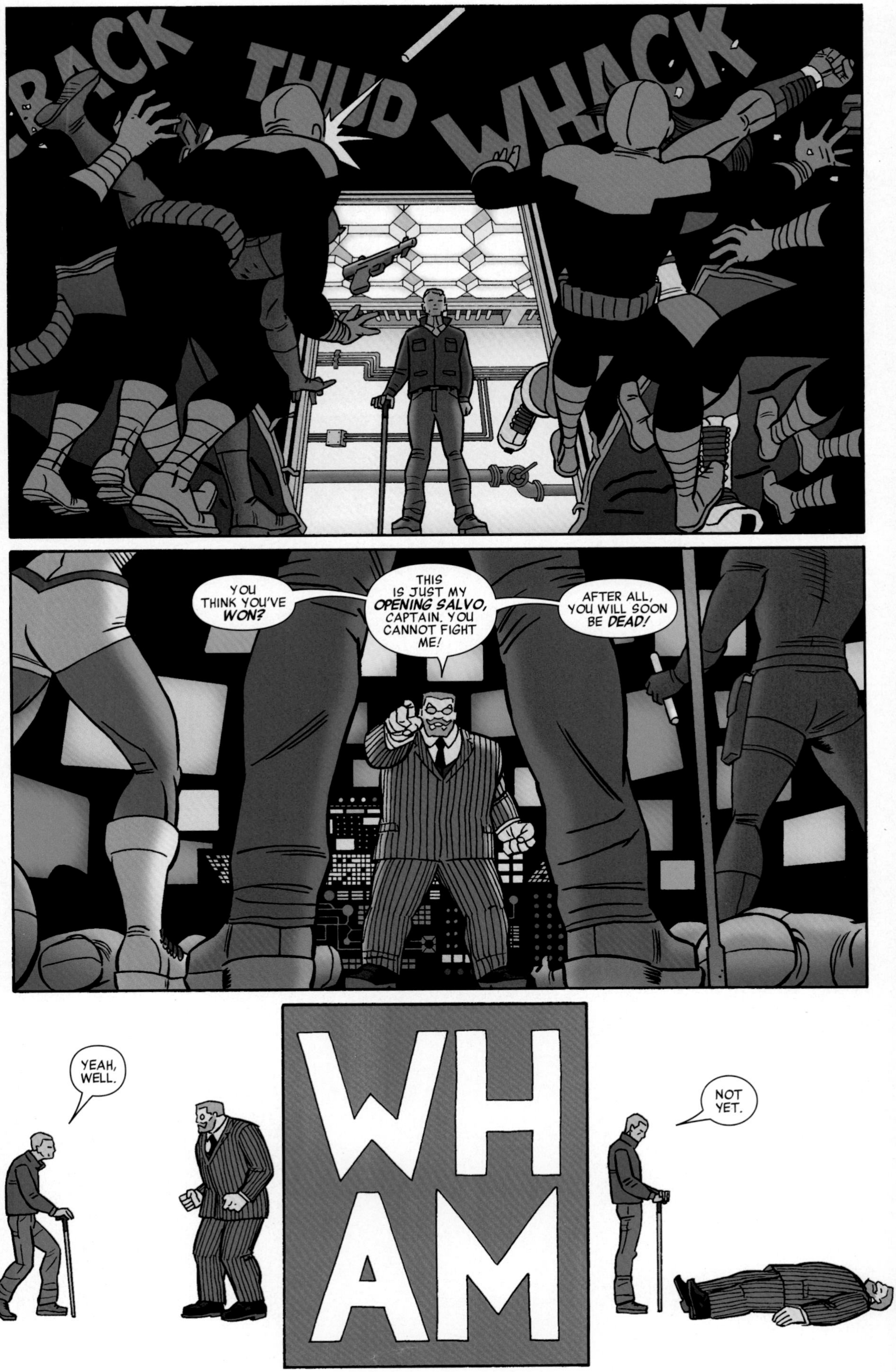
CRACK
THUD
WHACK
YOU THINK YOU'VE WON?
THIS IS JUST MY OPENING SALVO, CAPTAIN. YOU CANNOT FIGHT ME!
AFTER ALL, YOU WILL SOON BE DEAD!
YEAH, WELL.
WHAM
NOT YET.

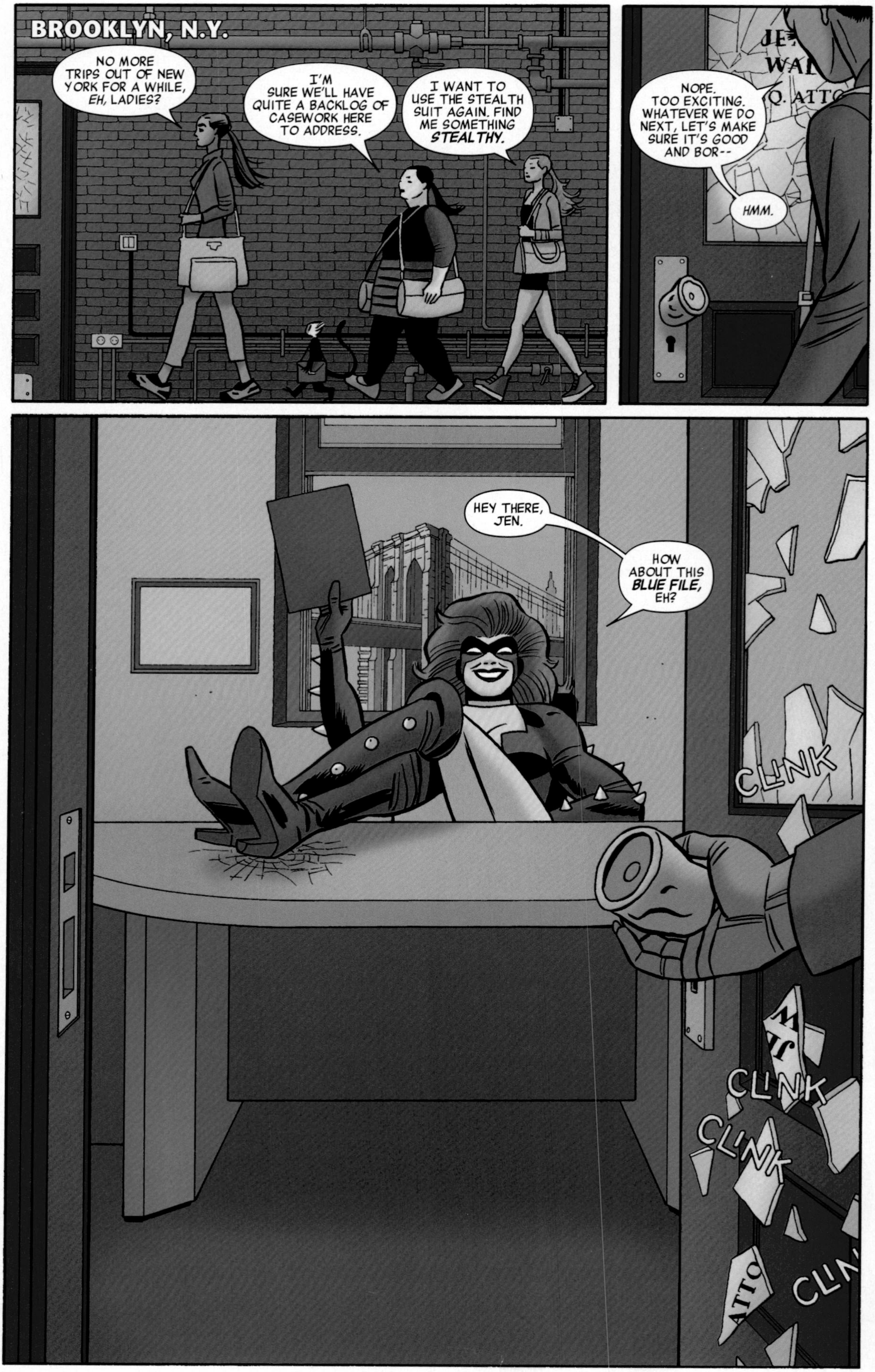
BROOKLYN, N.Y.
NO MORE TRIPS OUT OF NEW YORK FOR A WHILE, EH, LADIES?
I'M SURE WE'LL HAVE QUITE A BACKLOG OF CASEWORK HERE TO ADDRESS.
I WANT TO USE THE STEALTH SUIT AGAIN. FIND ME SOMETHING STEALTHY.
NOPE. TOO EXCITING. WHATEVER WE DO NEXT, LET'S MAKE SURE IT'S GOOD AND BOR--
HMM.
HEY THERE, JEN.
HOW ABOUT THIS BLUE FILE, EH?
CLINK
CLINK
CLINK
CLINK

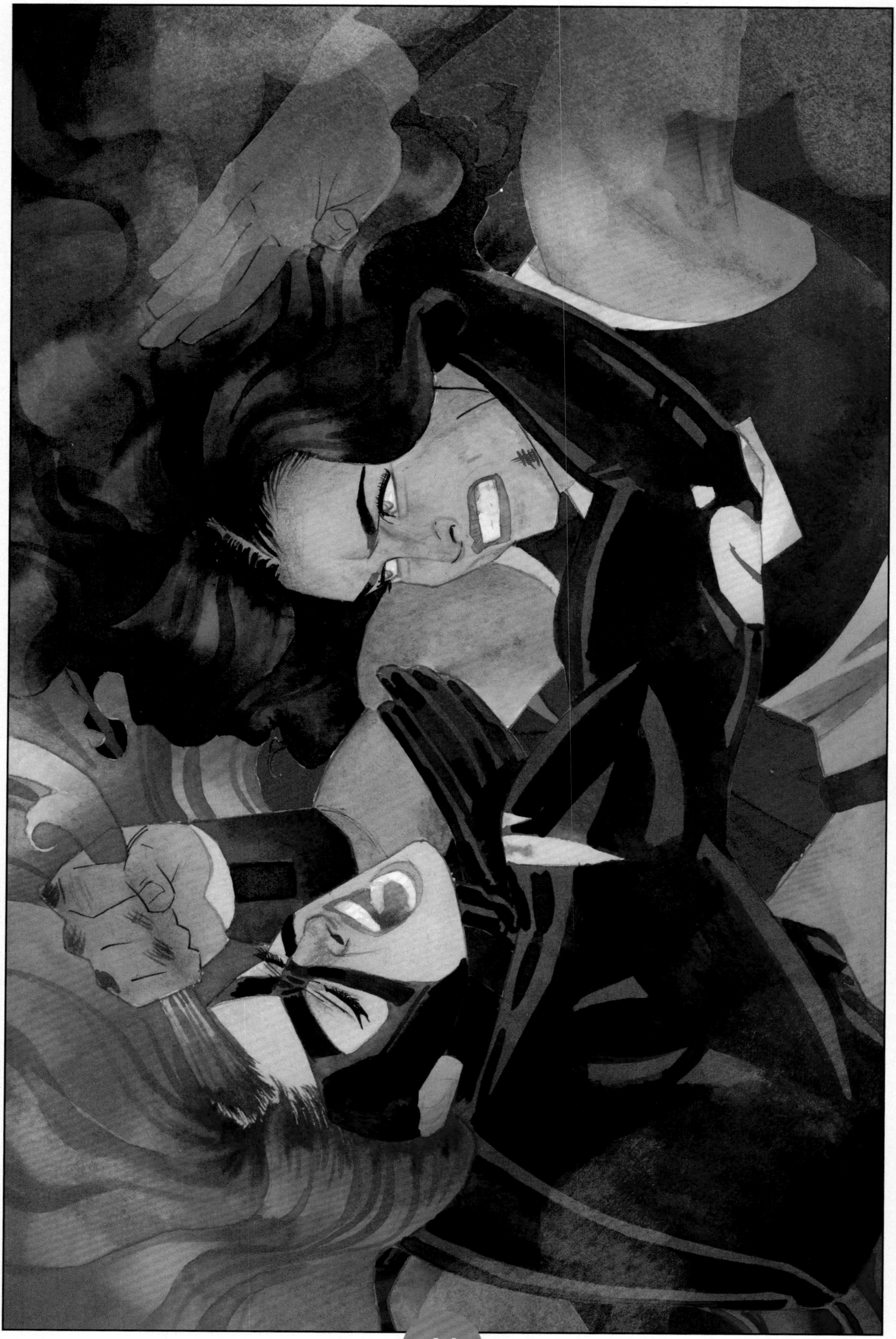

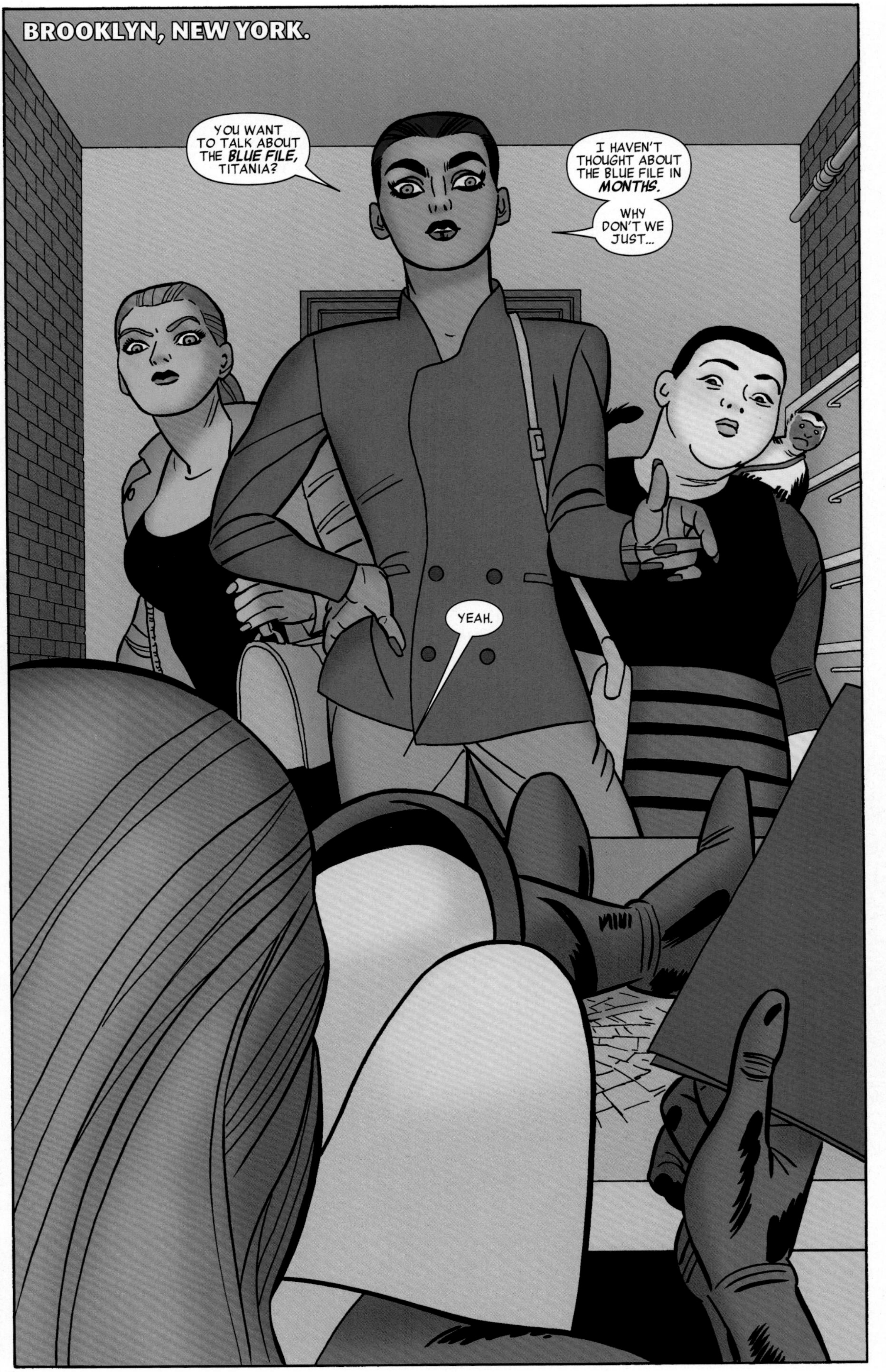
BROOKLYN, NEW YORK.
YOU WANT TO TALK ABOUT THE BLUE FILE, TITANIA?
I HAVEN'T THOUGHT ABOUT THE BLUE FILE IN MONTHS.
WHY DON'T WE JUST...
YEAH.

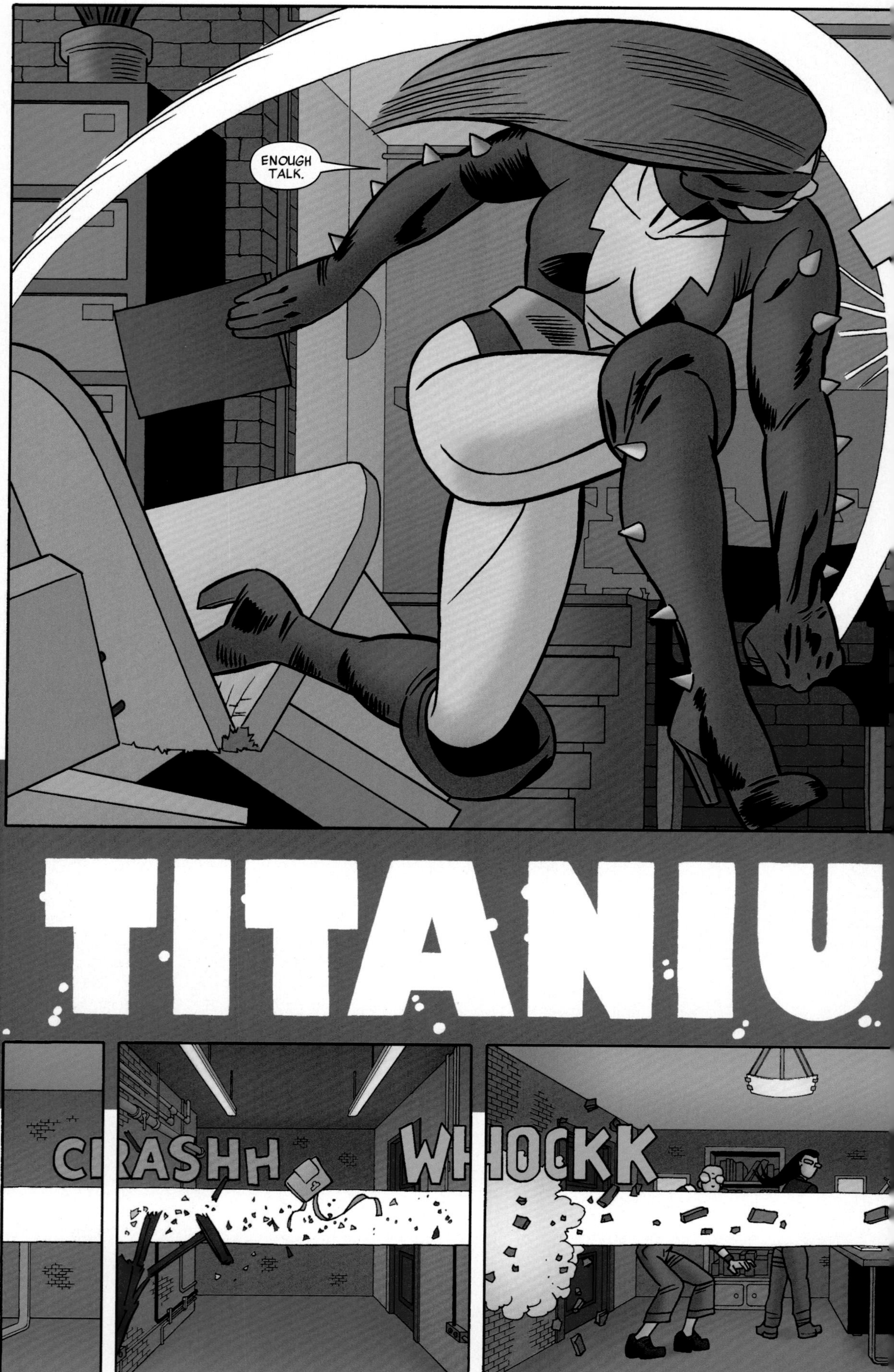
ENOUGH TALK.
TITANIU
CRASHH
WHOCKK

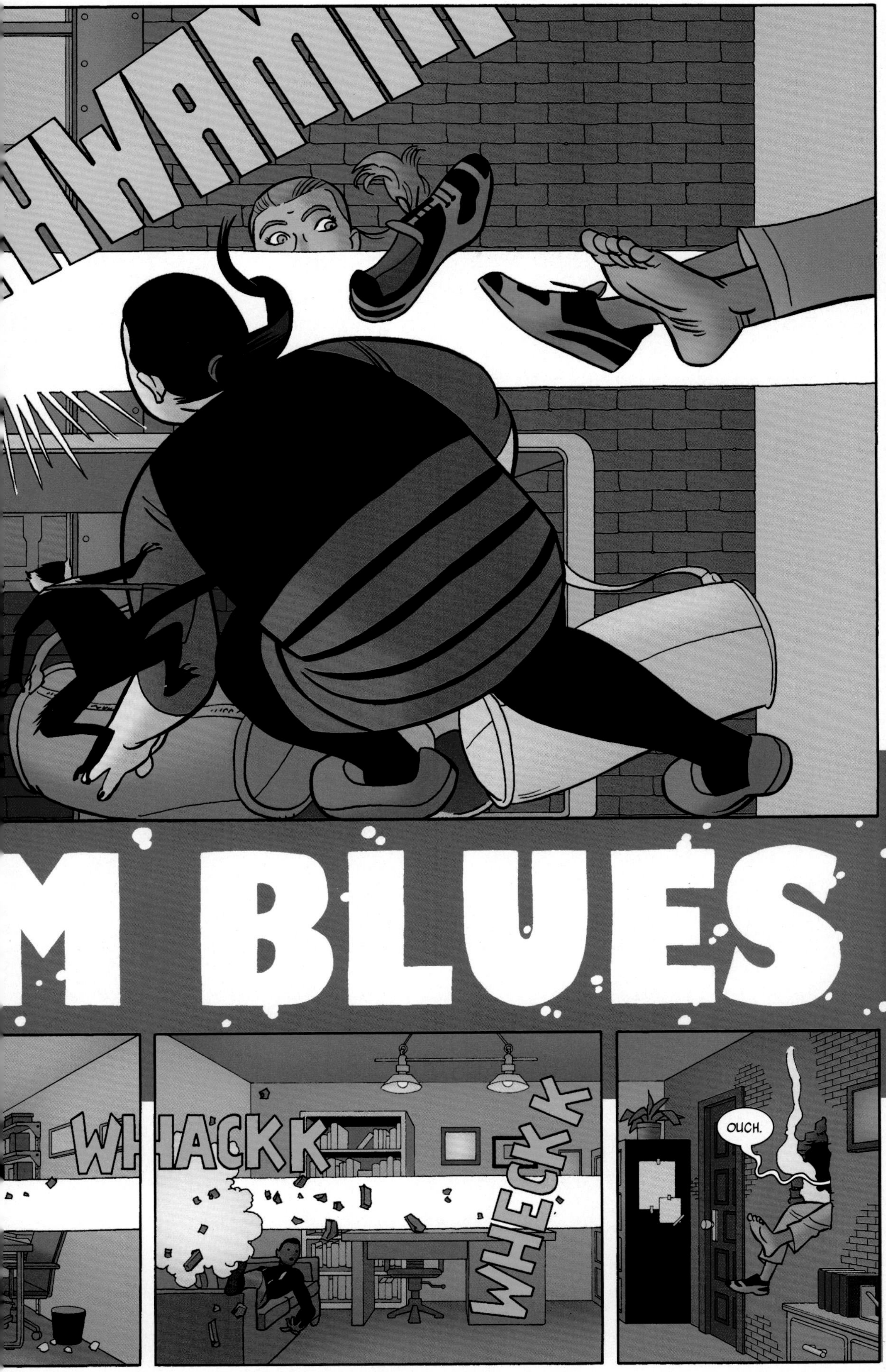

HWANNN
M BLUES
WHACKK
WHECK K
OUCH.

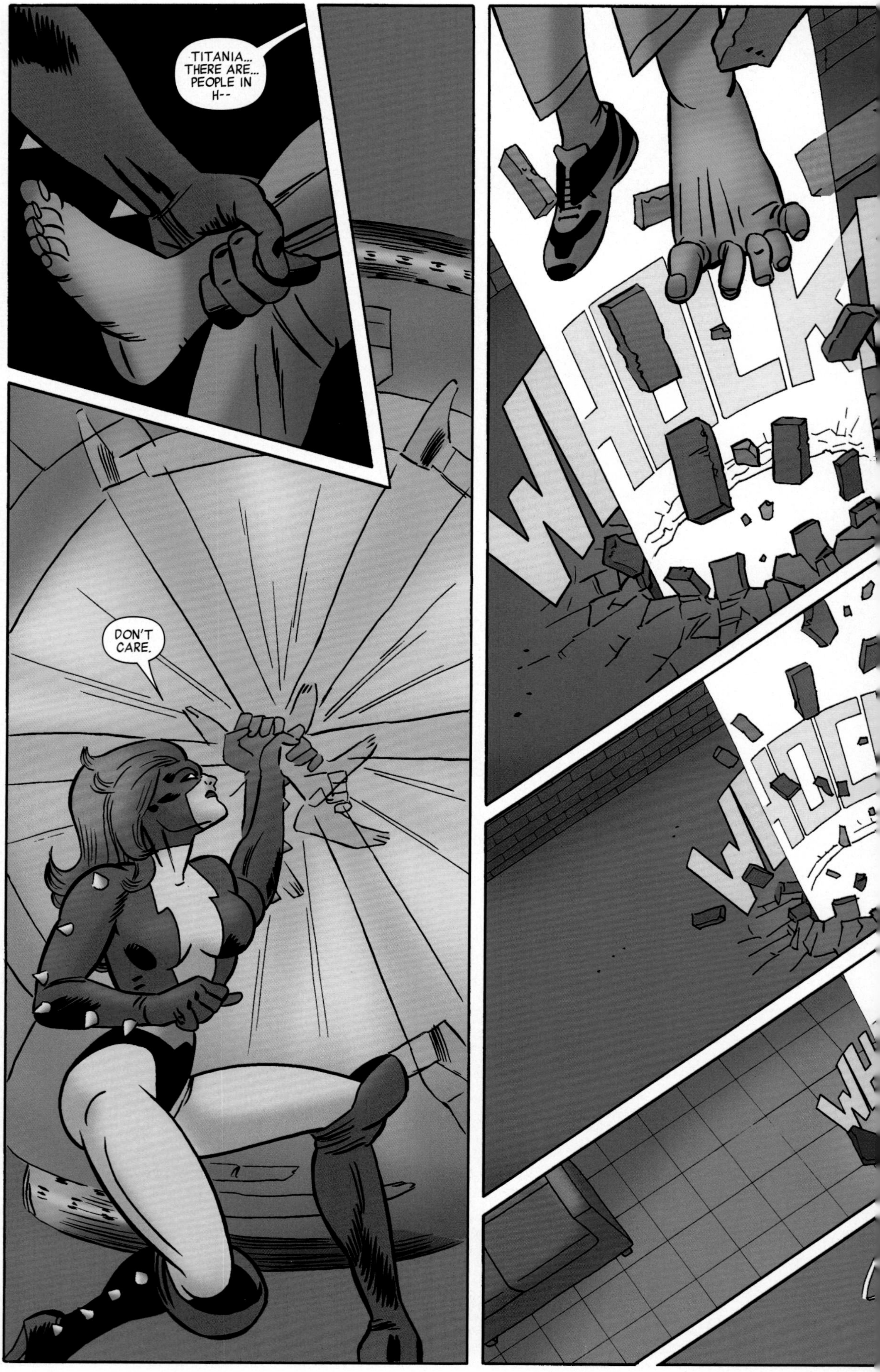
TITANIA... THERE ARE... PEOPLE IN H--
DON'T CARE.
WHACK
WHOO
WH

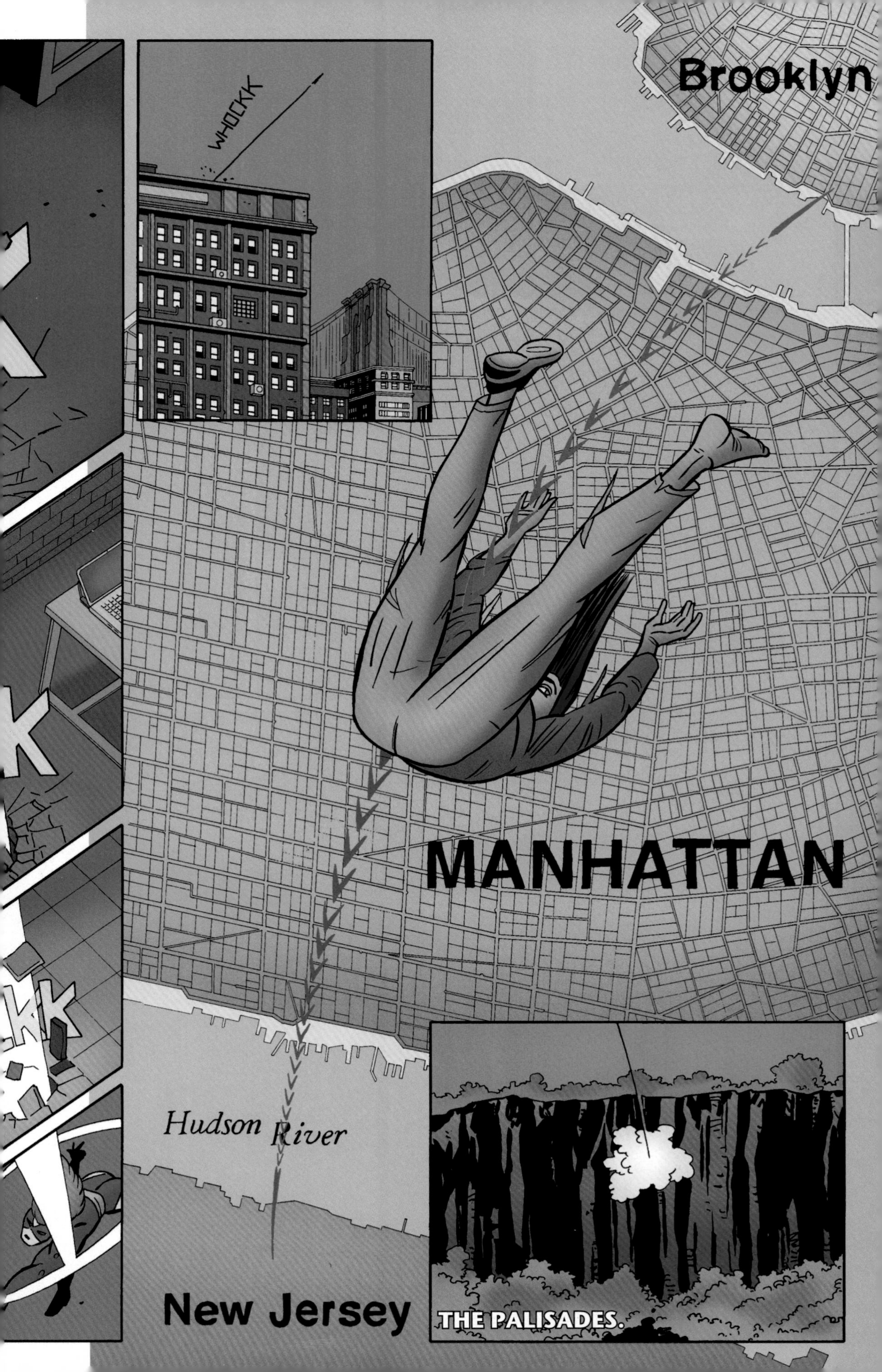
WHOCKK
Brooklyn
MANHATTAN
Hudson River
New Jersey
THE PALISADES.

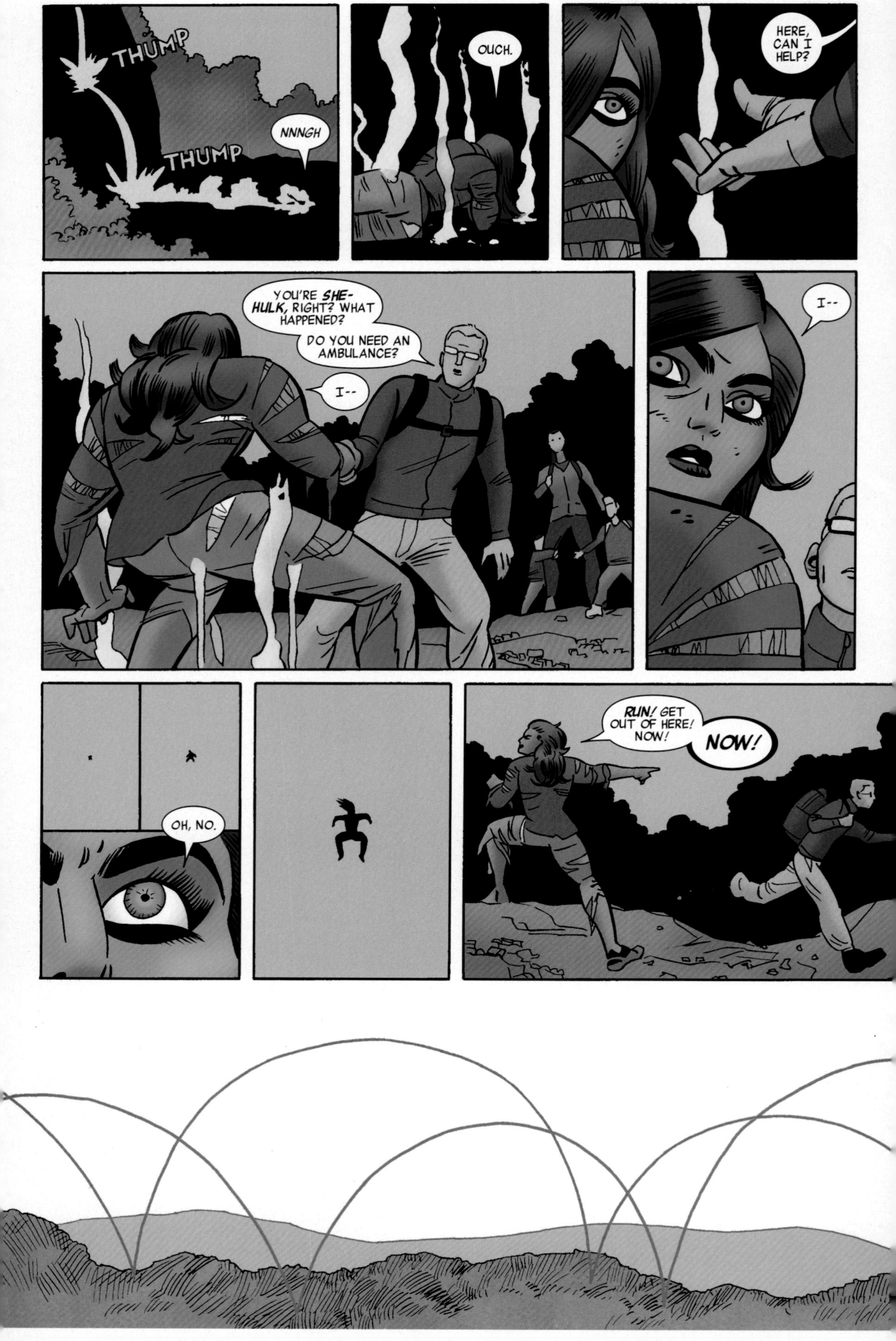
THUMP
THUMP
NNNGH
OUCH.
HERE, CAN I HELP?
YOU'RE SHE-HULK, RIGHT? WHAT HAPPENED?
DO YOU NEED AN AMBULANCE?
I--
I--
OH, NO.
RUN! GET OUT OF HERE! NOW!
NOW!

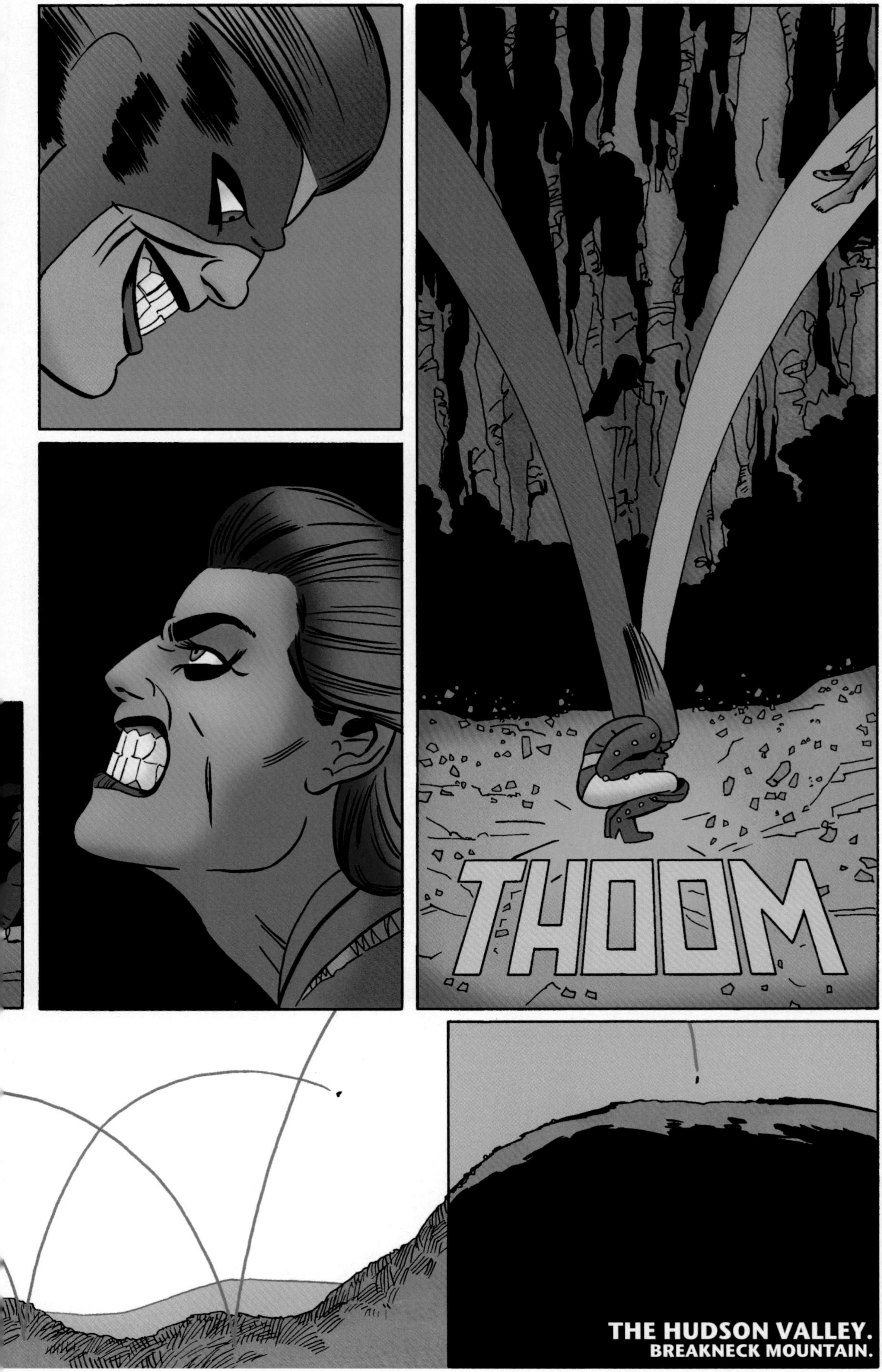
THOOM
THE HUDSON VALLEY.
BREAKNECK MOUNTAIN.

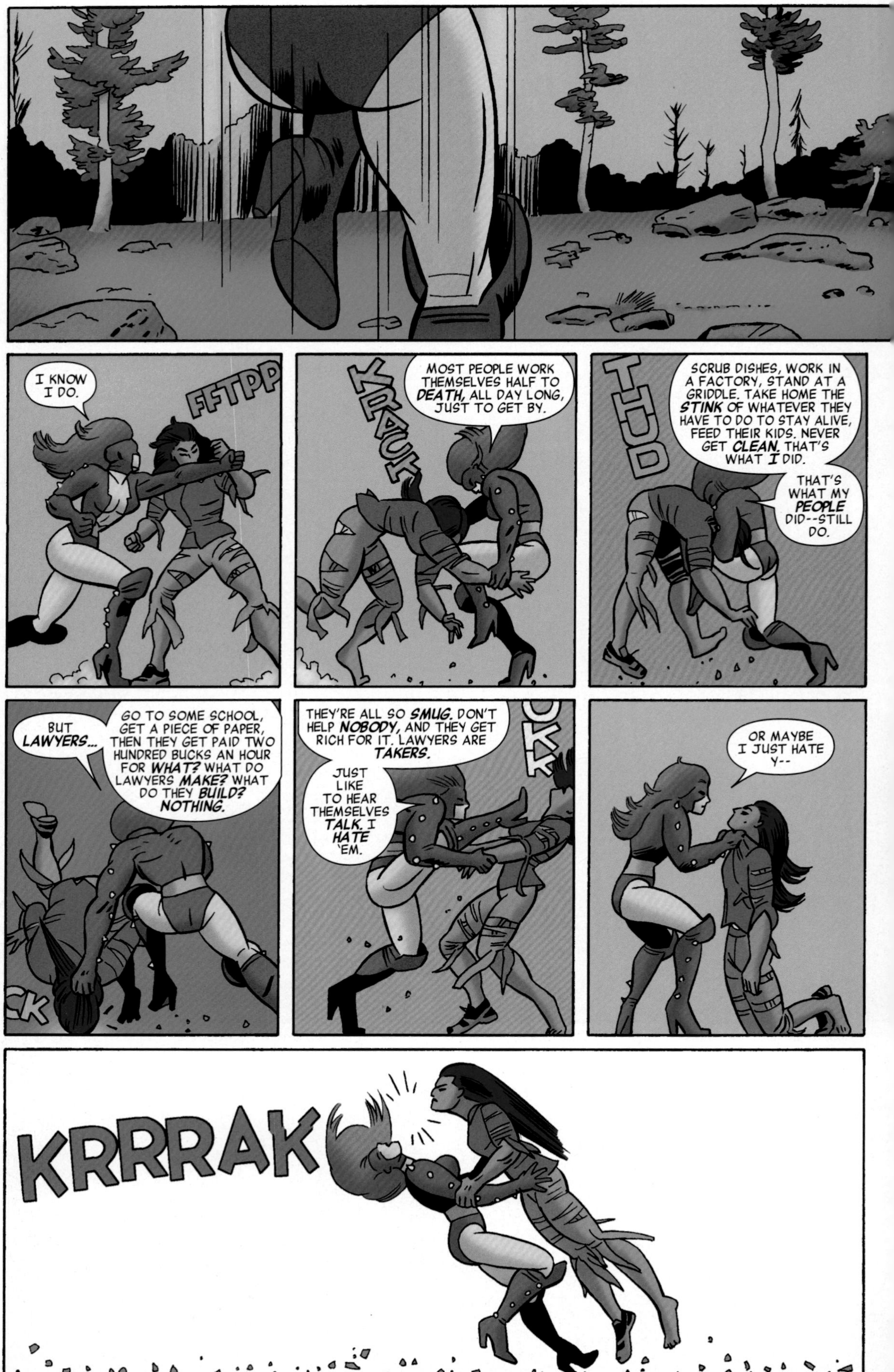

I KNOW I DO.
FFTPP
MOST PEOPLE WORK THEMSELVES HALF TO DEATH, ALL DAY LONG, JUST TO GET BY.
THUD
SCRUB DISHES, WORK IN A FACTORY, STAND AT A GRIDDLE. TAKE HOME THE STINK OF WHATEVER THEY HAVE TO DO TO STAY ALIVE, FEED THEIR KIDS. NEVER GET CLEAN. THAT'S WHAT I DID.
THAT'S WHAT MY PEOPLE DID--STILL DO.
BUT LAWYERS...
GO TO SOME SCHOOL, GET A PIECE OF PAPER, THEN THEY GET PAID TWO HUNDRED BUCKS AN HOUR FOR WHAT? WHAT DO LAWYERS MAKE? WHAT DO THEY BUILD? NOTHING.
THEY'RE ALL SO SMUG. DON'T HELP NOBODY, AND THEY GET RICH FOR IT. LAWYERS ARE TAKERS.
JUST LIKE TO HEAR THEMSELVES TALK. I HATE 'EM.
OR MAYBE I JUST HATE Y--
KRRRAK

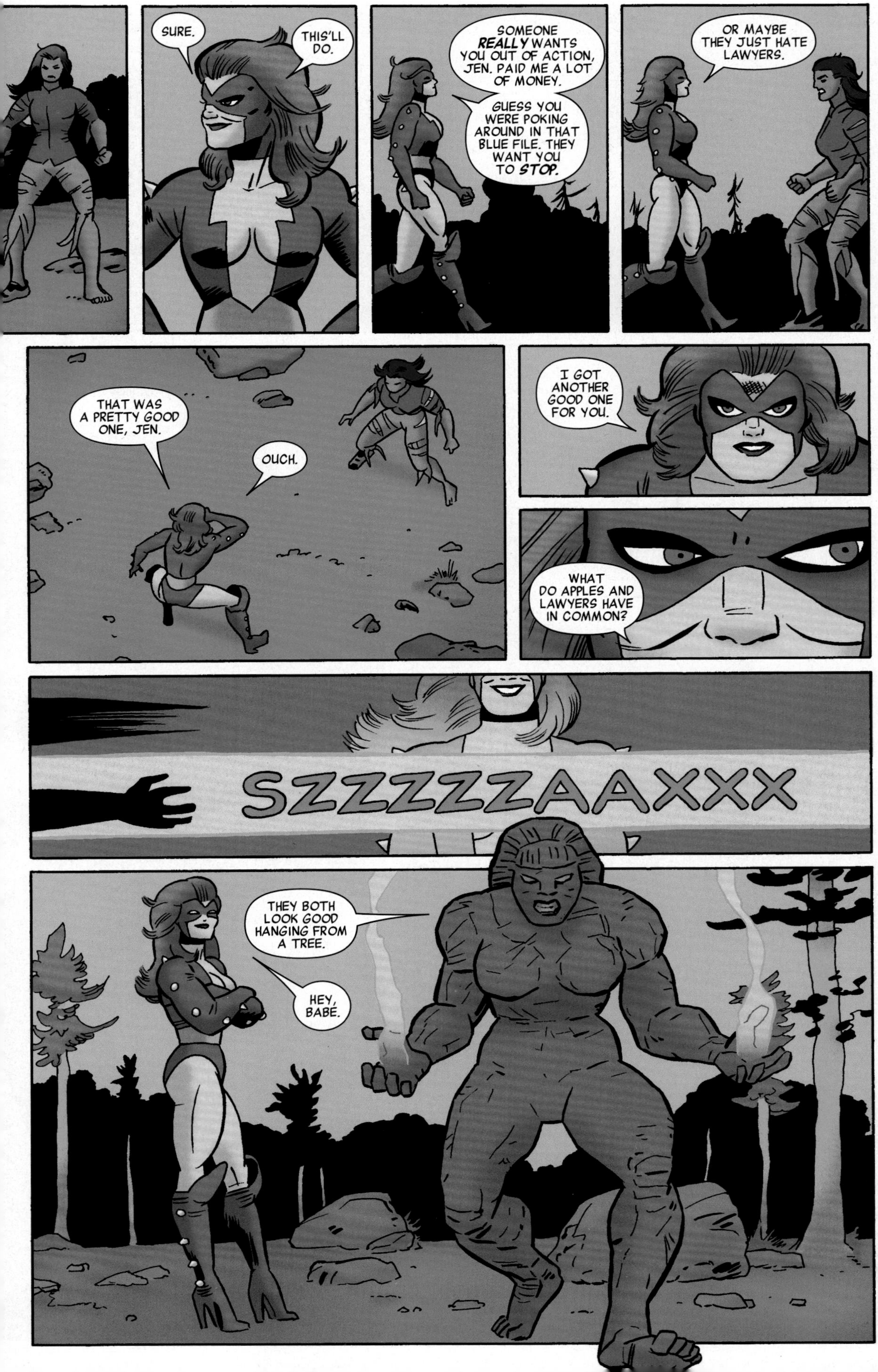
SURE.
THIS'LL DO.
SOMEONE REALLY WANTS YOU OUT OF ACTION, JEN. PAID ME A LOT OF MONEY.
GUESS YOU WERE POKING AROUND IN THAT BLUE FILE. THEY WANT YOU TO STOP.
OR MAYBE THEY JUST HATE LAWYERS.
THAT WAS A PRETTY GOOD ONE, JEN.
OUCH.
I GOT ANOTHER GOOD ONE FOR YOU.
WHAT DO APPLES AND LAWYERS HAVE IN COMMON?
SZZZZZZAAXXX
THEY BOTH LOOK GOOD HANGING FROM A TREE.
HEY, BABE.

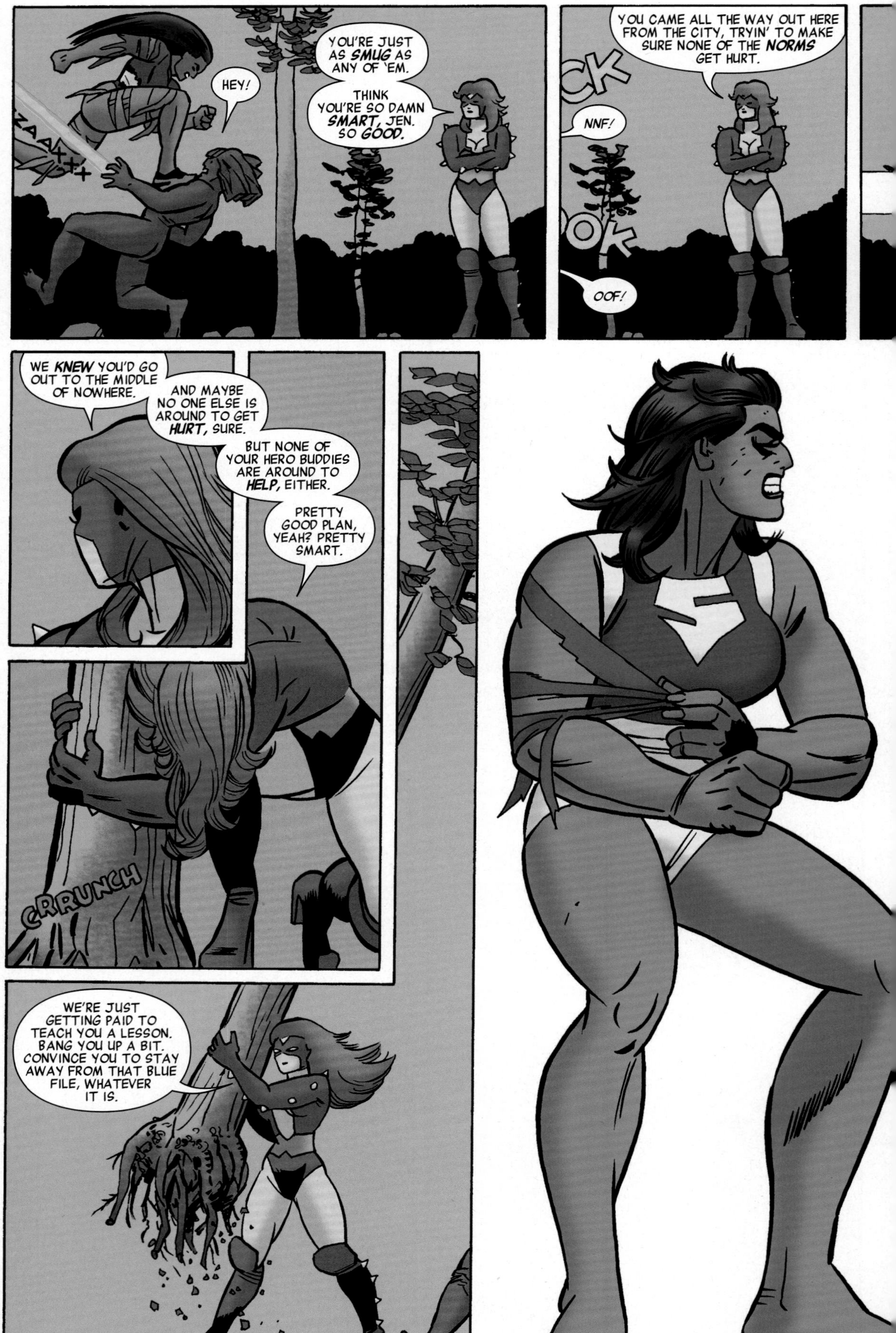

HEY!
ZAAAKX++
YOU'RE JUST AS SMUG AS ANY OF 'EM.
THINK YOU'RE SO DAMN SMART, JEN. SO GOOD.
YOU CAME ALL THE WAY OUT HERE FROM THE CITY, TRYIN' TO MAKE SURE NONE OF THE NORMS GET HURT.
NNF!
OOF!
WE KNEW YOU'D GO OUT TO THE MIDDLE OF NOWHERE.
AND MAYBE NO ONE ELSE IS AROUND TO GET HURT, SURE.
BUT NONE OF YOUR HERO BUDDIES ARE AROUND TO HELP, EITHER.
PRETTY GOOD PLAN, YEAH? PRETTY SMART.
CRRUNCH
WE'RE JUST GETTING PAID TO TEACH YOU A LESSON. BANG YOU UP A BIT. CONVINCE YOU TO STAY AWAY FROM THAT BLUE FILE, WHATEVER IT IS.

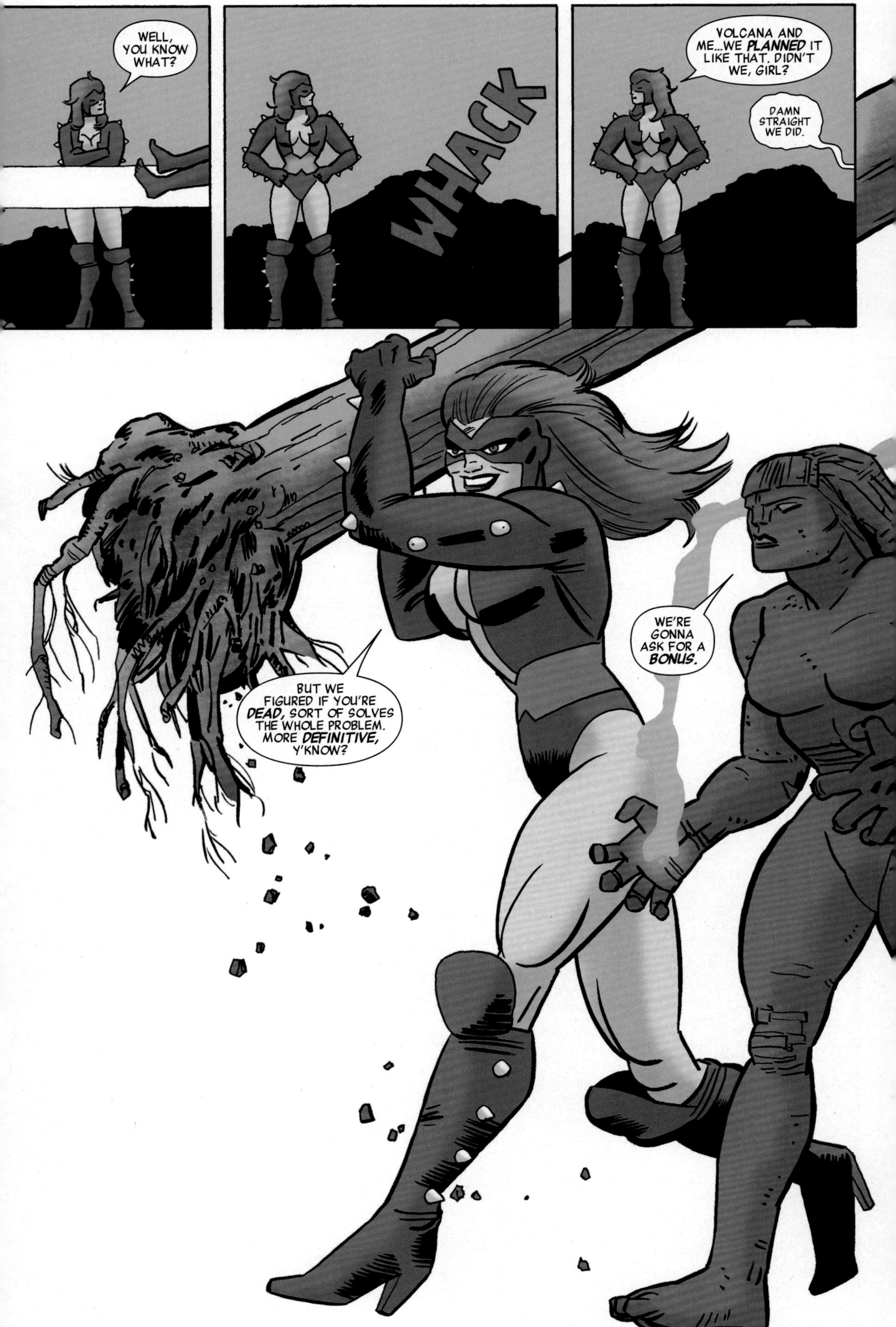
WELL, YOU KNOW WHAT?
WHACK
VOLCANA AND ME...WE PLANNED IT LIKE THAT. DIDN'T WE, GIRL?
DAMN STRAIGHT WE DID.
BUT WE FIGURED IF YOU'RE DEAD, SORT OF SOLVES THE WHOLE PROBLEM. MORE DEFINITIVE, Y'KNOW?
WE'RE GONNA ASK FOR A BONUS.

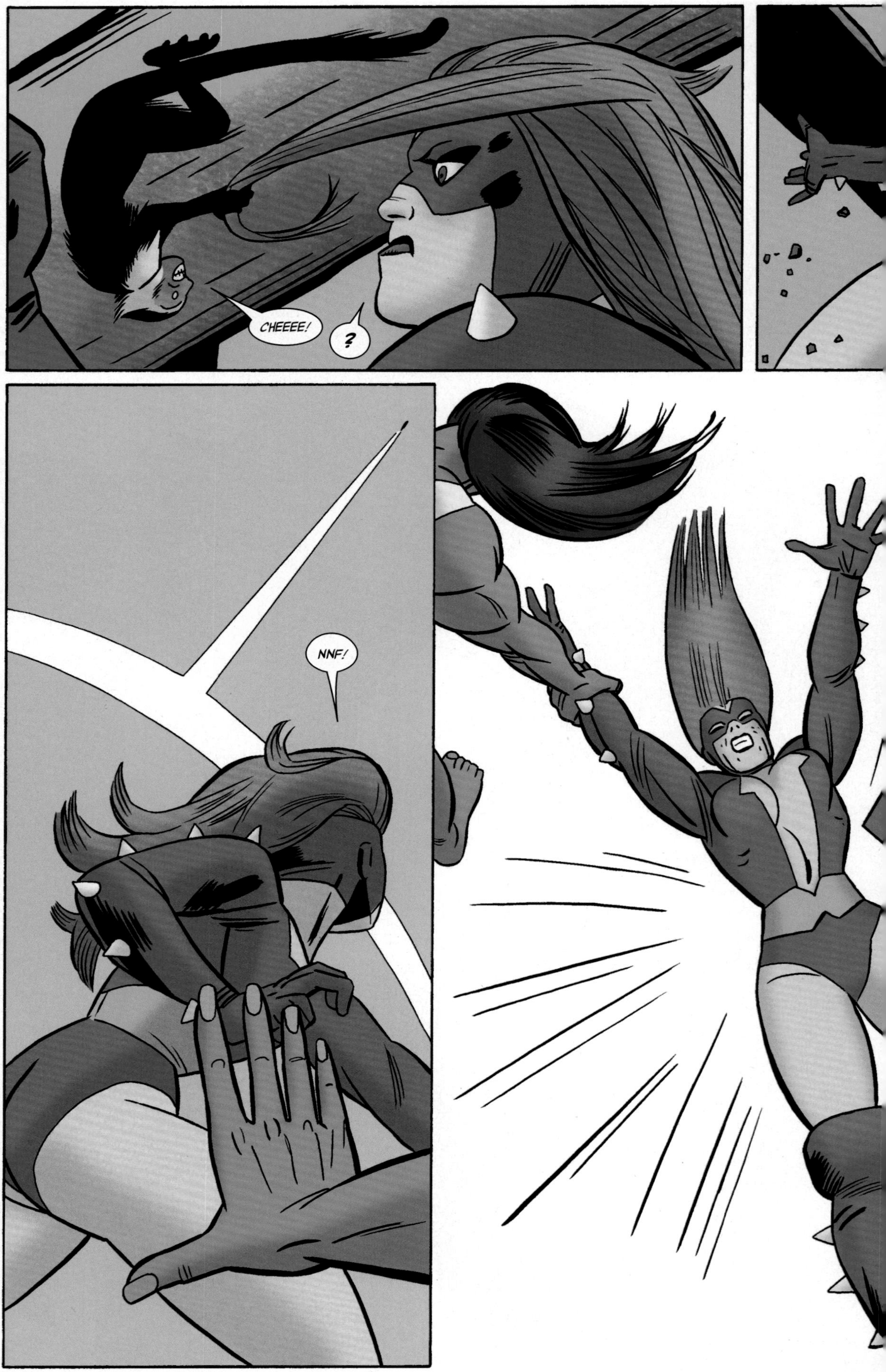
CHEEEE!
?
NNF!

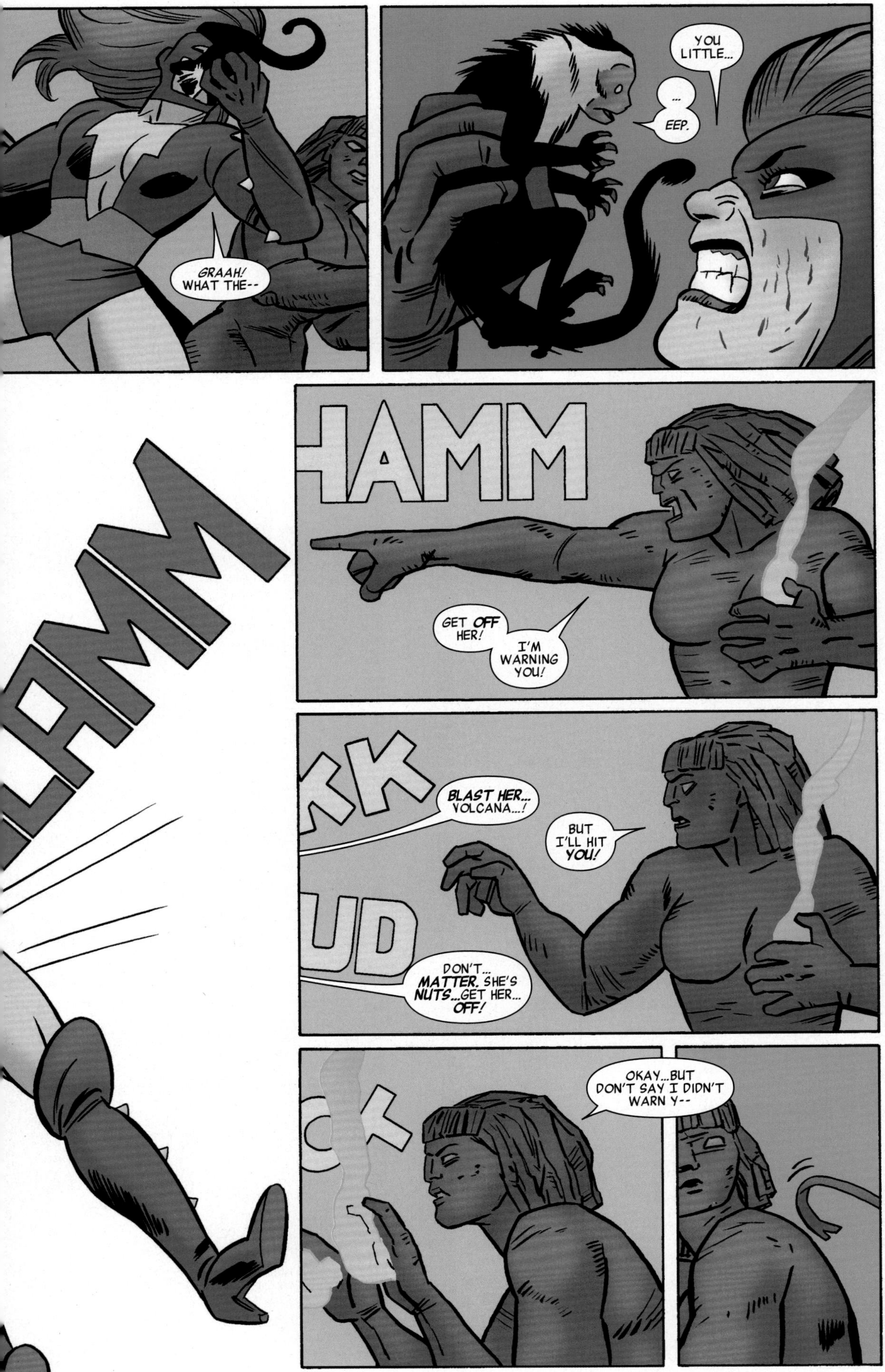
GRAAH! WHAT THE--
YOU LITTLE...
... EEP.
HAMM
GET OFF HER!
I'M WARNING YOU!
KK
BLAST HER... VOLCANA...!
BUT I'LL HIT YOU!
UD
DON'T... MATTER. SHE'S NUTS...GET HER... OFF!
OKAY...BUT DON'T SAY I DIDN'T WARN Y--

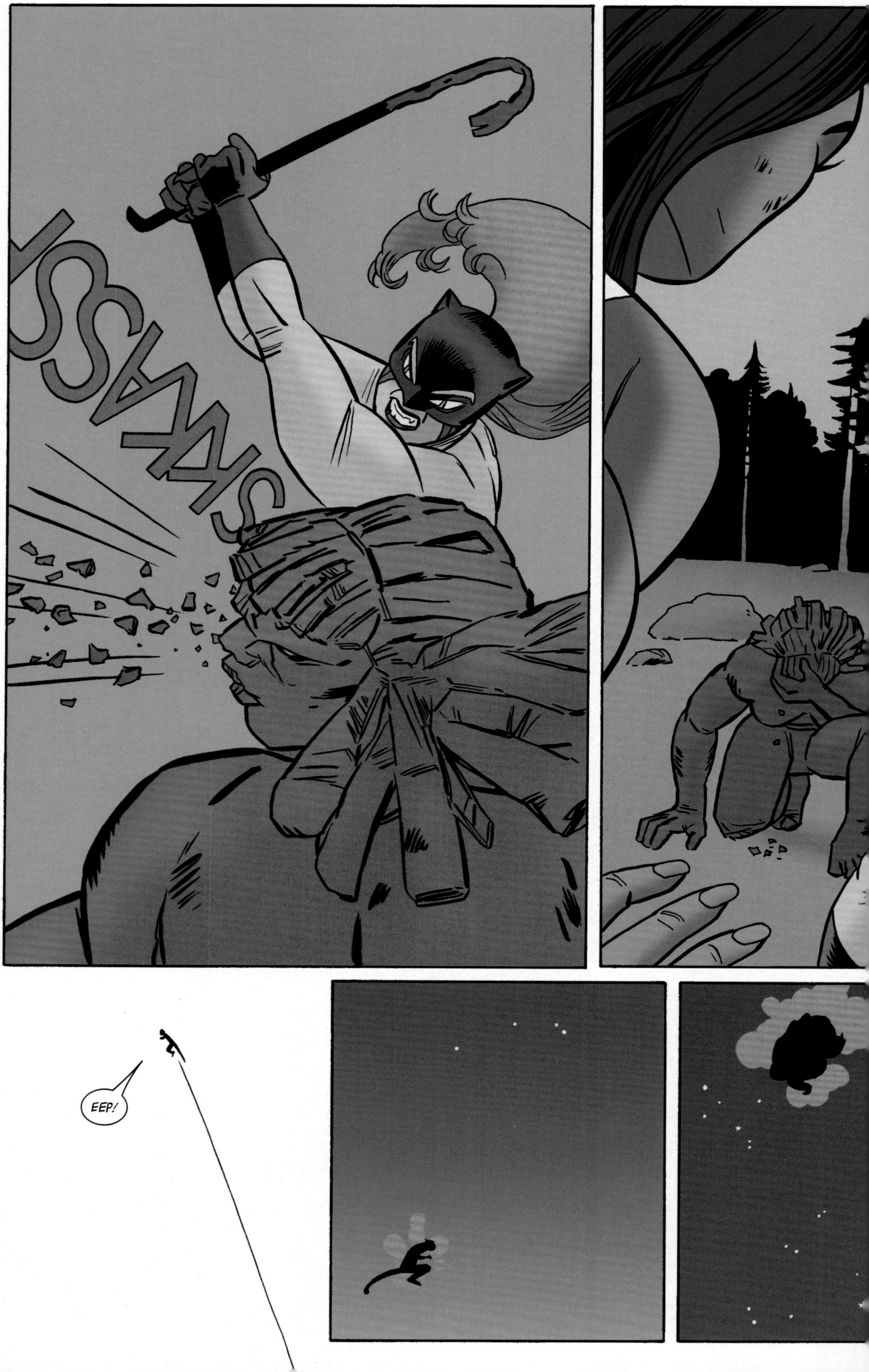
EEP!

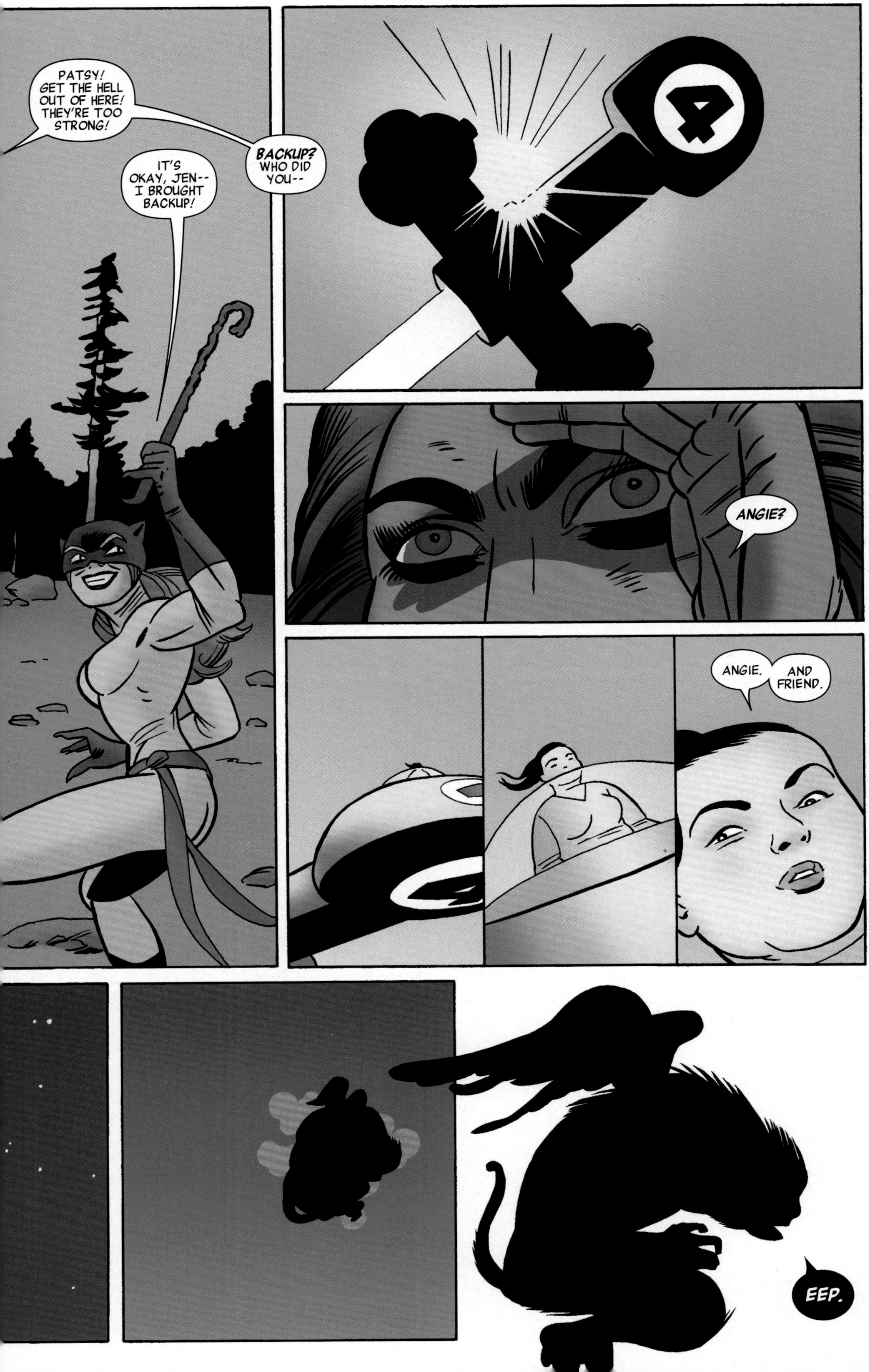
PATSY! GET THE HELL OUT OF HERE! THEY'RE TOO STRONG!
IT'S OKAY, JEN-- I BROUGHT BACKUP!
BACKUP? WHO DID YOU--
ANGIE?
ANGIE.
AND FRIEND.
EEP.

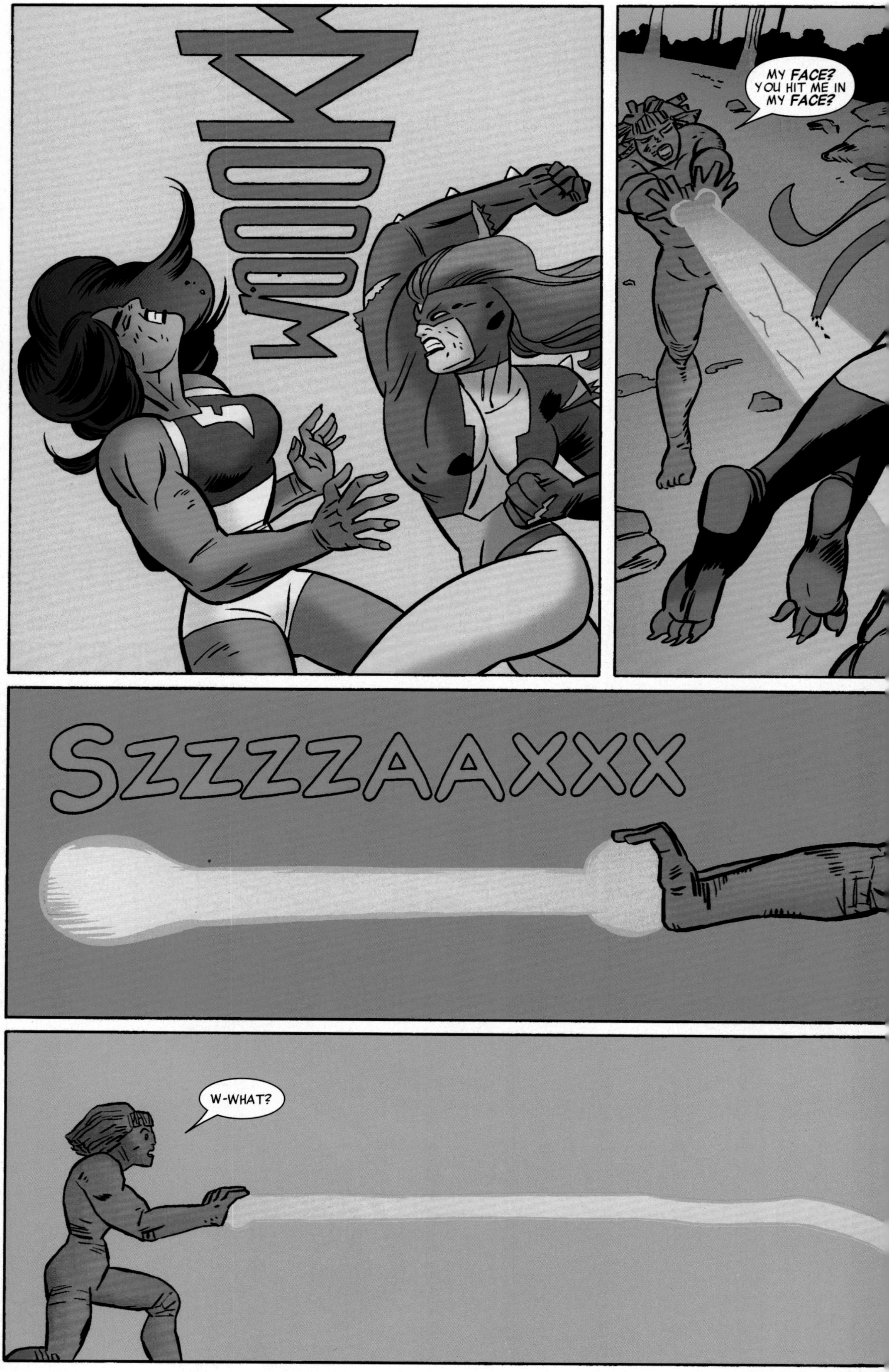
KRAKOOOOM
MY FACE? YOU HIT ME IN MY FACE?
SZZZZZAAXXX
W-WHAT?

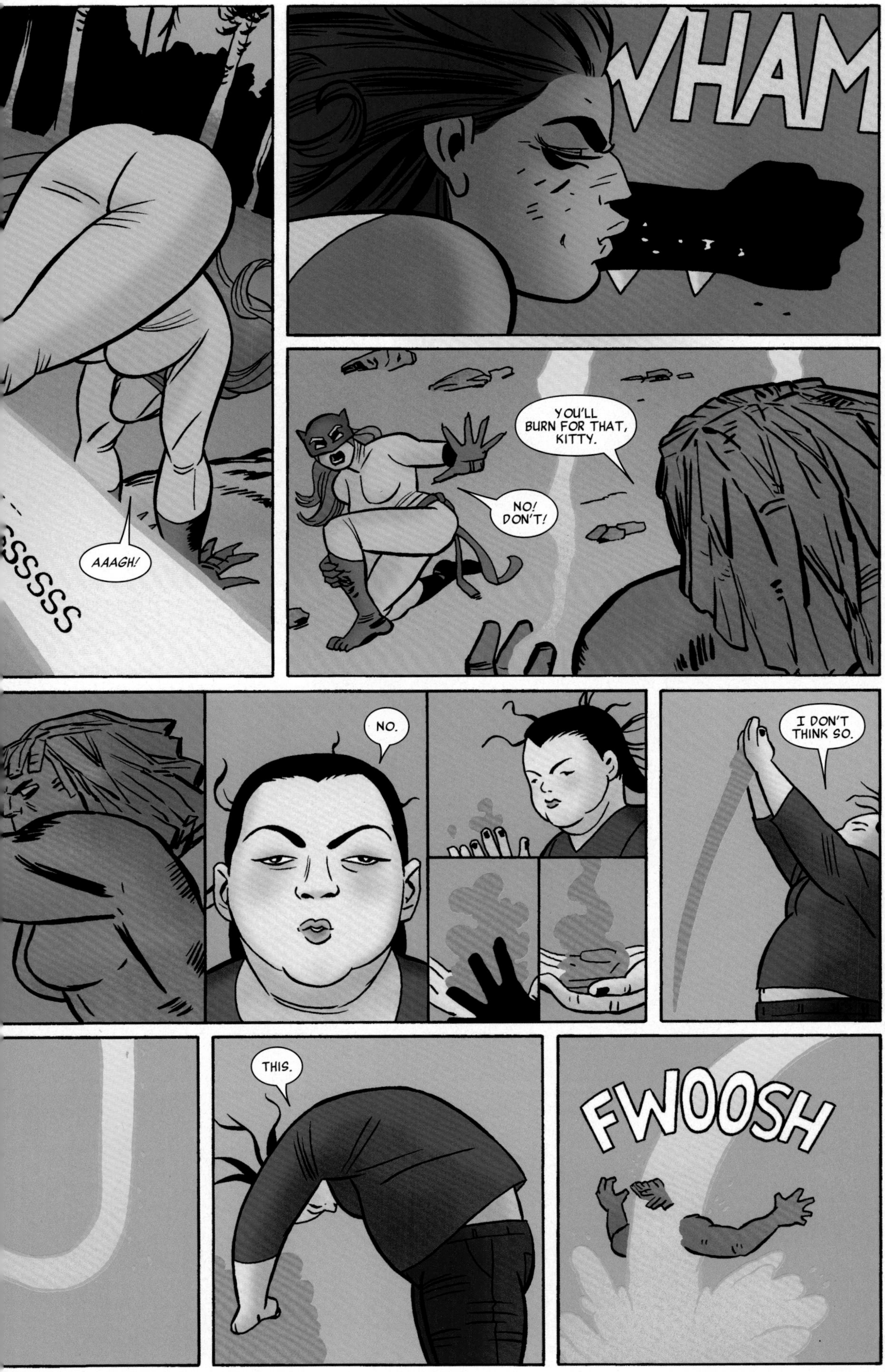
WHAM
SSSSSS
AAAGH!
YOU'LL BURN FOR THAT, KITTY.
NO! DON'T!
NO.
I DON'T THINK SO.
THIS.
FWOOSH

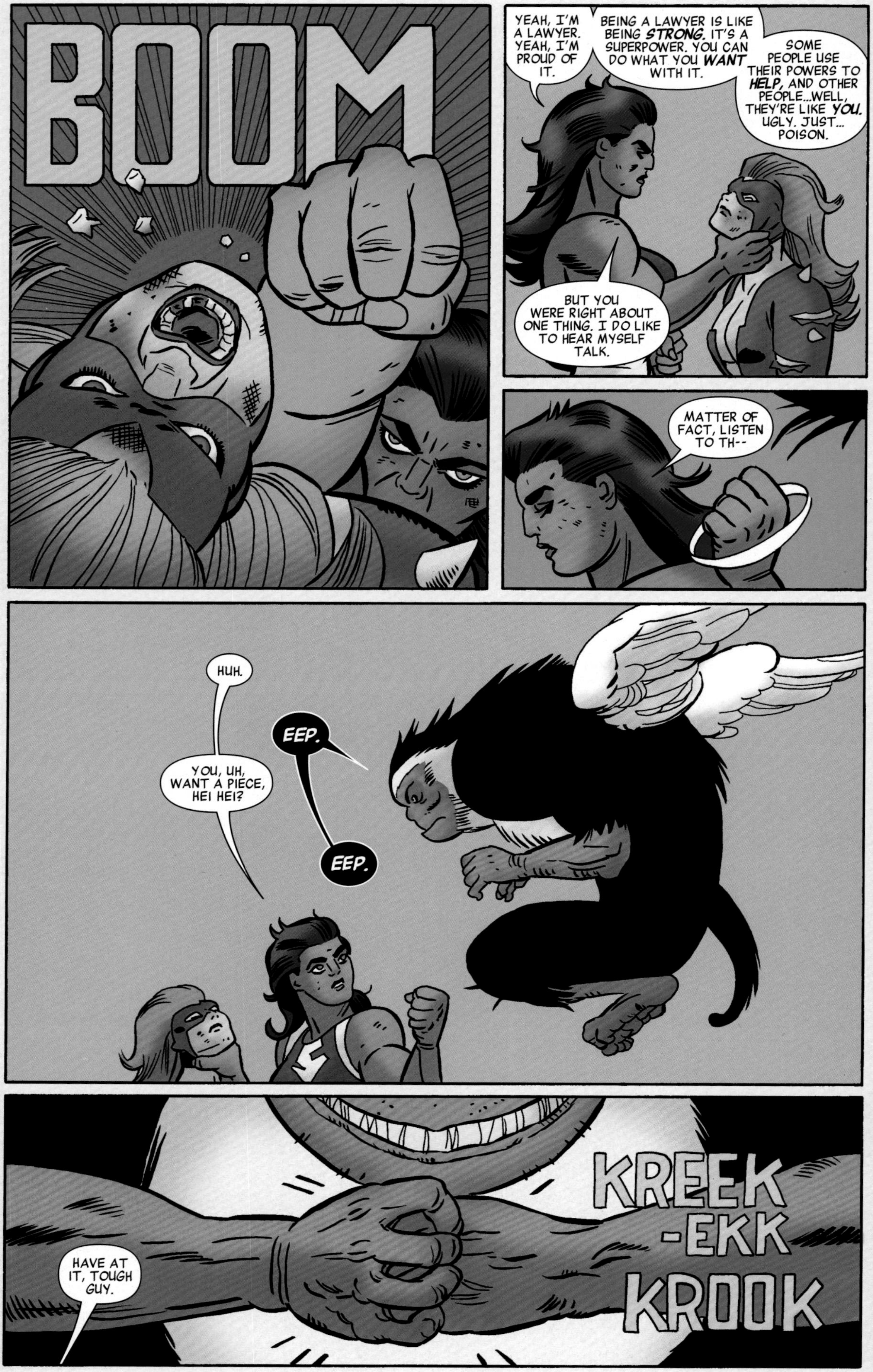
BOOM
YEAH, I'M A LAWYER. YEAH, I'M PROUD OF IT.
BEING A LAWYER IS LIKE BEING STRONG. IT'S A SUPERPOWER. YOU CAN DO WHAT YOU WANT WITH IT.
SOME PEOPLE USE THEIR POWERS TO HELP, AND OTHER PEOPLE...WELL, THEY'RE LIKE YOU. UGLY. JUST... POISON.
BUT YOU WERE RIGHT ABOUT ONE THING. I DO LIKE TO HEAR MYSELF TALK.
MATTER OF FACT, LISTEN TO TH--
HUH.
YOU, UH, WANT A PIECE, HEI HEI?
EEP.
EEP.
KREEK -EKK KROOK
HAVE AT IT, TOUGH GUY.

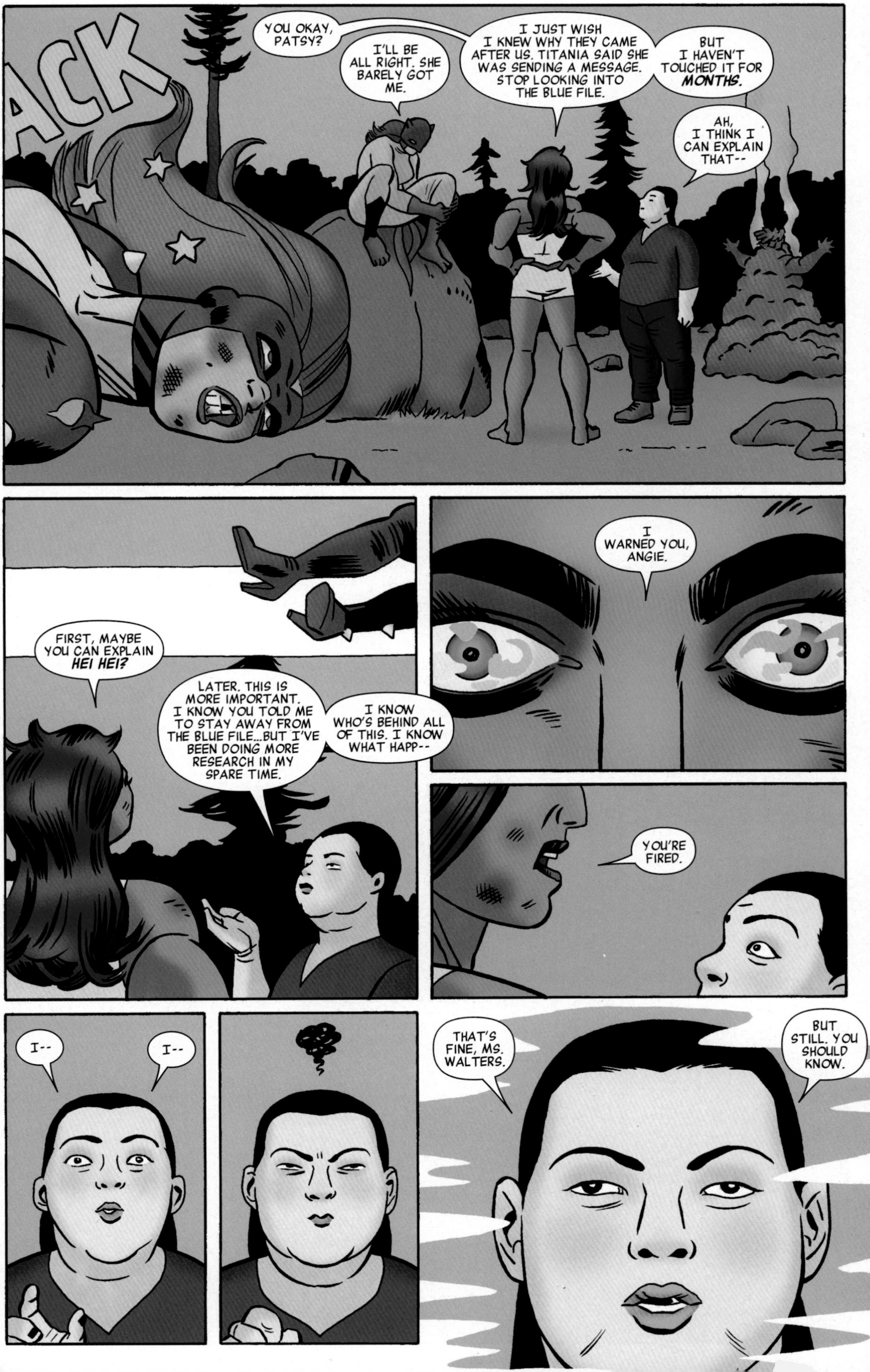
ACK
YOU OKAY, PATSY?
I'LL BE ALL RIGHT. SHE BARELY GOT ME.
I JUST WISH I KNEW WHY THEY CAME AFTER US. TITANIA SAID SHE WAS SENDING A MESSAGE. STOP LOOKING INTO THE BLUE FILE.
BUT I HAVEN'T TOUCHED IT FOR **MONTHS.**
AH, I THINK I CAN EXPLAIN THAT--
FIRST, MAYBE YOU CAN EXPLAIN **HEI HEI?**
LATER. THIS IS MORE IMPORTANT. I KNOW YOU TOLD ME TO STAY AWAY FROM THE BLUE FILE...BUT I'VE BEEN DOING MORE RESEARCH IN MY SPARE TIME.
I KNOW WHO'S BEHIND ALL OF THIS. I KNOW WHAT HAPP--
I WARNED YOU, ANGIE.
YOU'RE FIRED.
I--
I--
THAT'S FINE, MS. WALTERS.
BUT STILL. YOU SHOULD KNOW.

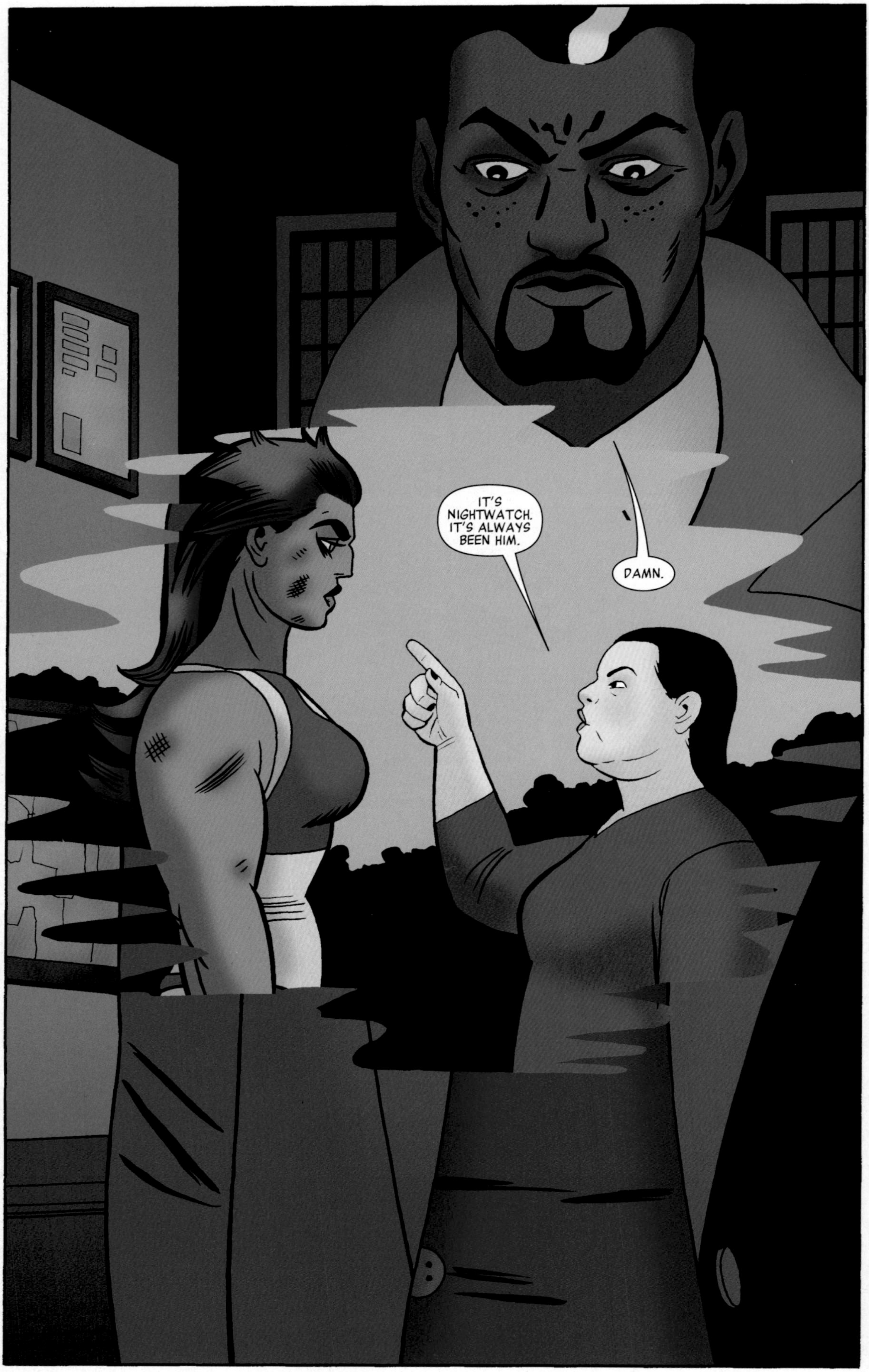
IT'S NIGHTWATCH. IT'S ALWAYS BEEN HIM.
DAMN.

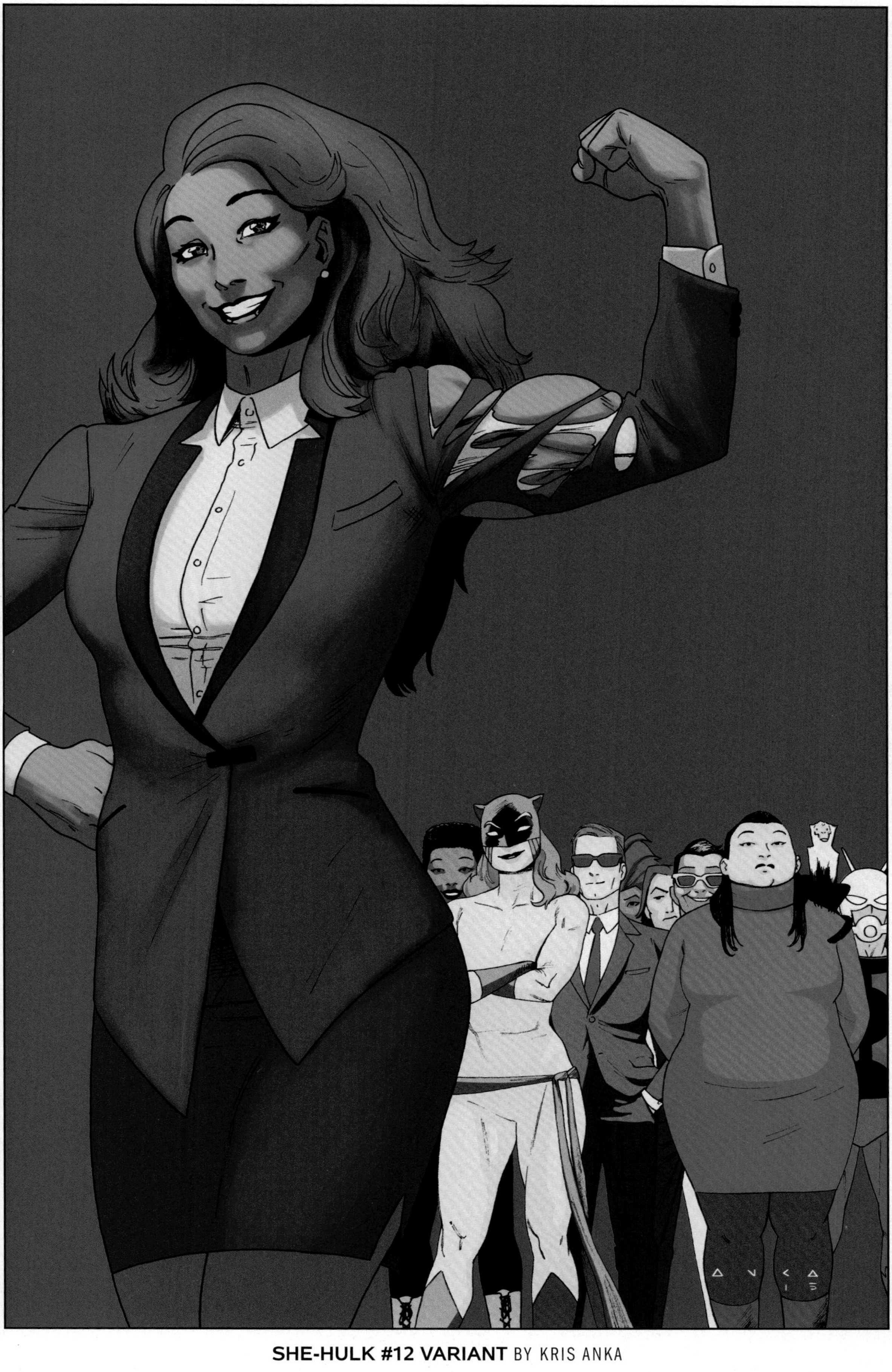
ANKA 15

SHE-HULK #12 VARIANT BY KRIS ANKA

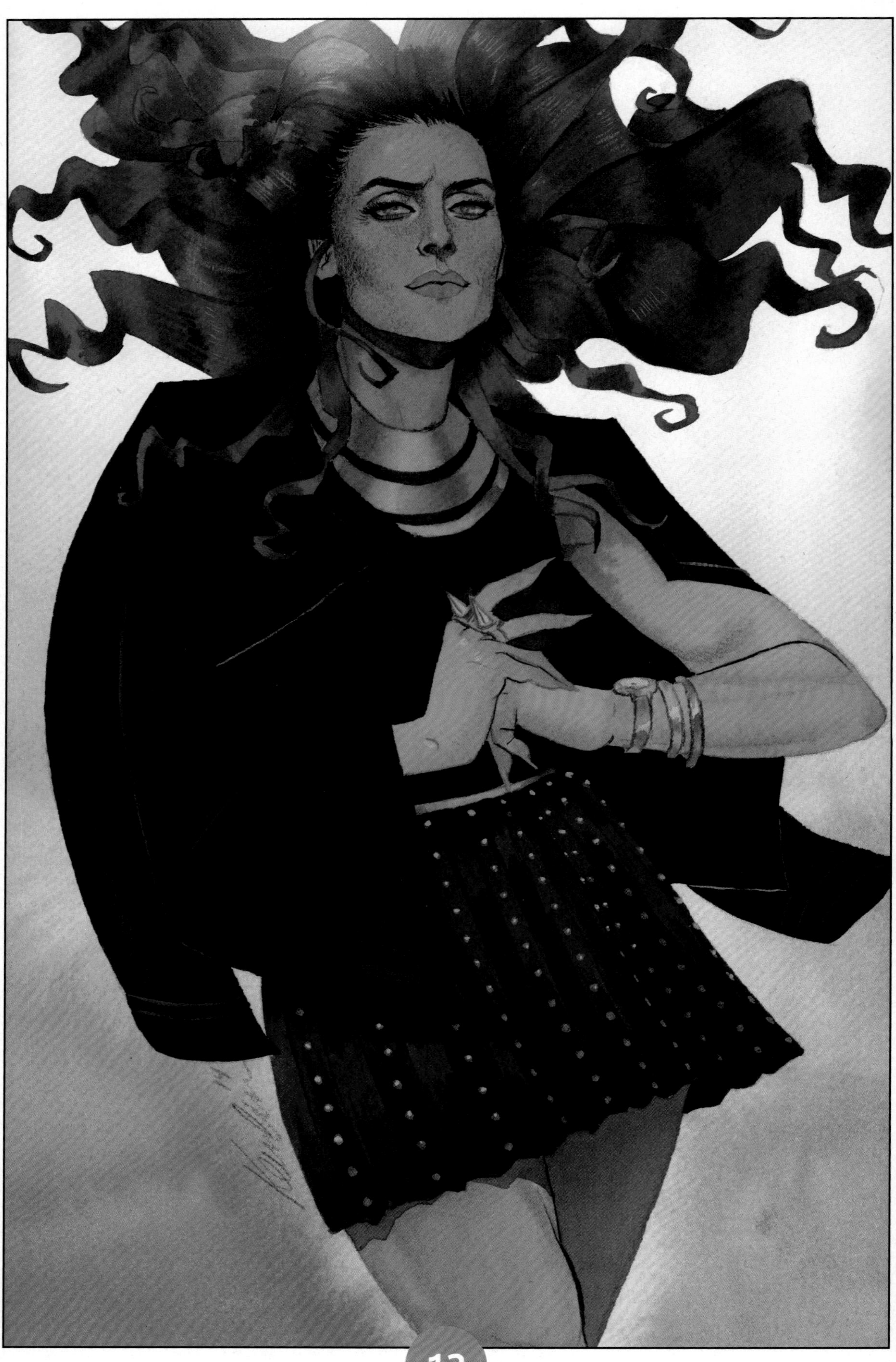

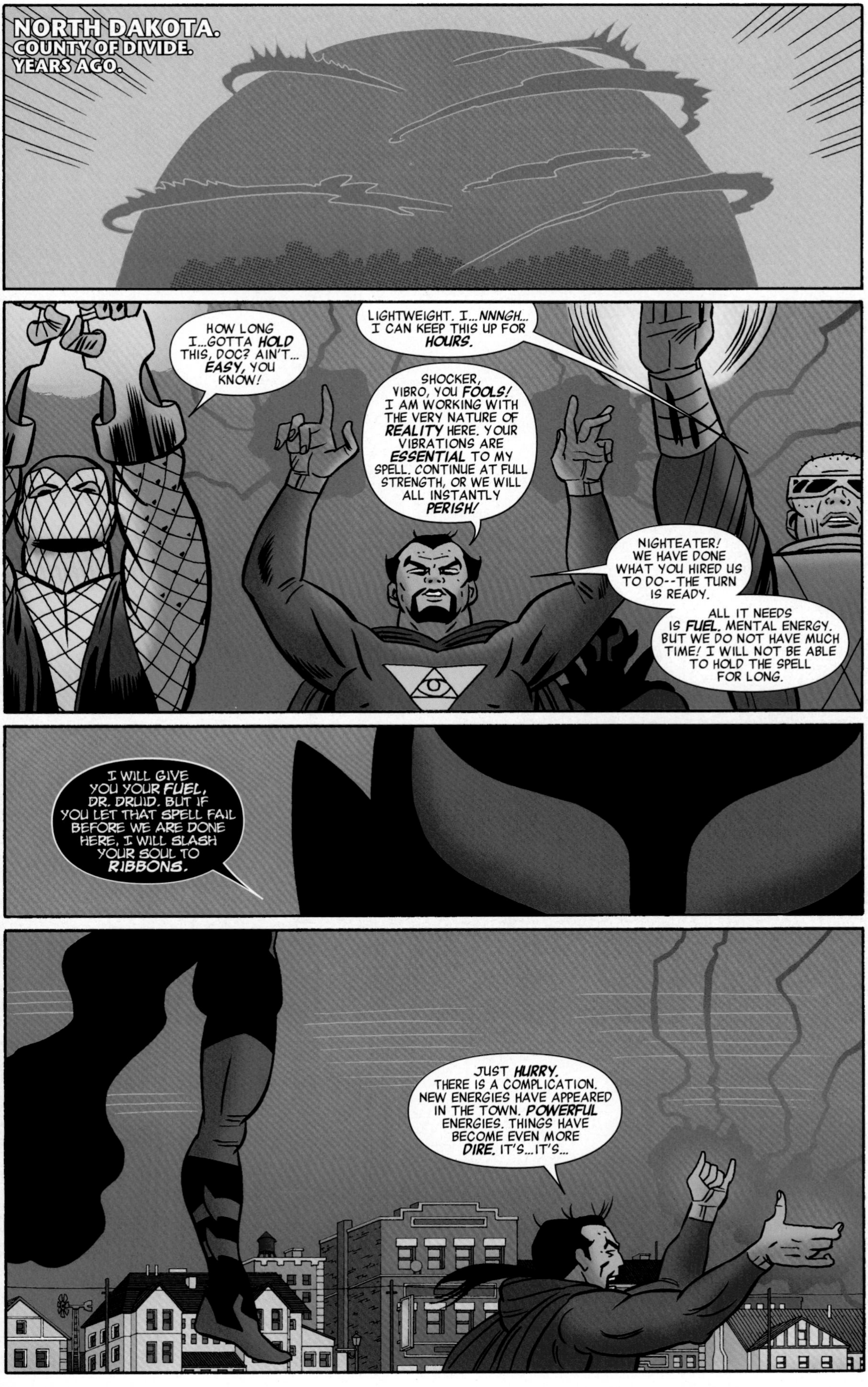
NORTH DAKOTA. COUNTY OF DIVIDE. YEARS AGO.
HOW LONG I...GOTTA HOLD THIS, DOC? AIN'T... EASY, YOU KNOW!
LIGHTWEIGHT. I...NNNGH... I CAN KEEP THIS UP FOR HOURS.
SHOCKER, VIBRO, YOU FOOLS! I AM WORKING WITH THE VERY NATURE OF REALITY HERE. YOUR VIBRATIONS ARE ESSENTIAL TO MY SPELL. CONTINUE AT FULL STRENGTH, OR WE WILL ALL INSTANTLY PERISH!
NIGHTEATER! WE HAVE DONE WHAT YOU HIRED US TO DO--THE TURN IS READY.
ALL IT NEEDS IS FUEL. MENTAL ENERGY. BUT WE DO NOT HAVE MUCH TIME! I WILL NOT BE ABLE TO HOLD THE SPELL FOR LONG.
I WILL GIVE YOU YOUR FUEL, DR. DRUID. BUT IF YOU LET THAT SPELL FAIL BEFORE WE ARE DONE HERE, I WILL SLASH YOUR SOUL TO RIBBONS.
JUST HURRY. THERE IS A COMPLICATION. NEW ENERGIES HAVE APPEARED IN THE TOWN. POWERFUL ENERGIES. THINGS HAVE BECOME EVEN MORE DIRE. IT'S...IT'S...

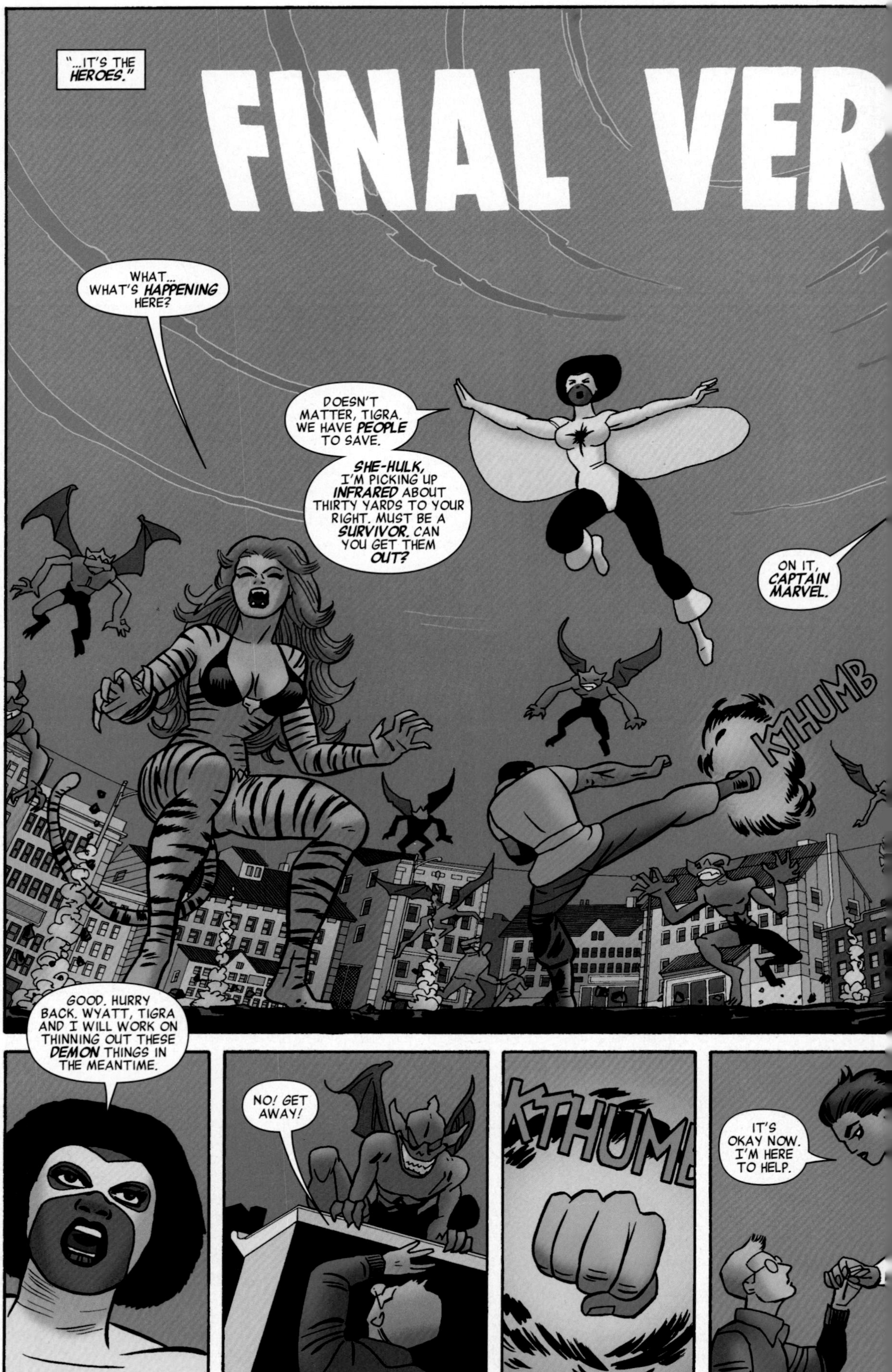
"...IT'S THE HEROES."
FINAL VER
WHAT... WHAT'S HAPPENING HERE?
DOESN'T MATTER, TIGRA. WE HAVE PEOPLE TO SAVE.
SHE-HULK, I'M PICKING UP INFRARED ABOUT THIRTY YARDS TO YOUR RIGHT. MUST BE A SURVIVOR. CAN YOU GET THEM OUT?
ON IT, CAPTAIN MARVEL.
KTHUMB
GOOD. HURRY BACK. WYATT, TIGRA AND I WILL WORK ON THINNING OUT THESE DEMON THINGS IN THE MEANTIME.
NO! GET AWAY!
KTHUMB
IT'S OKAY NOW. I'M HERE TO HELP.

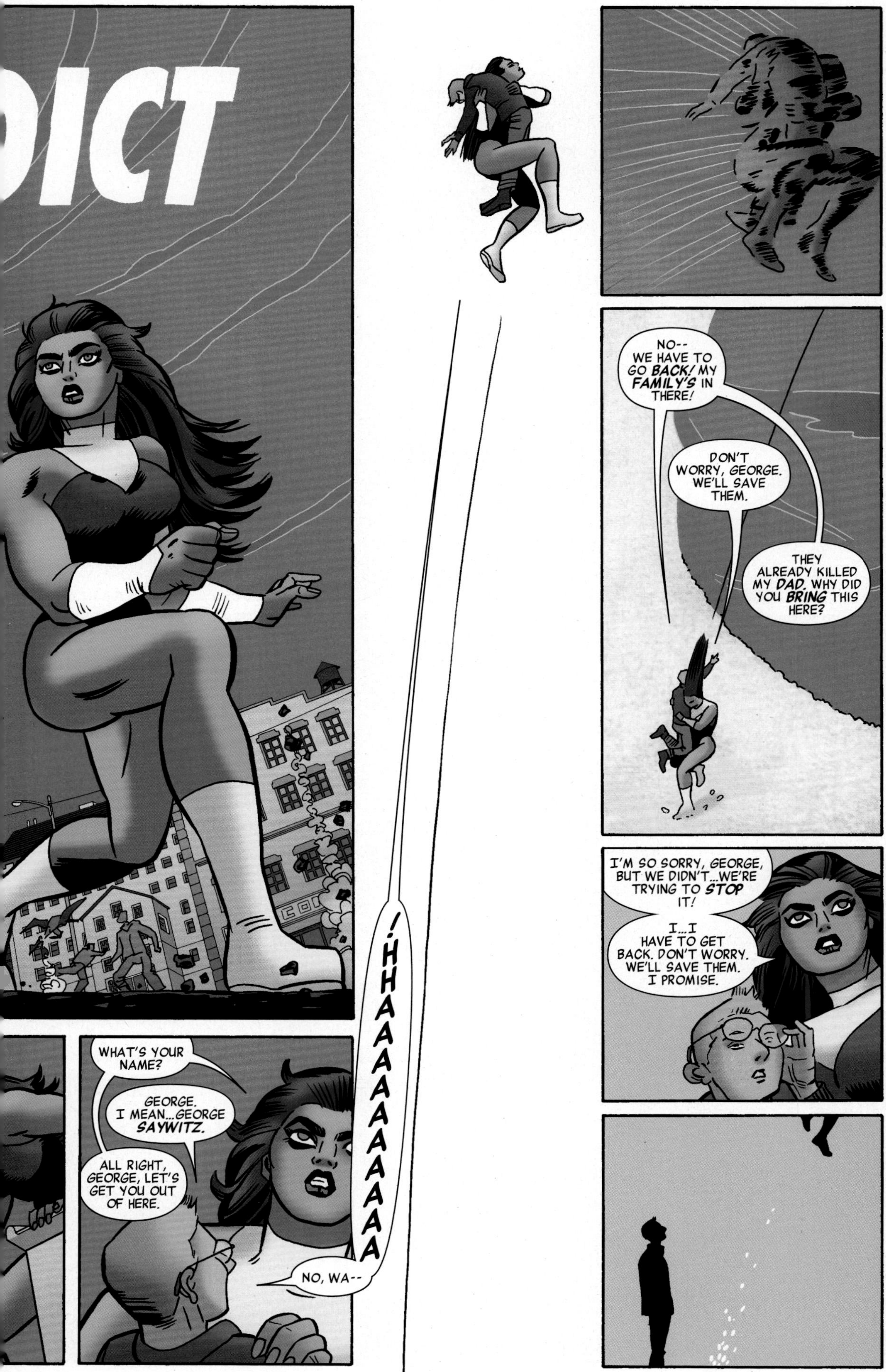
DICT
WHAT'S YOUR NAME?
GEORGE. I MEAN...GEORGE SAYWITZ.
ALL RIGHT, GEORGE, LET'S GET YOU OUT OF HERE.
NO, WA--
AAAAAAAAAAAAAHH!
NO-- WE HAVE TO GO BACK! MY FAMILY'S IN THERE!
DON'T WORRY, GEORGE. WE'LL SAVE THEM.
THEY ALREADY KILLED MY DAD. WHY DID YOU BRING THIS HERE?
I'M SO SORRY, GEORGE, BUT WE DIDN'T...WE'RE TRYING TO STOP IT!
I...I HAVE TO GET BACK. DON'T WORRY. WE'LL SAVE THEM. I PROMISE.

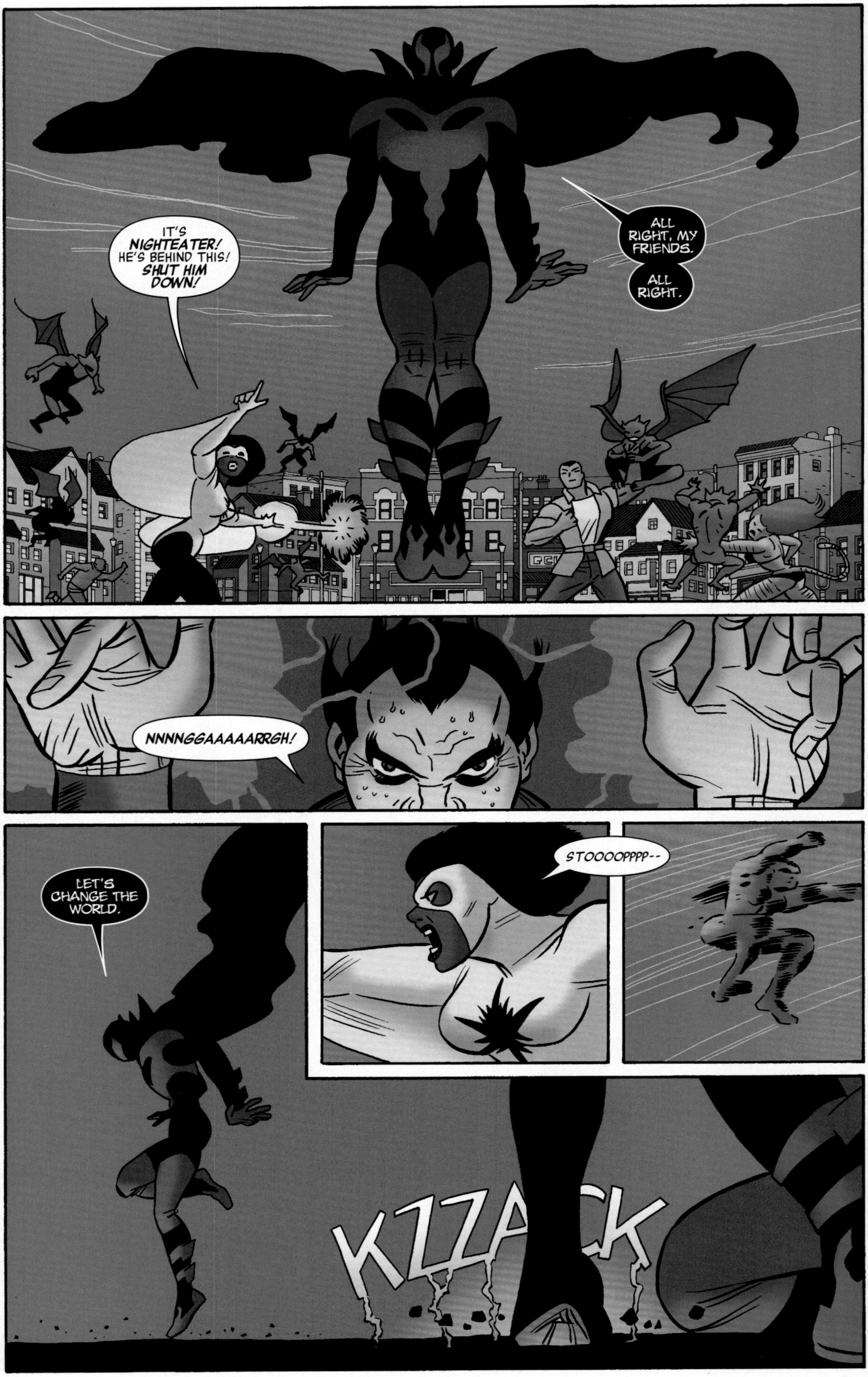
IT'S NIGHTEATER! HE'S BEHIND THIS! SHUT HIM DOWN!
ALL RIGHT, MY FRIENDS.
ALL RIGHT.
NNNNGGAAAAARRGH!
LET'S CHANGE THE WORLD.
STOOOOPPPP--
KZZACK

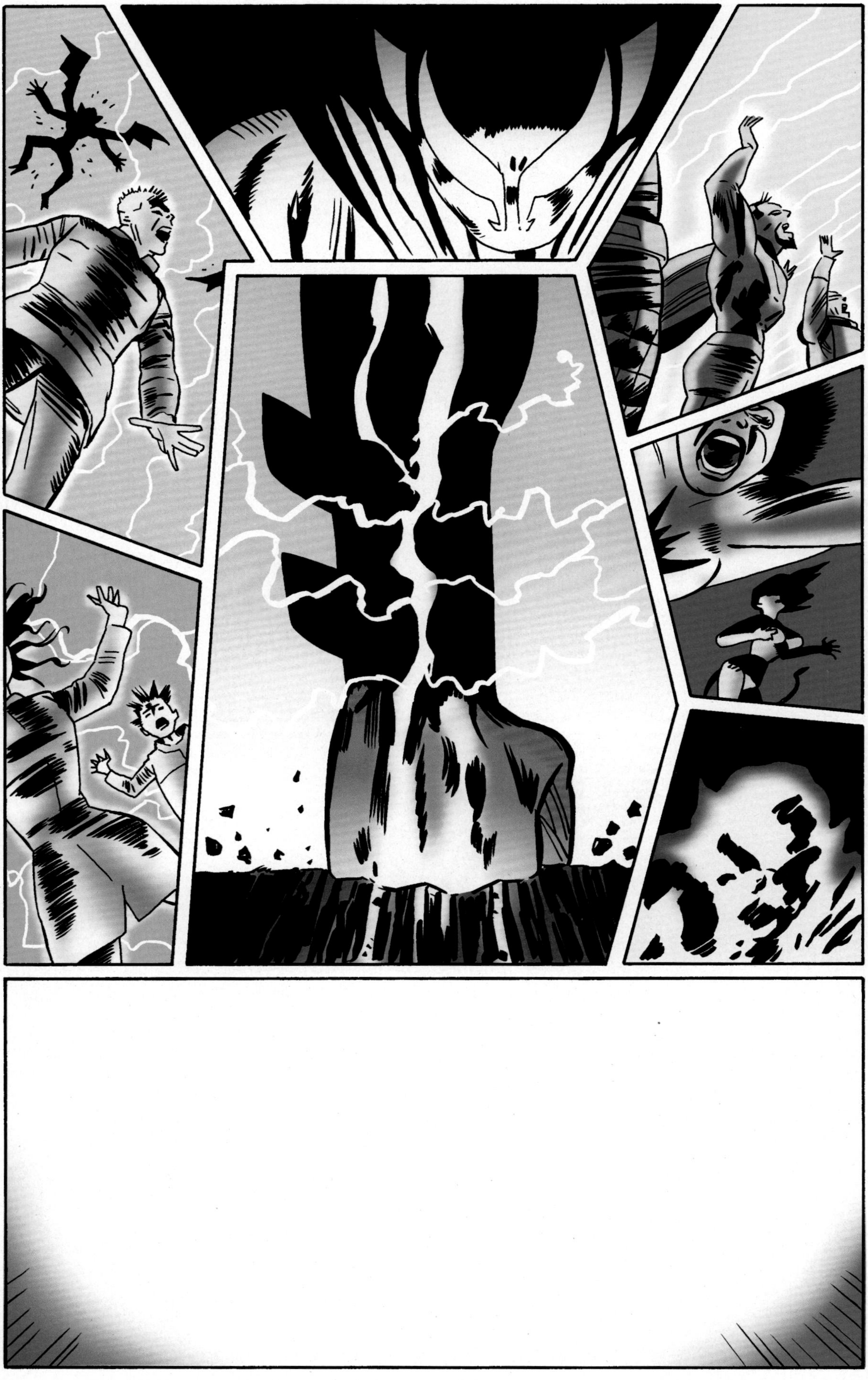

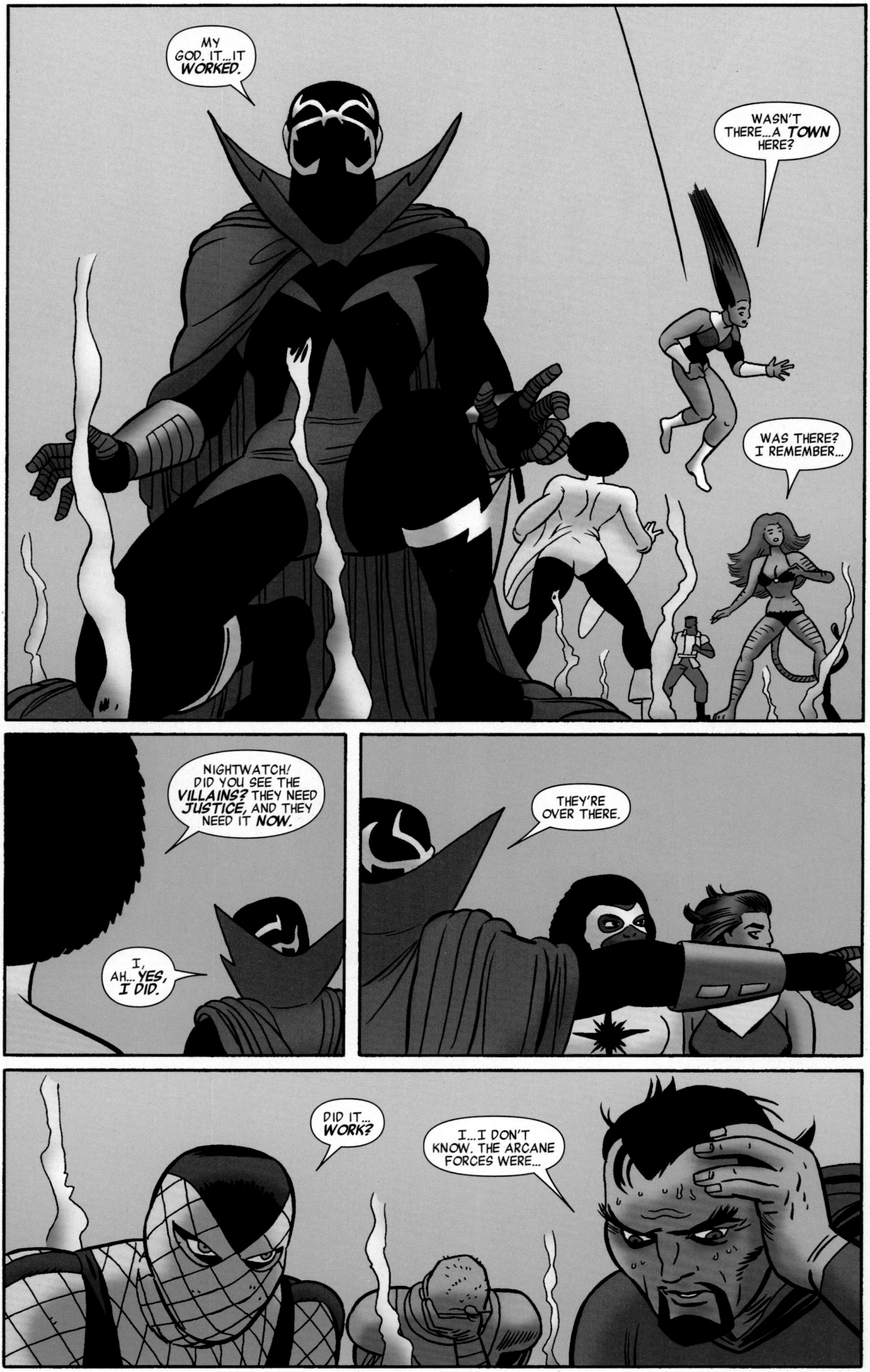
MY GOD. IT...IT WORKED.
WASN'T THERE...A TOWN HERE?
WAS THERE? I REMEMBER...
NIGHTWATCH! DID YOU SEE THE VILLAINS? THEY NEED JUSTICE, AND THEY NEED IT NOW.
I, AH... YES, I DID.
THEY'RE OVER THERE.
DID IT... WORK?
I...I DON'T KNOW. THE ARCANE FORCES WERE...

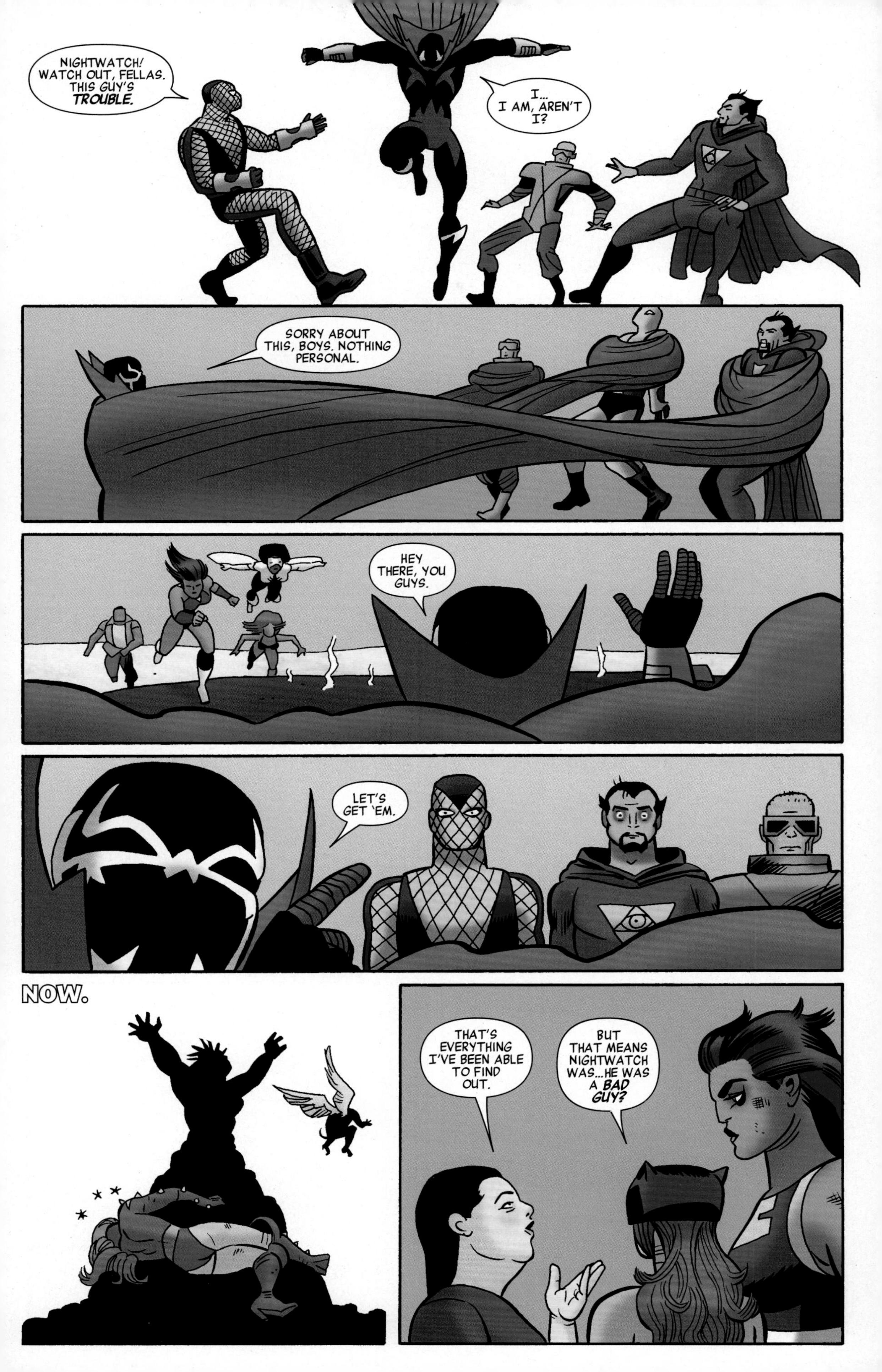
NIGHTWATCH! WATCH OUT, FELLAS. THIS GUY'S TROUBLE.
I... I AM, AREN'T I?
SORRY ABOUT THIS, BOYS. NOTHING PERSONAL.
HEY THERE, YOU GUYS.
LET'S GET 'EM.
NOW.
THAT'S EVERYTHING I'VE BEEN ABLE TO FIND OUT.
BUT THAT MEANS NIGHTWATCH WAS...HE WAS A BAD GUY?

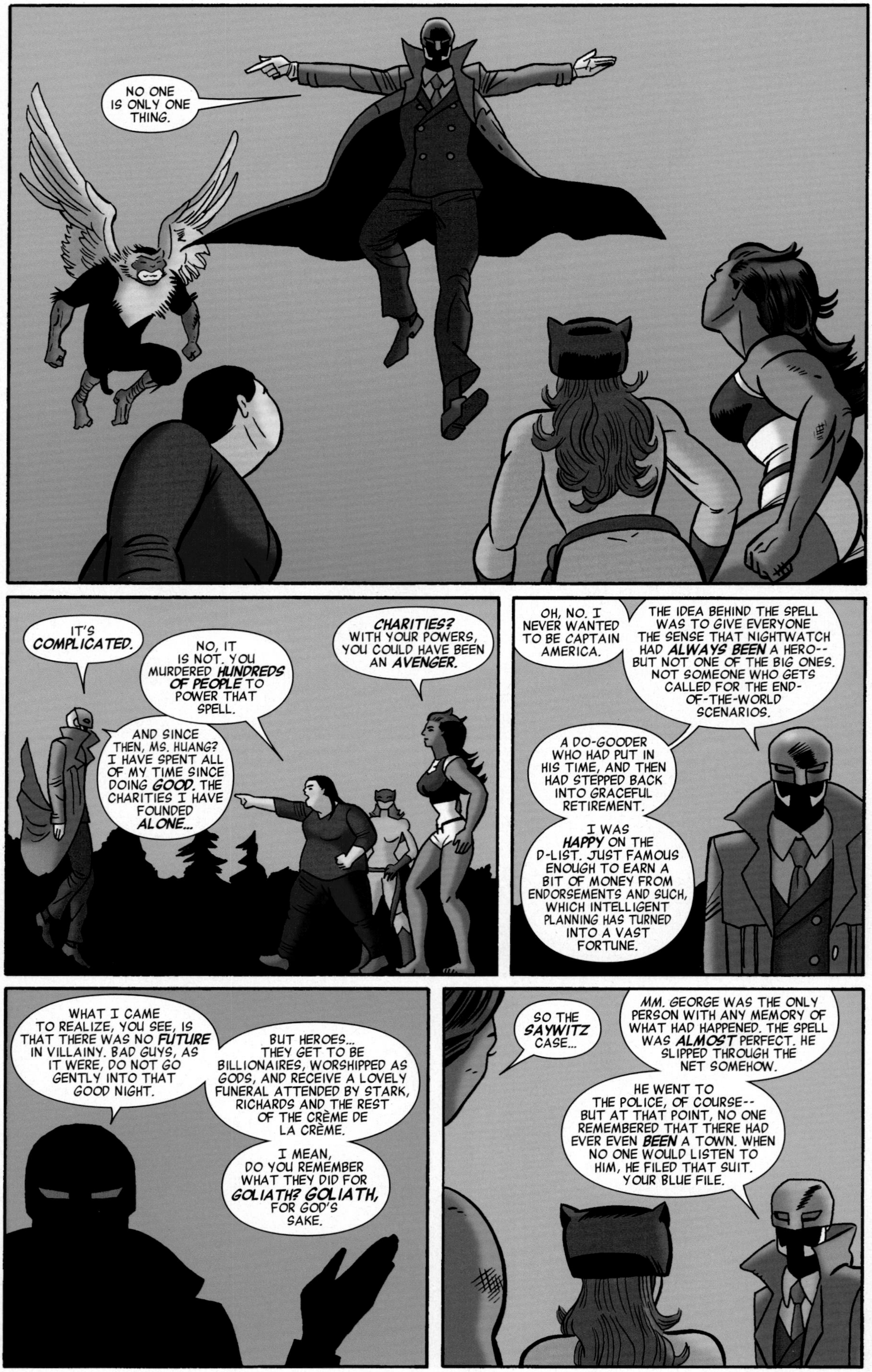

NO ONE IS ONLY ONE THING.
IT'S *COMPLICATED.*
NO, IT IS NOT. YOU MURDERED **HUNDREDS OF PEOPLE** TO POWER THAT SPELL.
CHARITIES? WITH YOUR POWERS, YOU COULD HAVE BEEN AN *AVENGER.*
AND SINCE THEN, MS. HUANG? I HAVE SPENT ALL OF MY TIME SINCE DOING **GOOD.** THE CHARITIES I HAVE FOUNDED **ALONE...**
OH, NO. I NEVER WANTED TO BE CAPTAIN AMERICA.
THE IDEA BEHIND THE SPELL WAS TO GIVE EVERYONE THE SENSE THAT NIGHTWATCH HAD ***ALWAYS BEEN*** A HERO-- BUT NOT ONE OF THE BIG ONES. NOT SOMEONE WHO GETS CALLED FOR THE END-OF-THE-WORLD SCENARIOS.
A DO-GOODER WHO HAD PUT IN HIS TIME, AND THEN HAD STEPPED BACK INTO GRACEFUL RETIREMENT.
I WAS ***HAPPY*** ON THE D-LIST. JUST FAMOUS ENOUGH TO EARN A BIT OF MONEY FROM ENDORSEMENTS AND SUCH, WHICH INTELLIGENT PLANNING HAS TURNED INTO A VAST FORTUNE.
WHAT I CAME TO REALIZE, YOU SEE, IS THAT THERE WAS NO ***FUTURE*** IN VILLAINY. BAD GUYS, AS IT WERE, DO NOT GO GENTLY INTO THAT GOOD NIGHT.
BUT HEROES... THEY GET TO BE BILLIONAIRES, WORSHIPPED AS GODS, AND RECEIVE A LOVELY FUNERAL ATTENDED BY STARK, RICHARDS AND THE REST OF THE CRÈME DE LA CRÈME.
I MEAN, DO YOU REMEMBER WHAT THEY DID FOR ***GOLIATH? GOLIATH,*** FOR GOD'S SAKE.
SO THE ***SAYWITZ*** CASE...
MM. GEORGE WAS THE ONLY PERSON WITH ANY MEMORY OF WHAT HAD HAPPENED. THE SPELL WAS ***ALMOST*** PERFECT. HE SLIPPED THROUGH THE NET SOMEHOW.
HE WENT TO THE POLICE, OF COURSE-- BUT AT THAT POINT, NO ONE REMEMBERED THAT THERE HAD EVER EVEN ***BEEN*** A TOWN. WHEN NO ONE WOULD LISTEN TO HIM, HE FILED THAT SUIT. YOUR BLUE FILE.

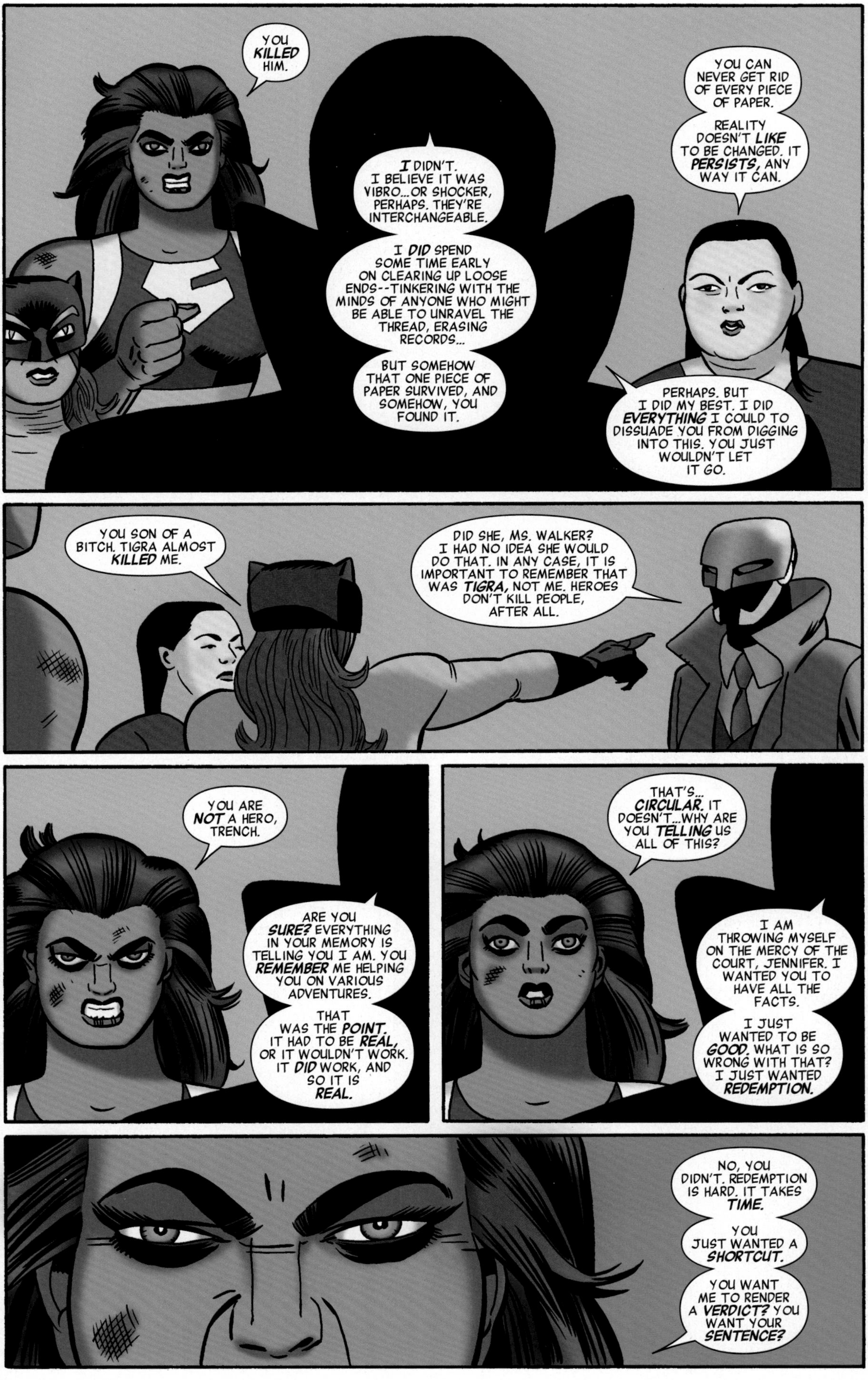

YOU KILLED HIM.
I DIDN'T. I BELIEVE IT WAS VIBRO...OR SHOCKER, PERHAPS. THEY'RE INTERCHANGEABLE.
I DID SPEND SOME TIME EARLY ON CLEARING UP LOOSE ENDS--TINKERING WITH THE MINDS OF ANYONE WHO MIGHT BE ABLE TO UNRAVEL THE THREAD, ERASING RECORDS...
BUT SOMEHOW THAT ONE PIECE OF PAPER SURVIVED, AND SOMEHOW, YOU FOUND IT.
YOU CAN NEVER GET RID OF EVERY PIECE OF PAPER.
REALITY DOESN'T LIKE TO BE CHANGED. IT PERSISTS, ANY WAY IT CAN.
PERHAPS. BUT I DID MY BEST. I DID EVERYTHING I COULD TO DISSUADE YOU FROM DIGGING INTO THIS. YOU JUST WOULDN'T LET IT GO.
YOU SON OF A BITCH. TIGRA ALMOST KILLED ME.
DID SHE, MS. WALKER? I HAD NO IDEA SHE WOULD DO THAT. IN ANY CASE, IT IS IMPORTANT TO REMEMBER THAT WAS TIGRA, NOT ME. HEROES DON'T KILL PEOPLE, AFTER ALL.
YOU ARE NOT A HERO, TRENCH.
ARE YOU SURE? EVERYTHING IN YOUR MEMORY IS TELLING YOU I AM. YOU REMEMBER ME HELPING YOU ON VARIOUS ADVENTURES.
THAT WAS THE POINT. IT HAD TO BE REAL, OR IT WOULDN'T WORK. IT DID WORK, AND SO IT IS REAL.
THAT'S... CIRCULAR. IT DOESN'T...WHY ARE YOU TELLING US ALL OF THIS?
I AM THROWING MYSELF ON THE MERCY OF THE COURT, JENNIFER. I WANTED YOU TO HAVE ALL THE FACTS.
I JUST WANTED TO BE GOOD. WHAT IS SO WRONG WITH THAT? I JUST WANTED REDEMPTION.
NO, YOU DIDN'T. REDEMPTION IS HARD. IT TAKES TIME.
YOU JUST WANTED A SHORTCUT.
YOU WANT ME TO RENDER A VERDICT? YOU WANT YOUR SENTENCE?

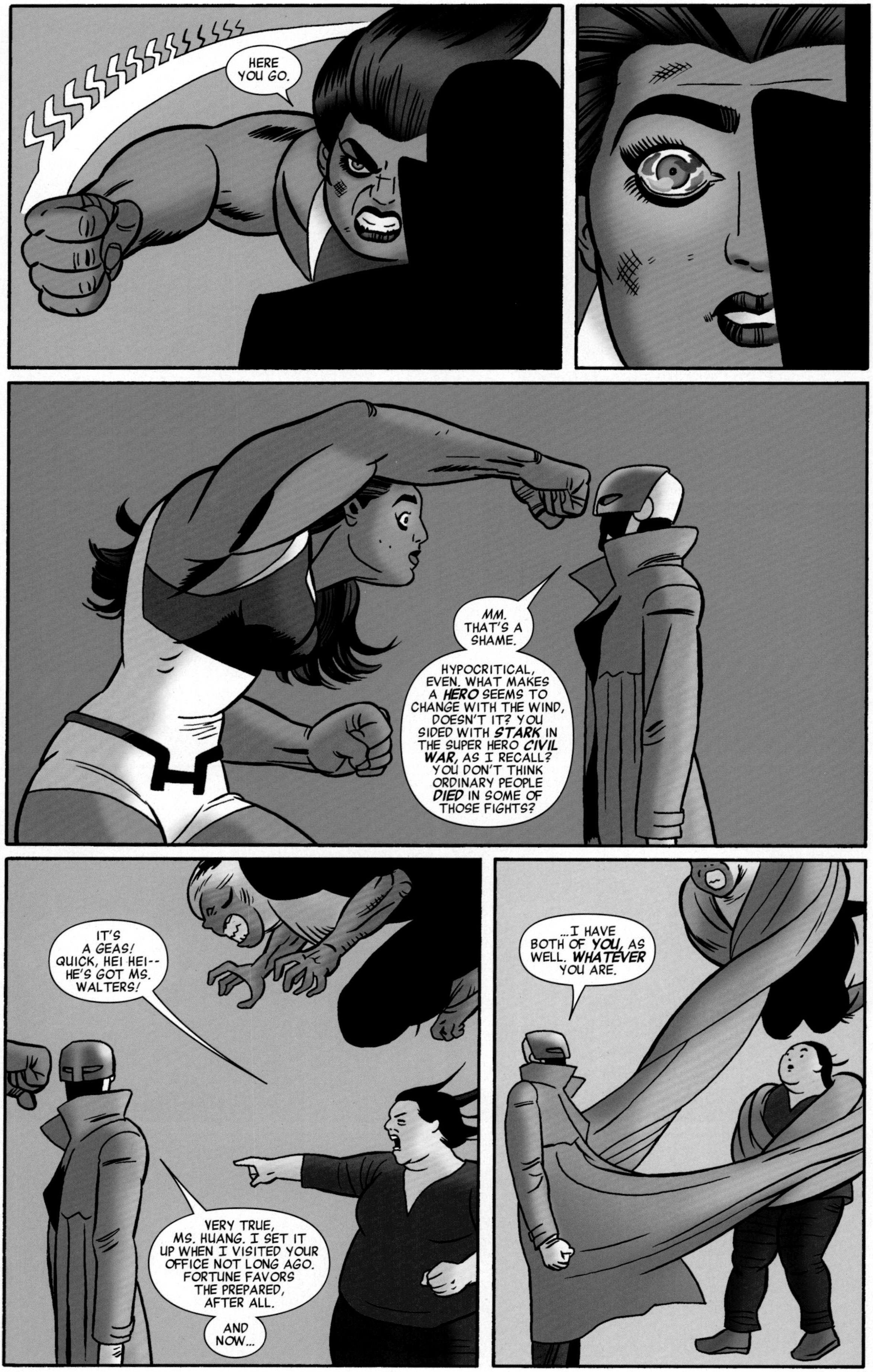
HERE YOU GO.
MM. THAT'S A SHAME.
HYPOCRITICAL, EVEN. WHAT MAKES A HERO SEEMS TO CHANGE WITH THE WIND, DOESN'T IT? YOU SIDED WITH STARK IN THE SUPER HERO CIVIL WAR, AS I RECALL? YOU DON'T THINK ORDINARY PEOPLE DIED IN SOME OF THOSE FIGHTS?
IT'S A GEAS! QUICK, HEI HEI--HE'S GOT MS. WALTERS!
VERY TRUE, MS. HUANG. I SET IT UP WHEN I VISITED YOUR OFFICE NOT LONG AGO. FORTUNE FAVORS THE PREPARED, AFTER ALL.
AND NOW...
...I HAVE BOTH OF YOU, AS WELL. WHATEVER YOU ARE.

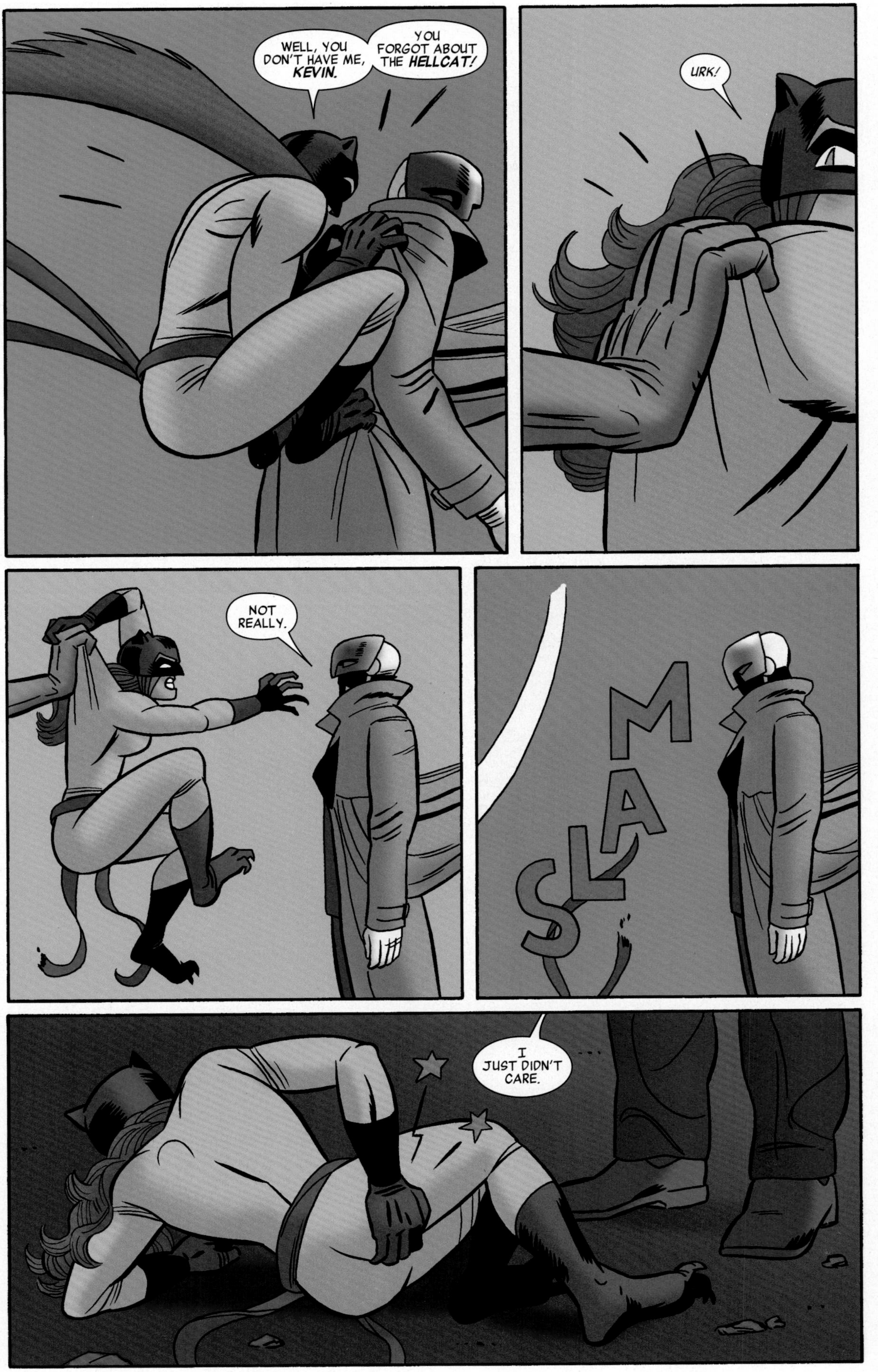
WELL, YOU DON'T HAVE ME, KEVIN.
YOU FORGOT ABOUT THE HELLCAT!
URK!
NOT REALLY.
SLAM
I JUST DIDN'T CARE.

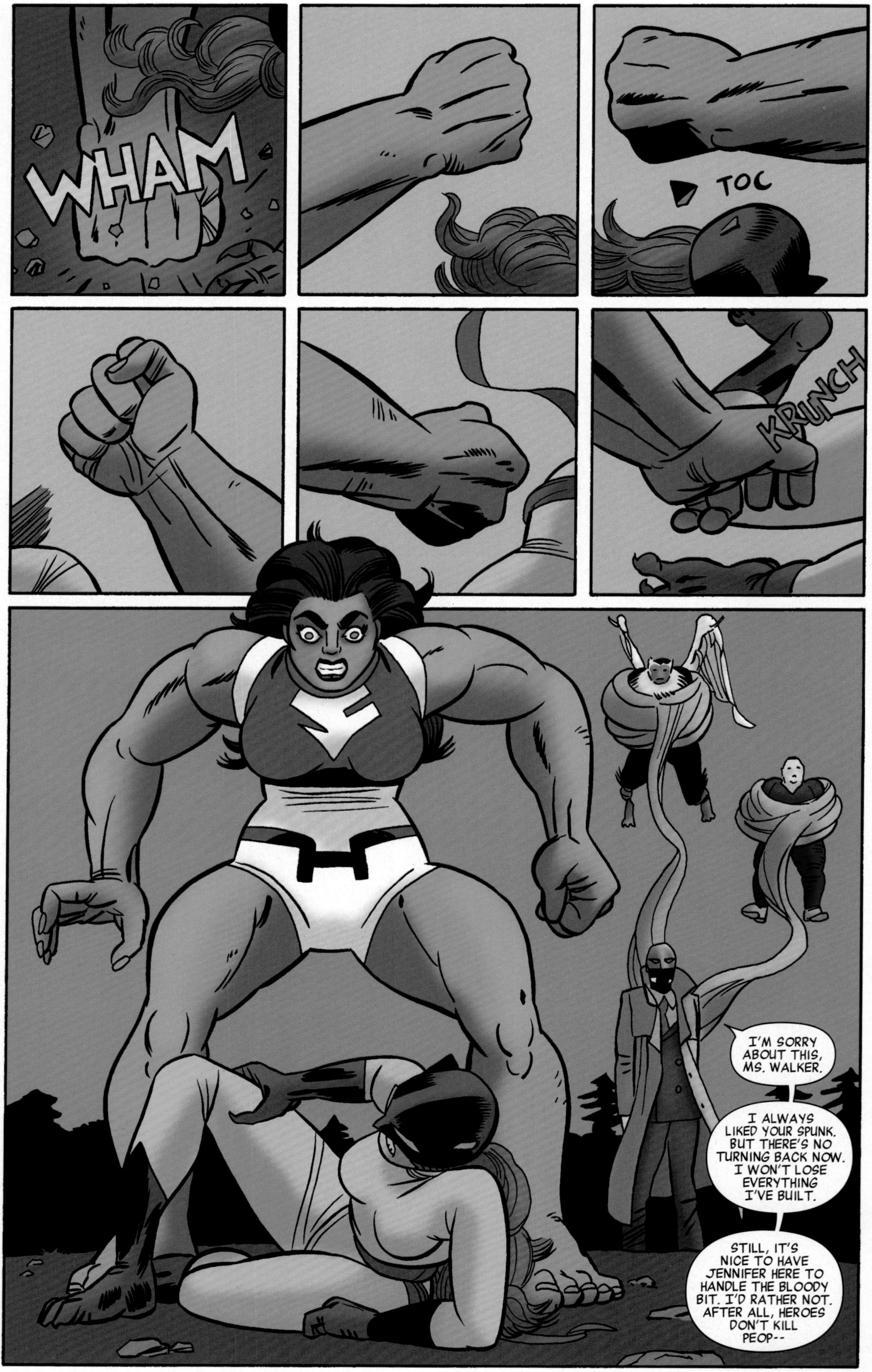
WHAM
TOC
KRUNCH
I'M SORRY ABOUT THIS, MS. WALKER.
I ALWAYS LIKED YOUR SPUNK. BUT THERE'S NO TURNING BACK NOW. I WON'T LOSE EVERYTHING I'VE BUILT.
STILL, IT'S NICE TO HAVE JENNIFER HERE TO HANDLE THE BLOODY BIT. I'D RATHER NOT. AFTER ALL, HEROES DON'T KILL PEOP--

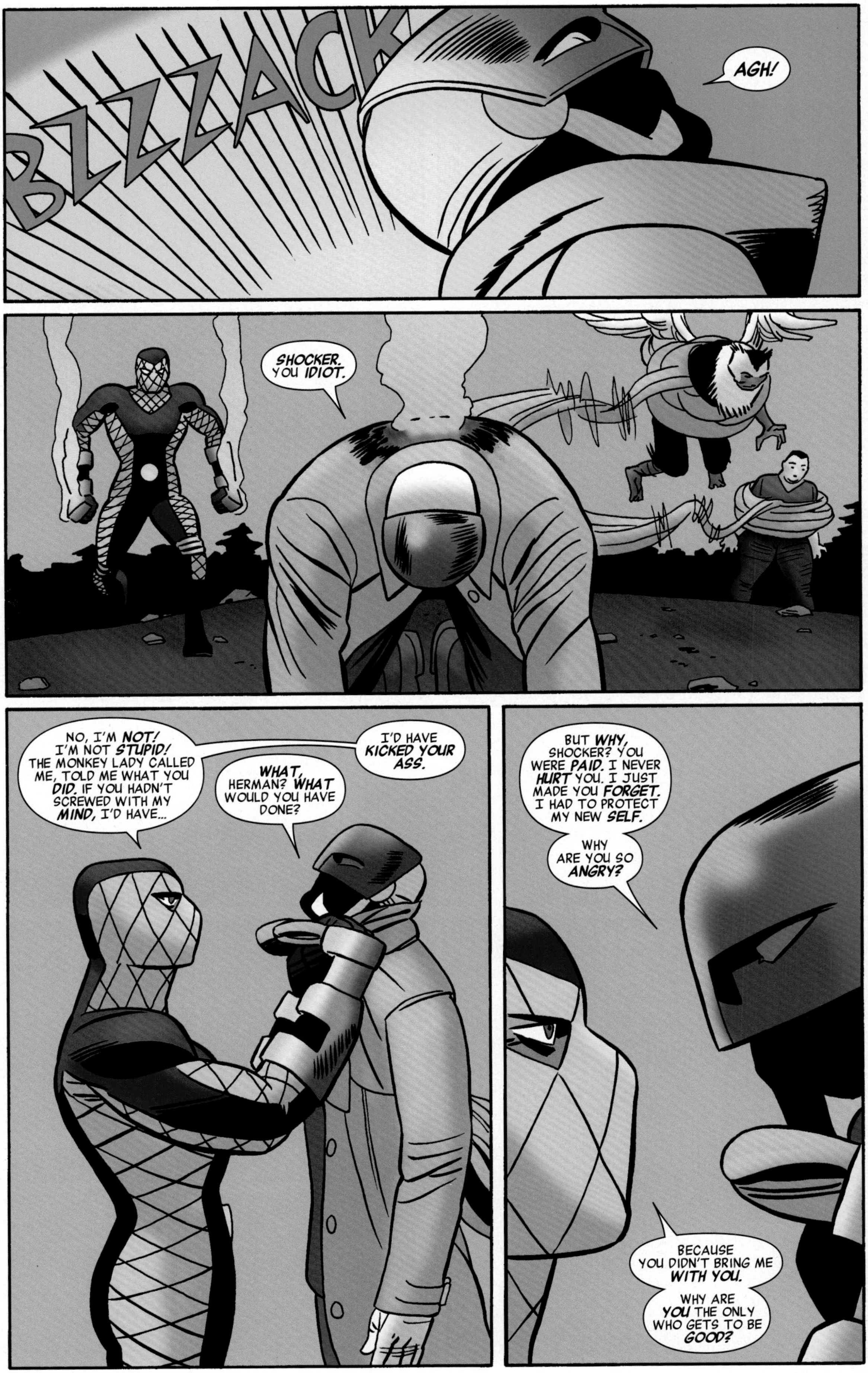
BZZZACK
AGH!
SHOCKER. YOU IDIOT.
NO, I'M NOT! I'M NOT STUPID! THE MONKEY LADY CALLED ME, TOLD ME WHAT YOU DID. IF YOU HADN'T SCREWED WITH MY MIND, I'D HAVE...
WHAT, HERMAN? WHAT WOULD YOU HAVE DONE?
I'D HAVE KICKED YOUR ASS.
BUT WHY, SHOCKER? YOU WERE PAID. I NEVER HURT YOU. I JUST MADE YOU FORGET. I HAD TO PROTECT MY NEW SELF.
WHY ARE YOU SO ANGRY?
BECAUSE YOU DIDN'T BRING ME WITH YOU.
WHY ARE YOU THE ONLY WHO GETS TO BE GOOD?

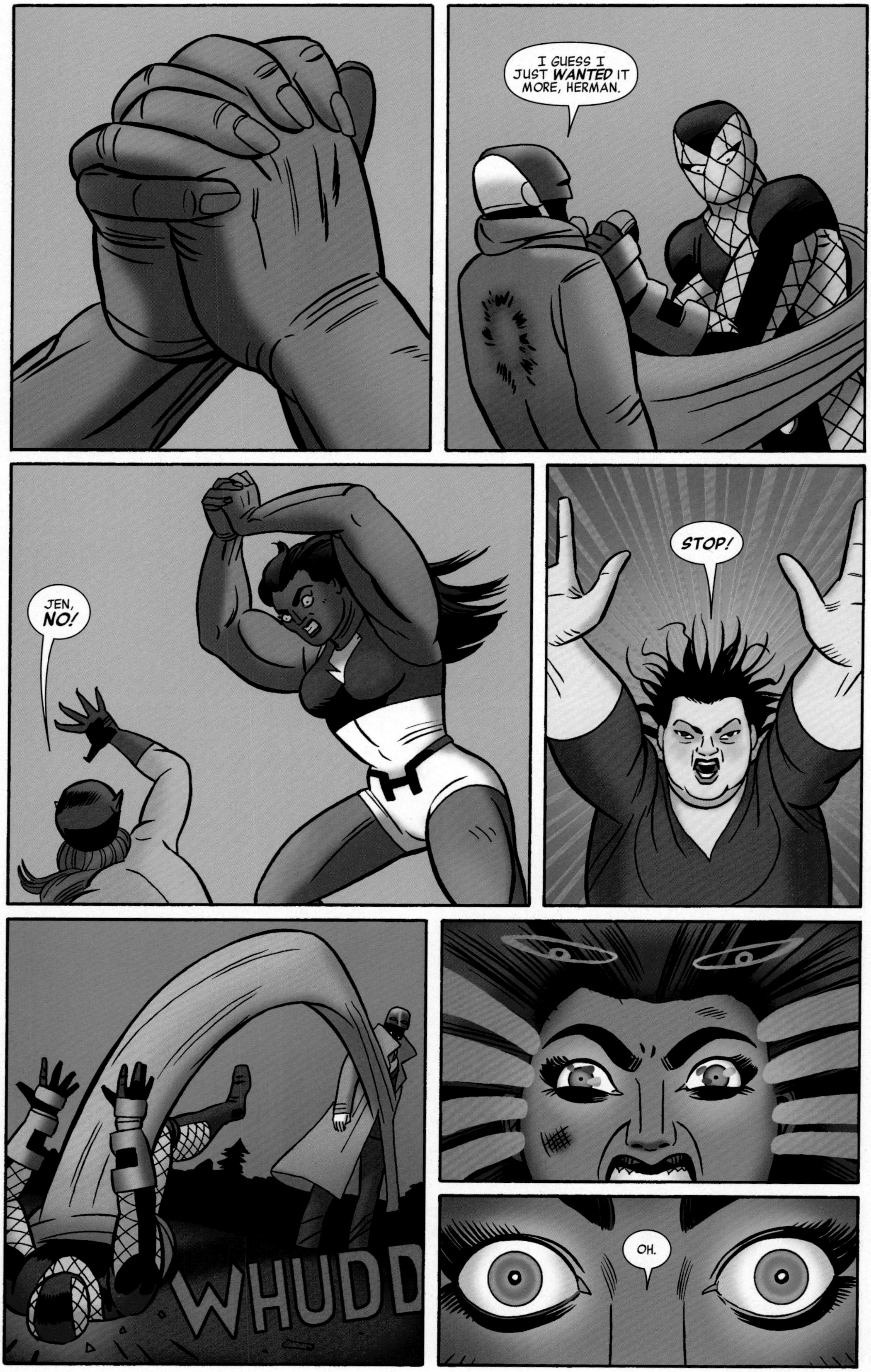
I GUESS I JUST WANTED IT MORE, HERMAN.
JEN, NO!
STOP!
WHUDD
OH.

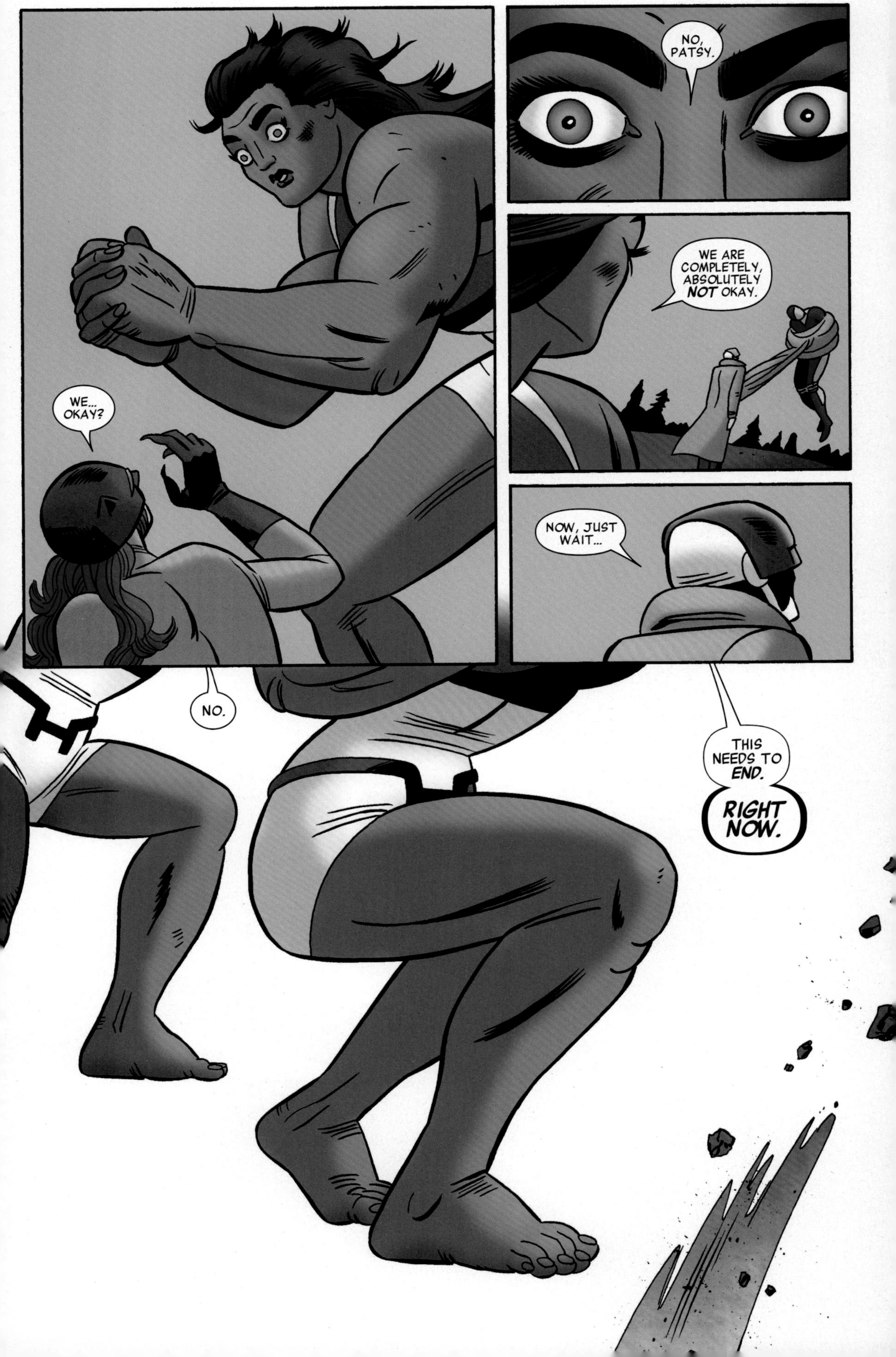
NO, PATSY.
WE... OKAY?
WE ARE COMPLETELY, ABSOLUTELY NOT OKAY.
NOW, JUST WAIT...
NO.
THIS NEEDS TO END.
RIGHT NOW.

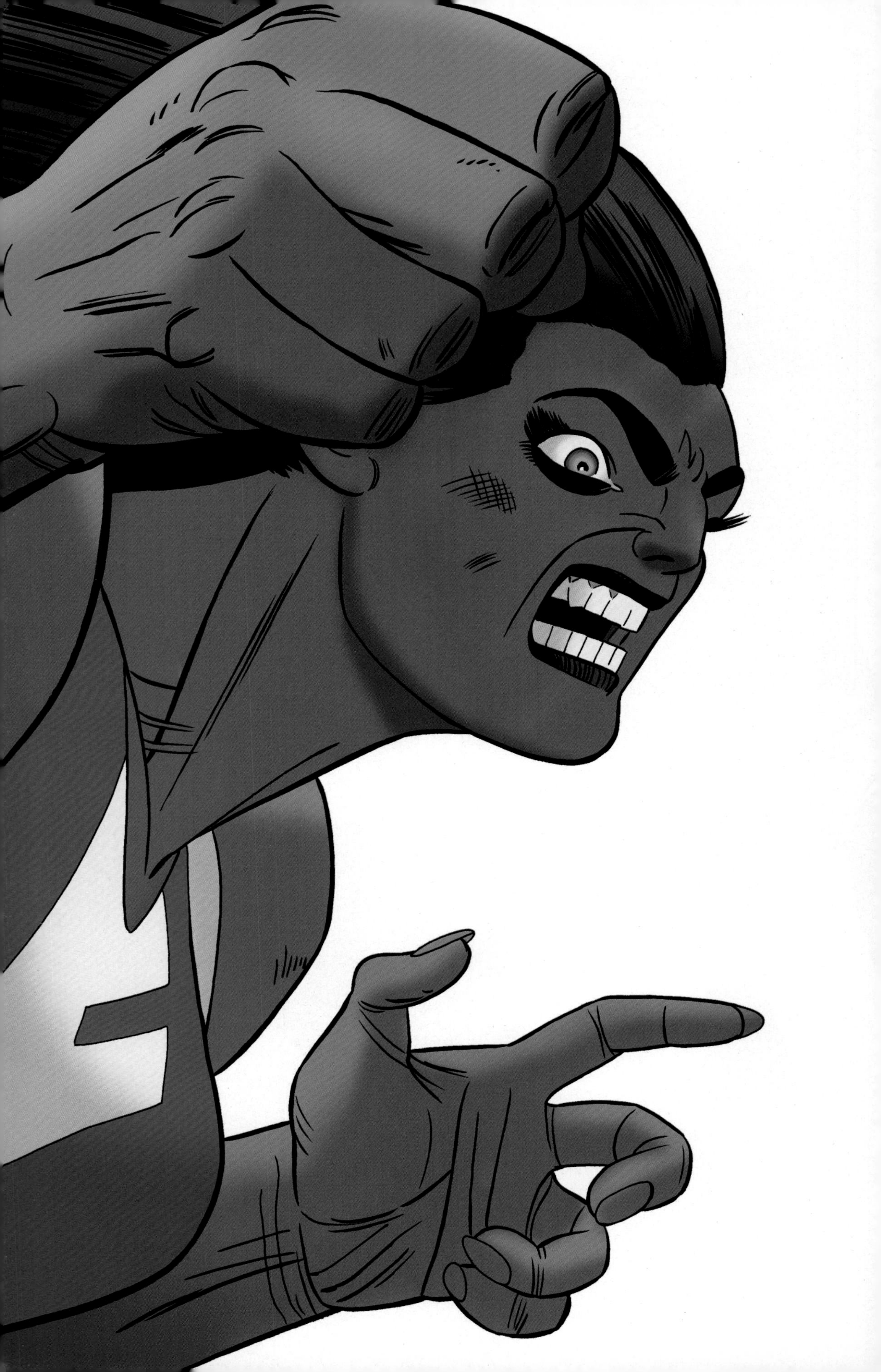

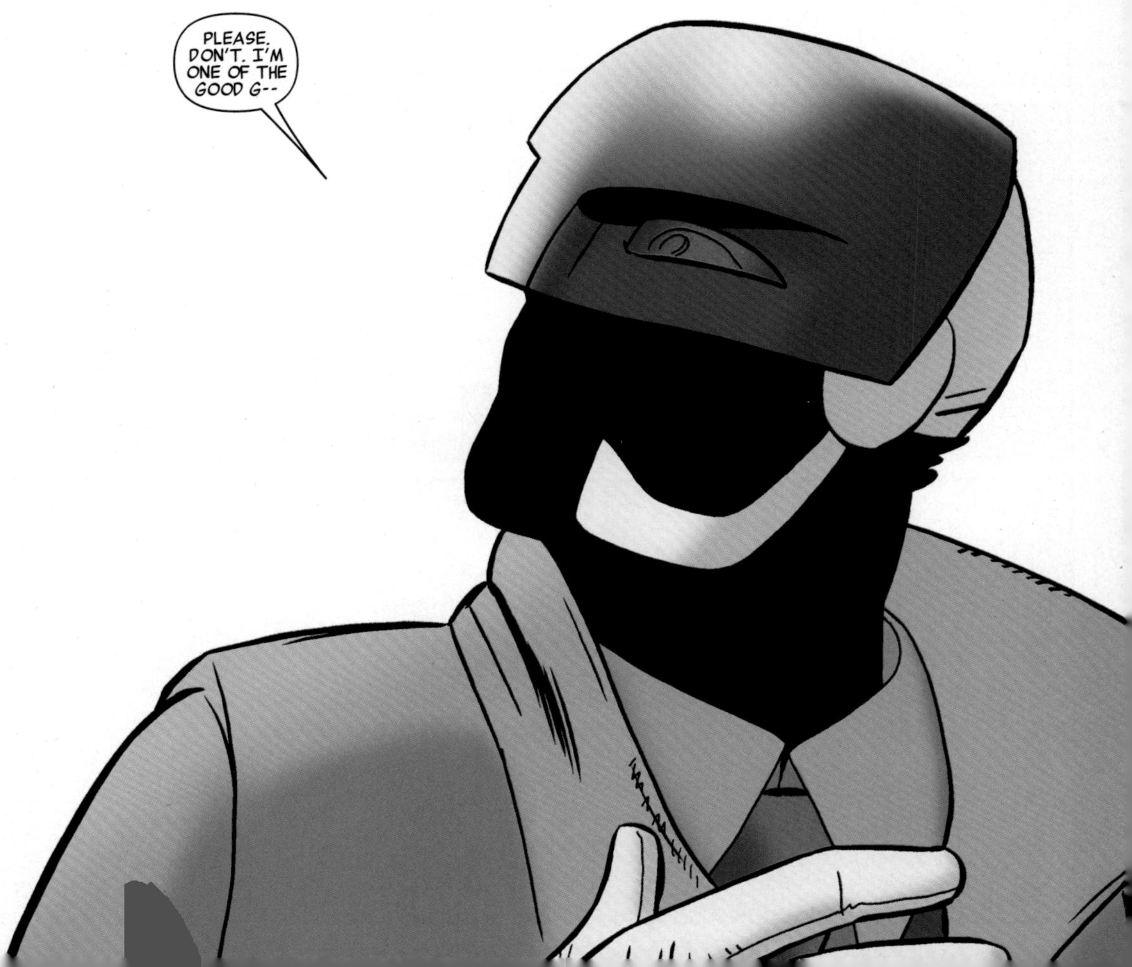
PLEASE. DON'T. I'M ONE OF THE GOOD G--

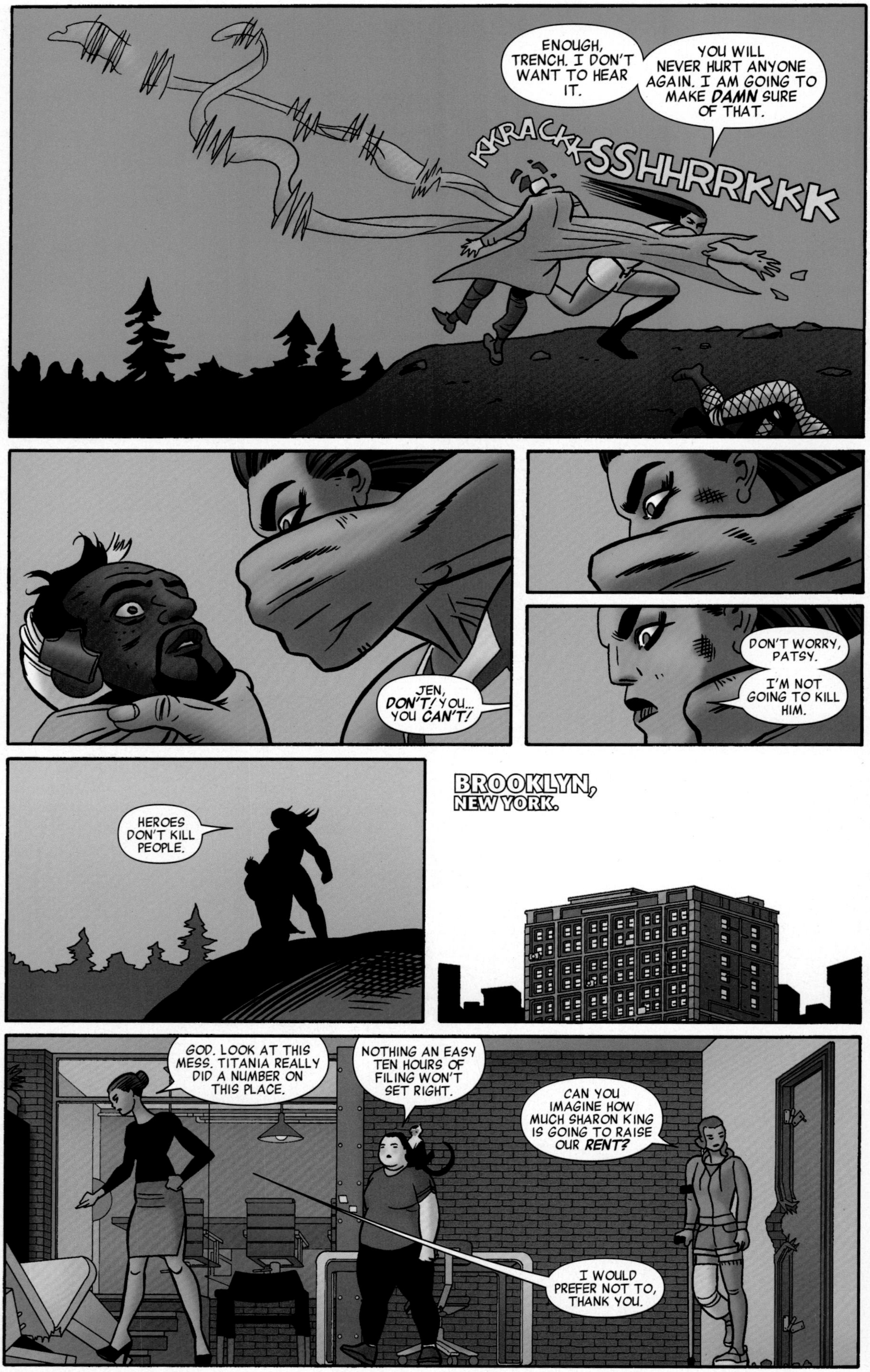
ENOUGH, TRENCH. I DON'T WANT TO HEAR IT.
YOU WILL NEVER HURT ANYONE AGAIN. I AM GOING TO MAKE DAMN SURE OF THAT.
KKRACKKSSHHRRKKK
JEN, DON'T! YOU... YOU CAN'T!
DON'T WORRY, PATSY.
I'M NOT GOING TO KILL HIM.
HEROES DON'T KILL PEOPLE.
BROOKLYN, NEW YORK.
GOD. LOOK AT THIS MESS. TITANIA REALLY DID A NUMBER ON THIS PLACE.
NOTHING AN EASY TEN HOURS OF FILING WON'T SET RIGHT.
CAN YOU IMAGINE HOW MUCH SHARON KING IS GOING TO RAISE OUR RENT?
I WOULD PREFER NOT TO, THANK YOU.

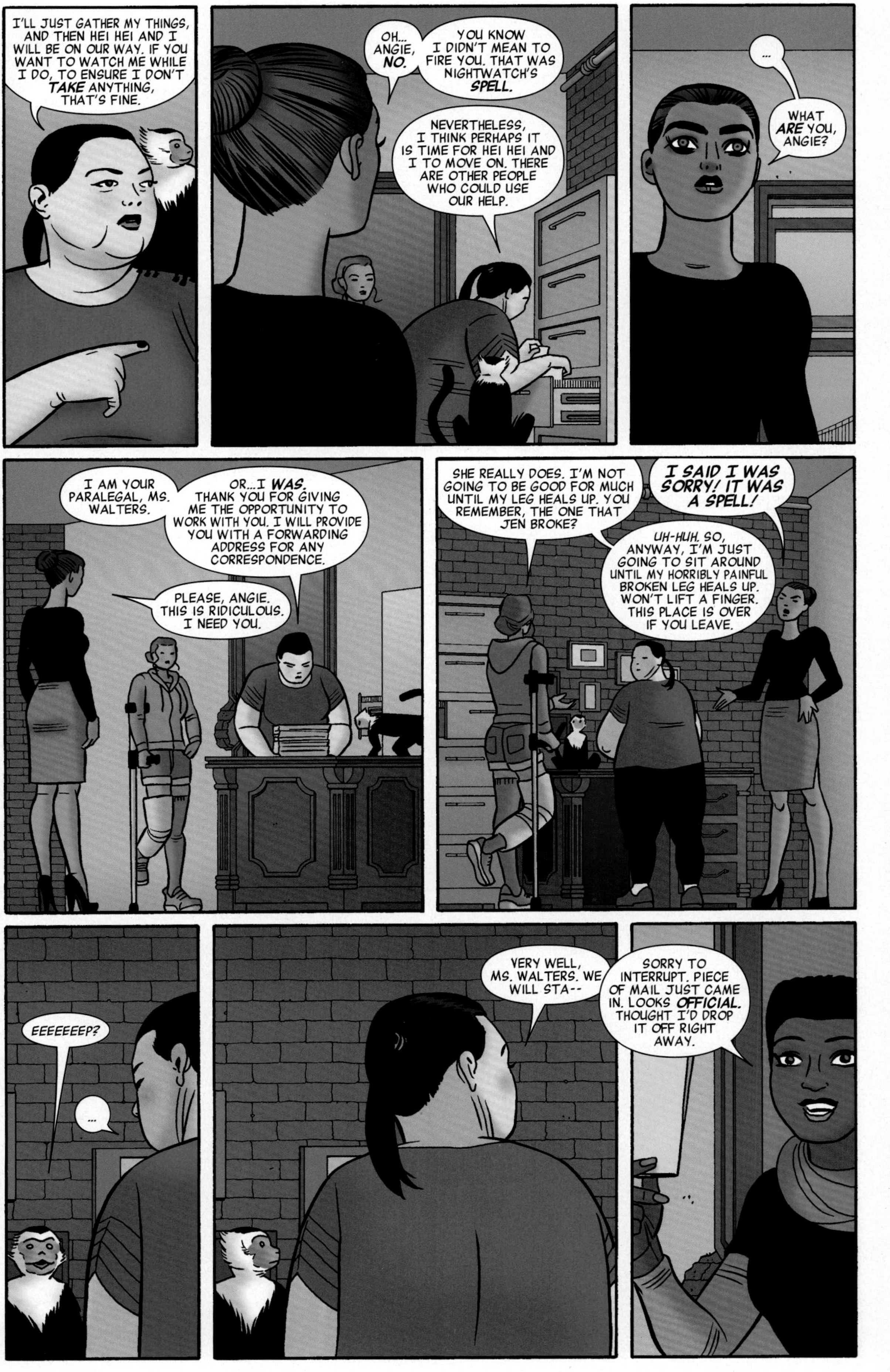
I'LL JUST GATHER MY THINGS, AND THEN HEI HEI AND I WILL BE ON OUR WAY. IF YOU WANT TO WATCH ME WHILE I DO, TO ENSURE I DON'T TAKE ANYTHING, THAT'S FINE.
OH... ANGIE, NO.
YOU KNOW I DIDN'T MEAN TO FIRE YOU. THAT WAS NIGHTWATCH'S SPELL.
NEVERTHELESS, I THINK PERHAPS IT IS TIME FOR HEI HEI AND I TO MOVE ON. THERE ARE OTHER PEOPLE WHO COULD USE OUR HELP.
...
WHAT ARE YOU, ANGIE?
I AM YOUR PARALEGAL, MS. WALTERS.
OR...I WAS. THANK YOU FOR GIVING ME THE OPPORTUNITY TO WORK WITH YOU. I WILL PROVIDE YOU WITH A FORWARDING ADDRESS FOR ANY CORRESPONDENCE.
PLEASE, ANGIE. THIS IS RIDICULOUS. I NEED YOU.
SHE REALLY DOES. I'M NOT GOING TO BE GOOD FOR MUCH UNTIL MY LEG HEALS UP. YOU REMEMBER, THE ONE THAT JEN BROKE?
I SAID I WAS SORRY! IT WAS A SPELL!
UH-HUH. SO, ANYWAY, I'M JUST GOING TO SIT AROUND UNTIL MY HORRIBLY PAINFUL BROKEN LEG HEALS UP. WON'T LIFT A FINGER. THIS PLACE IS OVER IF YOU LEAVE.
EEEEEEEP?
...
VERY WELL, MS. WALTERS. WE WILL STA--
SORRY TO INTERRUPT. PIECE OF MAIL JUST CAME IN. LOOKS OFFICIAL. THOUGHT I'D DROP IT OFF RIGHT AWAY.

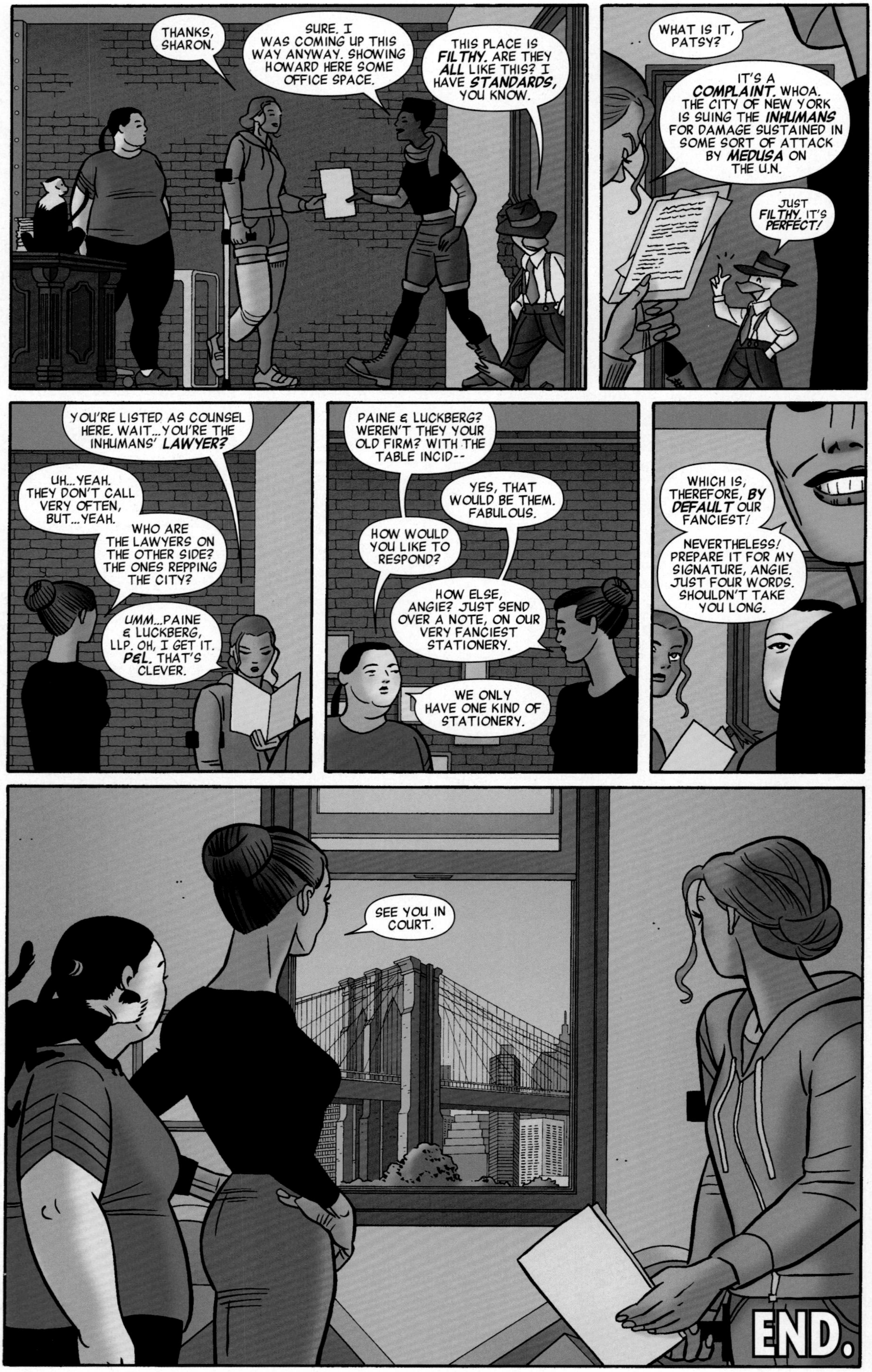
THANKS, SHARON.
SURE. I WAS COMING UP THIS WAY ANYWAY. SHOWING HOWARD HERE SOME OFFICE SPACE.
THIS PLACE IS FILTHY. ARE THEY ALL LIKE THIS? I HAVE STANDARDS, YOU KNOW.
WHAT IS IT, PATSY?
IT'S A COMPLAINT. WHOA. THE CITY OF NEW YORK IS SUING THE INHUMANS FOR DAMAGE SUSTAINED IN SOME SORT OF ATTACK BY MEDUSA ON THE U.N.
JUST FILTHY. IT'S PERFECT!
YOU'RE LISTED AS COUNSEL HERE. WAIT...YOU'RE THE INHUMANS' LAWYER?
UH...YEAH. THEY DON'T CALL VERY OFTEN, BUT...YEAH.
WHO ARE THE LAWYERS ON THE OTHER SIDE? THE ONES REPPING THE CITY?
UMM...PAINE & LUCKBERG, LLP. OH, I GET IT. PEL. THAT'S CLEVER.
PAINE & LUCKBERG? WEREN'T THEY YOUR OLD FIRM? WITH THE TABLE INCID--
YES, THAT WOULD BE THEM. FABULOUS.
HOW WOULD YOU LIKE TO RESPOND?
HOW ELSE, ANGIE? JUST SEND OVER A NOTE, ON OUR VERY FANCIEST STATIONERY.
WE ONLY HAVE ONE KIND OF STATIONERY.
WHICH IS, THEREFORE, BY DEFAULT OUR FANCIEST!
NEVERTHELESS! PREPARE IT FOR MY SIGNATURE, ANGIE. JUST FOUR WORDS. SHOULDN'T TAKE YOU LONG.
SEE YOU IN COURT.
END.

LEGAL BRIEFS

Well, here we are, dear readers. The end of our first new season of SHE-HULK. It's been a fun, emotional, sometimes crazy, always exciting ride, especially for me.

Because this is the last Marvel comic I'm editing.

It's also a comic whose first year almost exactly coincided with my daughter's first year; the first issue went to the printer the week after she was born. And this is what she looks like now:

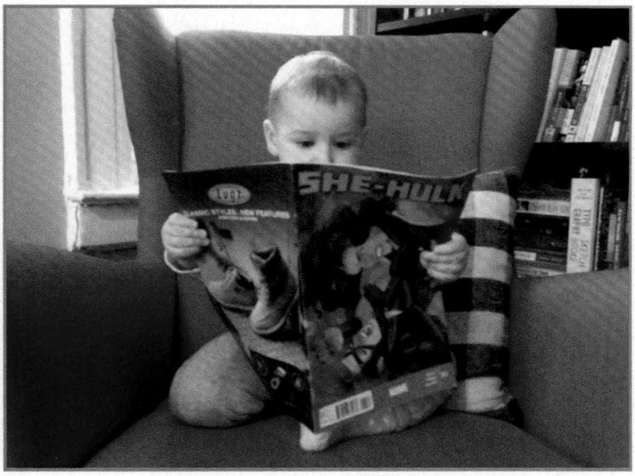
SHE-HULK

Working on a book with such a complex, real woman at its core at the same time as I was figuring out how to be a mother to a baby girl was huge for me. I've had the opportunity to work on so many amazing female characters through the years, and alongside so many amazing women: fellow editors, writers, artists, colorists, letterers, designers, bullpenners, proofreaders, lawyers, managers, producers, bloggers.... Every one of them has changed who I am for the better, and I never would have met them if it hadn't been for this crazy industry we all decided to dedicate ourselves to.

And not one of us, just like Jen Walters, is only one thing.

This is what I want for my daughter - to have a role model that she can see herself in, that she can identify with and look up to and ultimately find her own path alongside. I feel really lucky to have worked on this book, and to have been able to see it through to its end (at least for now).

I also feel really lucky to have met amazing fans who supported the book from go, who dressed up and emailed and introduced themselves at shows, who reviewed us and kept us honest and shared the book with friends. Thank you from the bottom of my heart.

And thank you to the team who worked on this: Charles, Javier, Muntsa, Clayton, Kevin, Ron, Tom, Frankie, Nick, Xander, and Sana.

I know Charles wants to say some words, too, so I'll, as gracefully as possible, hand it over to him now.

Thanks again. See you on the flip-side.

--J9,
January, 2015
New York, NY

Is this really the last SHE-HULK issue?

Oh no. Absolutely not. There will be more She-Hulk stories, whether I write them, whether Javier Pulido or Ron Wimberly draws them, whether they're covered and colored and lettered and edited by the extremely able folks who did all of that for the twelve issues we've put out in this most recent set of Jen Walters' solo adventures...or by other extremely talented people who love her just as much as all of us do.

This is just the end of this She-Hulk story - the twelfth part of a twelve-part story. What you've gotten in these issues is exactly the tale I wanted to tell. I pitched what you've read, and I was fortunate enough that Marvel decided that it might make a good story. And honestly, I think it speaks volumes that they're the kind of publisher who would get on board with a book like this in the first place.

Because let's face it, this volume of SHE-HULK has been sort of an idiosyncratic thing. It's a book starring a superhero who rarely super heroes. Instead of that, she *gulp* lawyers. She helps people, but the whole "punching bad guys" thing is pretty much a last resort. Instead, she uses her mind, her charm, her drive...

...which are things we all have, and which was always sort of the point of this book.

I think the best super hero stories are aspirational. They aren't just thrill rides - they're mirrors, showing us what we might be, if we become our best selves. And the best of the best super hero stories are the ones where the heroes themselves aspire to reach that same goal too...and every once in a while, after great sacrifice and incredible effort, they get there. That's Jennifer Walters to a T, if you ask me.

The response to this book has been straight up overwhelming. Thank you, thank you, thank you. I've heard from many parents who have introduced this book to their kids, professional women who like the idea that She-Hulk takes no guff from anyone and makes things work on her own terms, lawyers who dig the idea of their profession being celebrated in a comic (while still pulling exactly zero punches when it comes to pointing out any legal fudging on my part - which I always did solely for dramatic purposes, of course) and people who just like reading cool comics. You are all, every one of you, the best.

And speaking of that, I did my best on this book - I really tried to bring my A game - but so did you. Every tweet, every Tumblr or Facebook post, every email, every "hey, check out this cool book," every "hey, maybe I'll order an extra few copies for the shop..." all of that mattered, and continues to matter. You were all as much a part of this book as I was. I noticed, and Marvel noticed, and it matters. If we do see more stories with this creative team, it will be because of your support, and I can't tell you how much I appreciate it.

Thank you. So much.

**--Charles Soule
January, 2015
Brooklyn, NY**

P.S. I'm sneaking Jen and the gang into as many comics as I can - this series might be ending, but believe me, you'll see these folks again soon, one way or another!

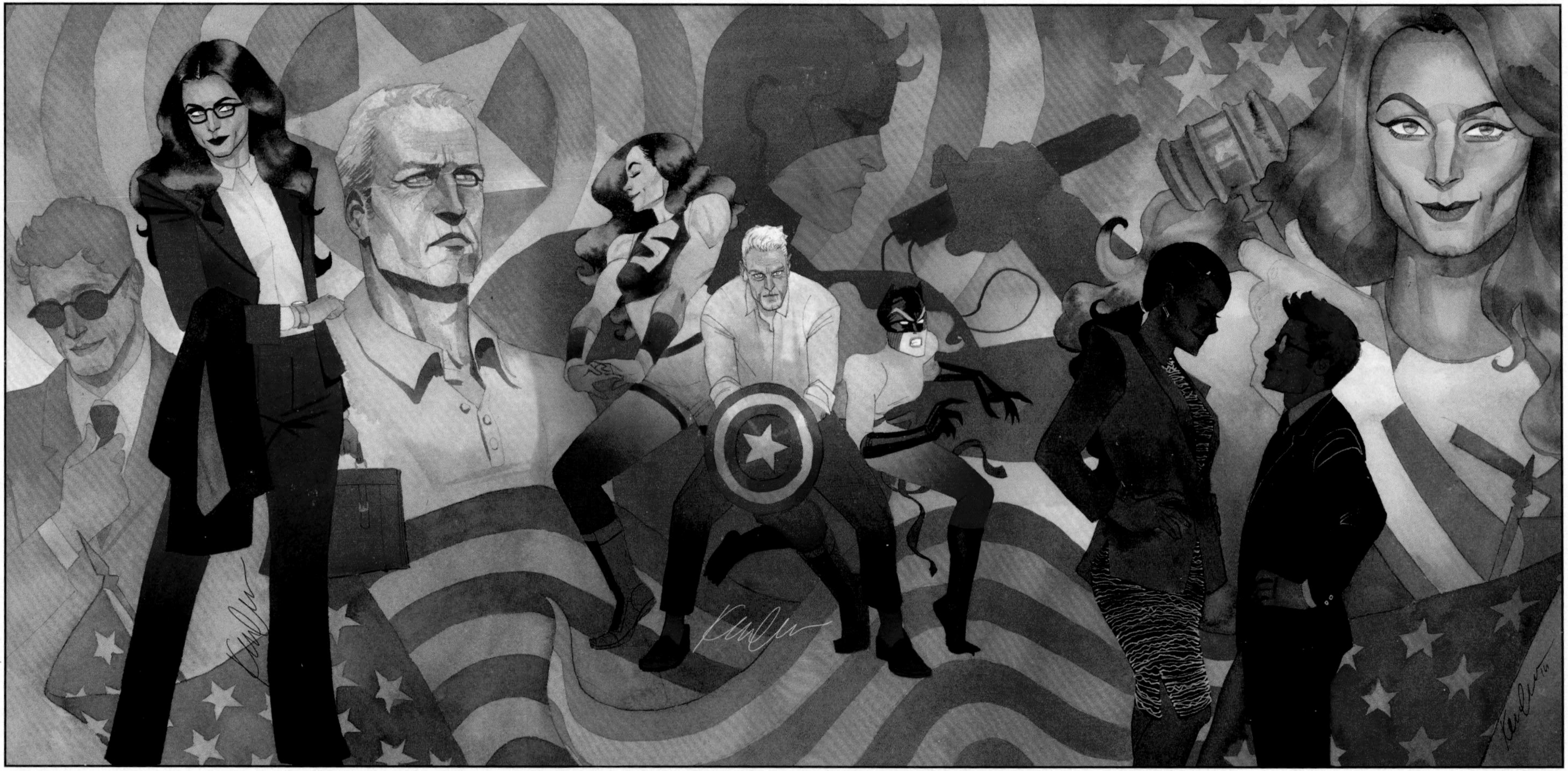

SHE-HULK #8-10 COMBINED COVERS BY KEVIN WADA